# Facilitating Young People's Development

## International perspectives on person-centred theory and practice

### edited by

### Michael Behr
### and
### Jeffrey H.D. Cornelius-White

*PCCS BOOKS*
Ross-on-Wye

First published in 2008

PCCS Books Ltd
2 Cropper Row
Alton Rd
Ross-on-Wye
Herefordshire
HR9 5LA
UK
Tel +44 (0)1989 763 900
www.pccs-books.co.uk

**Facilitating Young People's Development:
International perspectives on person-centred theory and practice**

A CIP catalogue record for this book is available from the British Library

ISBN 978 1 906254 00 1

Cover design by Old Dog Graphics
Printed by Athenæum Press, Gateshead, UK

# CONTENTS

SECTION 3

COUNSELLING, EDUCATION AND LEARNING IN SCHOOLS

# DEDICATION

## ANNE-MARIE AND REINHARD TAUSCH

Michael and Jef are happy to dedicate this book to Anne-Marie and Reinhard Tausch. They deeply influenced us in their never-resting efforts to bring humanity and relationship issues into schools and diverse work settings, practically combining person-centredness with other methods, always grounding person-centred work with empirical research, and never hesitating to be influenced by new research.

# ACKNOWLEDGEMENTS

'This will be a very complicated project.' This was the conclusion of Pete and Michael's first discussion of the plans for this book at the PCE Potsdam Conference in 2006. The book definitely turned out to be complicated. We are very grateful to Pete Sanders, Maggie Taylor-Sanders, Helen Dean, Sandy Green and Heather Allan at PCCS Books. We don't think any other publisher would have dared to embark on, let alone complete this enterprise given the challenge of cooperating with so many people writing outside of their first language across four continents of the world. We are thankful in addition for being always encouraged and facilitated by their professionalism in an unobtrusive but most effective way.

Our sincere appreciation is also extended to the organising committees of the conference from which most of these papers originated, particularly the staff of the Potsdam Conference and the German Association, GwG. We thank especially Elke Lambers, Germain Lietaer, Gerd-Walter Speierer, Karl-Otto Hentze, Michael Barg, Thomas Reckzeh-Schubert, Ursula Reinsch, and the GwG board: Helga Kühn Mengel, Gisela Borgmann-Schäfer, Sylvia Rasch-Owald, Alfons Bonus and Marion Locher.

As well we thank our authors. Most of them took on an immeasurable challenge to express themselves in another language for the sake of providing a worldwide network of person-centredness in the work with children, adolescents and parents. We acknowledge the energy and dedication with which they participated in the book's internal review process and repeatedly worked on revisions of their own chapters.

We also appreciated the support from our institutions and colleagues that has helped the authors and editors to bring this book to fruition, including the administration at University of Education Schwäbisch Gmünd, especially Karin Priem, Martin Weyer-Menkhoff, Edgar Buhl and Hans-Jürgen Albers and Missouri State University, especially Chuck Barké, David Hough, Belinda McCarthy, Don Keck, Lacey York, and finally, Carol Wolter-Gustafson.

Last but not least, we thank our spouses and family, particularly Michael's wife Naomi, Jef's wife Cecily, and Jef's kids Avery and Evan for their inspiration, listening and encouragement, which gave us all the extra energy needed to bring heart and meaning to such a book.

Michael Behr and Jeffrey H.D. Cornelius-White
March 2008

# ABSTRACTS

**Chapter 1    Relationship and Development: Concepts, practice and research in person-centred work with children, adolescents and parents**
Michael Behr and Jeffrey H.D. Cornelius-White

The original play therapy theory of Axline (1947) has been basically extended in two ways. The term 'play therapy' today often includes diverse intervention methods from all humanistic, family, gestalt and other related approaches. Also, person-centred play therapy has been subsumed by a more complex, internationally influenced, theoretically integrative, person-centered child and adolescent facilitative work with adolescents, parents and families. Major developments include adjusted concepts for different disorders or client groups; an interactive concept for the therapist–client relationship; the integration of experiential and other approaches, and the development of parent trainings and programmes of relationship enhancement within the family. Also, substantial developments have occurred in educational and school settings, including the development of teacher attitudes and behaviour, theoretical models and research on learner-centred instruction and special education. Research confirms person-centred work to be effective in most domains. International associations, disorder-specific treatments, meta-analyses and major reviews are listed.

**Chapter 2    Effective Factors in Child and Adolescent Therapy: Considerations for a meta-concept**
Klaus Fröhlich-Gildhoff

Grawe's (1998, 2004) concept of a 'general' or 'common factors' psychotherapy is the most discussed meta-concept in adult psychotherapy. There is no comparable concept in child and adolescent therapy, and there are no systematic reflections on the Grawe concept from the person-centred perspective. The chapter summarises psychotherapy research and also shows initial results of a research project based on a large-scale, hermeneutic, qualitative analysis of videotaped therapy sessions. The paper asserts that the 'effective factors' of the Grawe research (activation of resources; support in problem-solving; clarification; process activation) are also relevant in child/adolescent therapy. It also suggests a fifth factor: the increase of skills or competencies. Successful therapies are based on a supportive, therapeutic relationship marked by the skilled 'juggling' of the effective factors in synchrony with the status of the patient's development and therapeutic process.

## Chapter 3    What Happens in Child-Centred Play Therapy?
Else Döring

Children's play is a vehicle for cognitive, emotional, and social development. Attachment theory supports this assertion and provides hints for child-centred psychotherapy. This paper offers further principles for play therapy beyond Axline's concepts and illustrates the principles with case examples.

## Chapter 4    Sexually Abused Children and Adolescents: A person-centred play therapy protocol
Dorothea Hüsson

For many children and adolescents, sexual abuse is a reality in their life. Of course, their trauma is brought into therapy sessions. In the context of the person-centred approach, special problems arise. Some children show signs of abuse in direct or indirect ways through play therapy. Some adolescents are able to address, directly, being abused. If children and adolescents are not able to face their abuse, if they cannot discuss or symbolise it in play, the therapist has to consider how to allow this topic its place in therapy. Another challenge is the therapeutic proceeding in the play therapy sessions; for example, how the therapist can interact when children make imitations of sexually violent acts in the role of the victim or the offender. Likewise, to protect the child, the therapist sometimes has to offer additional interventions. Several possible interventions are described. Topics like boundaries, guilt and secrets are dealt with in the therapeutic work with sexually abused children in a special empathic and careful way because they mostly represent an emotionally charged and fragile experience for the young people.

## Chapter 5    Freeing Children to Tell Their Stories: The utilisation of person-centred and experiential psychotherapy in child welfare investigations
Frances Bernard Kominkiewicz

The application of person-centred and experiential psychotherapy in child welfare investigations has not been thoroughly studied. This chapter addresses the conceptual formulation of person-centred therapy in the investigative process of the child's experience of maltreatment. As children begin to process their abuse during the investigative process, the focus can also be placed on their ability to begin healing through the utilisation of person-centred and experiential psychotherapeutic concepts.

## Chapter 6    Focusing Training for Adolescents with Low Self-Confidence and a Negative Self-Image
Erwin Vlerick

This programme teaches adolescents (aged 15–18) with little self-confidence and/or a negative self-image to use focusing in their daily lives. Starting from the core concepts of focusing – the finding of and listening to your felt sense and the listening to each other in a focusing way – the young people are invited to explore their own problems and to handle inner critics. They learn to be more connected with their feelings and to make use of them in daily situations. As a result, they develop their self-confidence, intuition and power to make good decisions. This chapter describes some of the ingredients of the programme. After an introduction of the working model and a description of the profile of the adolescents who followed the training, an overview of the training sessions is given. The chapter concludes with some results of the programme's evaluation.

### Chapter 7   Person-Centred Interventions with Violent Children and Adolescents
Klaus Fröhlich-Gildhoff

This chapter proposes a disorder-specific conceptualisation for person-centred therapeutic work with violent children and adolescents. The first part of the chapter summarises empirical results, exploring the causes of aggressive/violent behaviour, based on an integrated biopsychosocial explanation model fundamental for considerations of disorder-specific interventions. The second part of the chapter shows five central principles for an extension or specification of the person-centred approach in the work with the specific target group.

### Chapter 8   Peer Group Counselling: A person-centred and experiential treatment for stressed adolescents
Ulrike Bächle-Hahn

Peer group counselling is a highly structured treatment primarily for stressed and disadvantaged adolescents in residential programmes with roots in the ideas of a positive peer culture (Vorrath & Brendtro, 1985; Brendtro & Ness, 1983). This contribution gives an overview of the positive peer culture (PPC) tenets and describes the course of the peer group counselling (PGC) meetings at St. Augustinusheim with male adolescents (aged 12–20). As various therapeutic experiences with aggressive and violent adolescents show (Fröhlich-Gildhoff, 2006), giving structure is a necessary task in therapeutic contact and pedagogic settings with this clientele. Peer group counselling can be combined with person-centred work as a skill-acquisition approach. Adolescents benefit from counselling in various ways. They experience themselves as helpful to others, learn strategies to solve problems and conflicts while being helped and supported by others, and experience how it feels to trust and be trusted by others (Steinebach & Steinebach, 2007). PPC/PGC and person-centred education both have roots in basic beliefs of personal growth, unconditional positive regard and orientation, valuing the person's inherent resourcefulness.

### Chapter 9   The Effectiveness of Humanistic Counselling in UK Secondary Schools: Literature review
Mick Cooper

This paper summarises the findings of five recent studies that evaluate person-centred and humanistic counselling in UK secondary schools. Counselling was found to be associated with significant improvements in levels of psychological well-being, with around two-thirds of clients rating the service as moderately to very helpful. Both young people and teachers expressed high levels of satisfaction with the services. Improvements were greatest at the emotional and interpersonal level, with lowest levels of change at the behavioural level. The aspects of therapy cited by clients as most helpful were generally consistent with person-centred theory – having an opportunity to talk and be listened to, getting things off one's chest, and confidentiality – although some young people did cite guidance and advice as one of the most helpful aspects of their counselling. Children and young people expressed a preference for counselling that was one-to-one and based at their school.

## Chapter 10    Japanese Person-Centred School Counselling: Case studies with school non-attendees and Japanese-Koreans
Akira Kanazawa and Satoko Wakisaka

The chapter explains the stance and viewpoint which therapists are required to adopt in the work with children, parents and teachers in schools in Japan. It also refers to the importance of therapist intervention in school institutions with individuals and the importance of the acceptance of maladjusted students by school institutions. We discuss, with special attention, issues related to non-attendance and working with Japanese-Korean children and adolescents.

## Chapter 11    Reflections on Person-Centred Classroom Discipline
Bernie Neville

Teachers who identify themselves as student-centred may be confused or conflicted when confronted with issues of classroom control or classroom management. Carl Rogers' theory of personality and behaviour provides a framework for resolving this confusion. This chapter explores this framework in its concrete application to a 'difficult student', with a view to exploring the ways in which a student-centred teacher may resolve the paradox of 'person-centred control' theoretically and in practice.

## Chapter 12    The Use of the Person-Centred Approach for Parent–Teacher Communication: A qualitative study
Dagmar Hölldampf, Gernot Aich, Theresa Jakob and Michael Behr

This chapter discusses a person-centred approach to communication between parents and teachers based on a study of needs and problems in communication, as perceived in parent–teacher interviews and surveys. The study provides a qualitative content analysis using Mayring's method of semi-structured interviews with 17 teachers and 17 representatives of parents from 14 schools. The study focuses on the following: favourable conditions for conversations, problem-orientated strategies in the process of communication, power conflicts between parents and teachers, and the impact of the interview context and whether it is initiated by the parent or the teacher. The results suggest that teachers need to improve both their communication skills and adopt a more person-centred approach in parent–teacher dialogues.

## Chapter 13  The Dialogue between Teachers and Parents: Concepts and outcomes of communication training

Susanne Mühlhäuser-Link, Gernot Aich, Simone Wetzel, Georg Kormann and Michael Behr

This paper introduces and presents studies on a communication training especially developed for teachers and student teachers in parent–teacher conferences. The duration of the training is about 60 hours, and the aim is to improve the teachers' communication skills. The training is based on approaches of person-centred counselling, transactional analysis and systems theory. Study I analyses student teachers in an experimental setting on their improvement during the training. In Study II, the techniques of field studies are used to examine 14 professionally experienced teachers in real teacher–parent conferences. The evaluations show significant and relevant effects regarding the use of communication skills, as well as positive statements by the participating parents.

## Chapter 14  Can Person-Centred Encounter Groups Contribute to Improving Relationships and Learning in Academic Environments?

Renate Motschnig-Pitrik

Recent educational values encourage the development of attitudes and skills as a basis for knowledge development. This paper investigates how person-centred education, including encounter groups, structured workshops, and the use of new media for online communication, can contribute to significant, whole-person learning. We take an action-research view on an academic course on person-centred communication. Action research and a quantitative study on students' perceptions on the effects of the course confirmed that the vast majority of students learned significantly on the level of personal attitudes, social skills, and intellect. Likewise, their interpersonal relationships improved as a result of the course. Online communication and support played a considerable though not prominent role in students' learning.

## Chapter 15  Themes and Continuing Challenges in Person-Centred Work with Young People

Jeffrey H.D. Cornelius-White and Michael Behr

The editors invite critical evaluation of the contributions to this volume on person-centred work with young people. They identify four themes that weave throughout the contributions and leave room for further investigation: (1) exploring the question of the necessity, sufficiency, or optimality of the core conditions; (2) the perceived need for competency and skill development; (3) communication, compromise, and reciprocal contribution between people in varied contexts; and (4) evidence of the effectiveness of person-centred work with young people in educational, familial, therapeutic and other settings.

# FOREWORD

## BRIAN THORNE

In 2007 a report by UNICEF, the UN children's agency, published a survey which showed that UK schoolchildren were the unhappiest of 21 countries surveyed in the Western world. More recently, major research studies from Cambridge University expressed the same concern and spoke of a 'loss of childhood' among today's young people. The National Association of Head Teachers and the Association of Lecturers and Teachers have attacked the school curricula and there is a widespread lament from teachers, children and parents that the repeated insistence on constant testing is undermining the love of learning at all levels of education. The government's response to this flood of protest is to ignore it and to maintain that the majority of Britain's children are gloriously happy.

It was against this background that I read Michael Behr and Jef Cornelius-White's edited book on 'Facilitating Young People's Development'. It proved a splendid antidote to the prevailing gloom. In its pages I found encouraging evidence from four different continents of the dedicated efforts of person-centred practitioners to work effectively with children and young people and to bring hope and healing into lives which had already been badly damaged or were in danger of becoming grossly dysfunctional. The extent of this work is impressive as are the attempts to research and evaluate the outcomes of interventions with individuals, groups and even whole environments. Teachers and parents as well as the children themselves often feature in the projects discussed and there is an overall sense of purposefulness and of deep concern for the well-being of the world's future generations.

Carl Rogers would have been wholly delighted by the evidence of such endeavours. The first part of his professional life was spent working with adolescents and their families and his first book, published in 1939, was entitled *The Clinical Treatment of the Problem Child*. Many of his contemporaries considered him odd in the extreme to have devoted his energies for 12 years to such work when, in their view, he could have been profitably employed in a prestigious university and making his name in academia. Rogers, however, believed that his early experience as a child psychologist working for the Rochester Society for the Prevention of Cruelty to Children gave him the necessary grounding for the rest of his therapeutic work. It was also at Rochester that he learned the disciplined commitment to his clients and the endless patience which were to characterise the subsequent stages of his career. When later he turned his attention to the application of the person-centred approach to the classroom and to whole school systems it is not difficult to imagine that he was often reminded of the adolescents he had met at Rochester who had suffered not only from abusive families but also from schools which threatened to stifle children's spirits rather than liberating them.

If Rogers would be heartened to know that there are now those in the person-centred community whose primary concern it is to care for the children and young people of the world, he would perhaps be a little surprised at some of the methods which they deploy both in practice and research. For some readers this book will prove to be highly controversial, for many of its contributors unashamedly adopt a thoroughly pragmatic view of the mental health scene in their respective cultures and, while preserving what they believe to be a person-centred attitude to their work, they are at pains to incorporate ideas and practices from other traditions and to accept the need for diagnosis and for structured processes. For me, they most frequently achieve a creative compromise and there is little doubt of the beneficial results for their young clients. Rogers always stated that he was interested in 'what works' and in this respect he would assuredly be encouraged by much that is reported in these pages. Others may sniff treachery and a sell-out to a materialistic and driven culture interested only in cost-cutting and economic progress. This is a book, then, which will stir emotions. It will assuredly have its admirers but it may have its sceptics and even its detractors. What cannot be doubted is the determination of the contributors to make a difference. In a world which seems all too often to have capitulated to lassitude and a quiet despair, this book is a beacon of hope.

Brian Thorne
Norwich
March, 2008

# CHAPTER 1

# RELATIONSHIP AND DEVELOPMENT

## CONCEPTS, PRACTICE AND RESEARCH IN
## PERSON-CENTRED WORK WITH CHILDREN,
## ADOLESCENTS AND PARENTS

MICHAEL BEHR
JEFFREY H.D. CORNELIUS-WHITE

Rogers' (1959) theory of personality describes how a more or less congruent and healthy self emerges through a facilitative developmental process. Within this process, experiences of interpersonal relationships are viewed as the decisive condition for the welfare and development of young people and for the individual's strong, yet flexible, self-experience and awareness (Rogers, 1963). Within his theory of personality Rogers thus created, implicitly, a theory of both development and interpersonal relationships; unsurprisingly, his theory has evolved into more than a concept for working with adults.

For Rogers' colleagues, working with young people and their parents was a challenge from the beginning (Ellinwood, 1959/2005), which perhaps can be dated from the late 1940s with the publication of the significant books of Virginia Axline (about play therapy; 1947) and Dorothy Baruch (about education; 1949). Rogers' strong connection to the field of work with young people can be recognised in his personal development as a practitioner and researcher; he began his career as a psychologist in a child guidance clinic in Rochester, New York, where he worked for 12 years (Hinz & Behr, 2002; Kirschenbaum, 1979, 2007; Rogers, Cornelius-White & Cornelius-White, 2005) and, as far as we know, he mainly worked with parents and adolescents during this time, especially diagnostically (Rogers, 1939). The origins of the person-centred framework thus naturally show a unique fit with practice, concepts and research about young people, parents, education and school.

In this article we will give an overview of the diverse branches, concepts, developments and research which have emerged since then. Criteria for inclusion are references to a humanistic understanding of the person and of personal development, meaning mainly that self-directed self-exploration is regarded as a most significant factor of personal development, and a well-balanced, mainly non-directive interpersonal relationship based on the Rogerian core conditions (1957) is the most significant facilitating factor within this process.

# GAINING A COMPREHENSIVE VIEWPOINT
## ECLECTIC PLAY THERAPY AND PERSON-CENTRED PSYCHOTHERAPY WITH CHILDREN, ADOLESCENTS, PARENTS AND FAMILIES

Today, the original psychotherapeutic concept of Virginia Axline, which mainly focused on non-directive play therapy, has gained two extensional perspectives.

### THE USE OF PLAY

Play therapy has evolved from an orthodox basis of a non-directive approach. It mostly integrates ideas from humanistic concepts, including gestalt techniques, hypnotherapy, psychodrama, or sand-tray work. Eclectic concepts have numerous rationales of development, personality, disorder and/or health underlying their therapeutic ideas.

### EXTENDING THE RESPONSIBILITY OF THE THERAPIST

Play therapy is viewed as one part (or option) of working therapeutically with young people and families within the emerging person-centred framework. Adolescents, parents and families are frequently involved as well. Disorder-specific approaches have been developed. Overall, the person-centred therapist is usually the all-encompassing 'child and adolescent psychologist/counsellor'. Though integrative, this developing work is clearly based on the person-centred theory of personality, disorder and relationships. When extending the responsibility of the therapist towards the complete development of the young person within their family, home environment, school and supplemental social contacts, the therapist is the person who monitors all interventions and coordinates all helping initiatives in which the family is involved. The therapist is not just a play therapist: he or she is a professional responsible for providing holistic person-centred facilitation with children, adolescents, parents and families and several countries have accredited professions (with titles such as 'child and adolescent psychotherapist') that involve work with parents and families. Textbooks relevant to this subject have been written by Schmidtchen (2001b), Goetze (2002), Thompson (2007) and Weinberger (2005).

# MORE RESPONSIBILITY, COMPETENCE AND CHALLENGE FOR THE CHILD AND ADOLESCENT PSYCHOTHERAPIST

This development has led to an increase in responsibility and to a need for additional competencies in the child and adolescent psychotherapist – perhaps the most challenging of these being diagnosis. This is not merely a problem of technique and special competence – these can be trained. For the person-centred therapist, diagnosis offers a basic conceptual problem: for an approach that follows the fundamental idea that each individual's experience is unique and their perspective as valid as the therapist's, it may be regarded as a conceptual and practical violation to force a child's or family's problem into a diagnostic category and to be the person who defines this.

However, within today's micro-managed health-care system, an orthodox Rogerian (e.g. purist or classical) position, steadfastly refraining from a diagnosis that could potentially interfere with the unique progress in personal growth and gaining congruence, has mostly become unacceptable. Meanwhile, many person-centred therapists (almost all, in some countries, such as Germany) are convinced that their work on diagnosis or process considerations, leading to an adjusted design of therapeutic actions, is not only necessary to interact with health-care systems but likely to improve treatment without significantly interfering with self-directed growth; therefore, a considerable number of concepts and manuals for diagnosis within the person-centred paradigm have been created (Jürgens-Jahnert, 1997; Behr, Ruprecht, Aubele, Sonnentag & Jakob, 2004; Behr, 2006; Landreth & Bratton, 2005; Perry & Landreth, 2001; Schmidtchen, von Ondarza & Dahme, 1974; Schmidtchen, 1982, 1995).

A diagnosis, whether by the *International Classification of Disease* (*ICD-10*) (WHO, 1992), *Diagnostic and Statistical Manual* (*DSM-IV-TR*) (APA, 2000) or, more subtly, through levels of processing found in experiential approaches, is a prerequisite for client- and disorder-specific therapeutic action. Current health-care systems mostly demand the fit of diagnosis and therapeutic methods. Person-centred child and adolescent psychotherapy meets this demand with an array of specialised concepts, reflections or case studies about the person-centred way of understanding and healing for nearly every disorder listed in the *ICD-10*. For young people, the ICD categories (F80–89 Developmental Disorders and F90–98 Behavioural and Emotional Disorders) are generally used. The second and third category levels of F80–89 include: diverse language disorders, F80; developmental disabilities of school performance, F81; motoric disorders, F82; and autism, F84. The sublevels of F90–98 include: hyperkinesis, F90; conduct disorders, F91; combined disorder of conduct and emotions, F92; emotional disorders, F93; disorders of social functioning, mutism, attachment disorders, F94; tic disorders, F95; and other disorders, F98; anorexia and bulimia are coded under F50. Personality disorders and further disorders are also coded within the categories for adults.

In addition, consideration has been given to and concepts created for work with two groups of clients not listed in the ICD categories. Contributions in this volume include:

- traumatised and abused children (e.g. Hüsson, Chapter 4)
- young people from specific cultures outside the dominant culture of a country (e.g. Kanazawa & Wakisaka, Chapter 10).

Thus, a considerable amount of concept construction and research has been accomplished in the last 60 years. Person-centred play therapy has grown into a well-established and complete psychotherapeutic approach with wide potential to facilitate growth for a young person, including all social and environmental aspects. While the therapist has gained the potential to manage and coordinate this process, the person-centred child and adolescent psychotherapist often has to fight (through advocacy and research) for this position, especially when working with so-called multi-problem families and with multidisciplinary teams.

# STREAMS OF CONCEPTUAL DEVELOPMENT
## THE DIFFERENTIATION AND INTEGRATION OF METHODS

Within the work of the therapy room, we might distinguish four major areas of development:

1. The specialisation of methods according to client groups.
2. Handling the interpersonal relationship, including the alter-ego concept and interactive approach.
3. The combination or integration of person-centred child and adolescent psychotherapy with other major approaches or methods.
4. Training parents to be person-centred co-therapists or to build relationships with their children.

## 1. SPECIALISING METHODS ACCORDING TO CLIENT GROUPS

In addition to the already mentioned disorder-specific work (see Table 1, pp. 18–23), skills concepts have been developed according to client and age groups.

### DIFFERENTIATION OF PLAY AS A THERAPEUTIC MEDIUM
Through these developments, methods of play therapy have been greatly enriched – many salient concepts have been developed (e.g. Moustakas, 1959; Landreth, 2001, 2002; West, 1996; Goetze, 2002; Norton & Norton, 2002; Weinberger, 2005; Wilson & Ryan, 2006) and numerous publications offer eclectic listings of methods.

### PSYCHOTHERAPY WITH ADOLESCENTS
Axline's (1947) original approach did not exclude adolescents – nor did it address them explicitly – and it has been supplemented by contemporary concepts for working with young people (e.g. Sywulak, 1984; Monden-Engelhardt, 1997; Schmidtchen, 2003; Gallo-Lopez & Schaefer, 2005; Fehringer, 2006; Holzer, 2006; Weinberger & Papastefanou, 2008); a crucial development, since play therapy with adolescents must be mixed and modified in special ways.

### COUNSELLING PARENTS AND FAMILIES
For work with parents, concepts for a parallel counselling process have been developed (Behr, 2006; Crane, 2001; Ellinwood, 1959/2005; Fröhlich-Gildhoff, 2003; Killough-McGuire & McGuire, 2001), and concepts for person-centred work with families have also emerged (Anderson, 1989, 2001; Bott, 2001; Gaylin, 2001; McPherrin, 2005; Moon & Pildes, 2007; Levant, 1978; O'Leary, 1999; Raskin & van der Veen, 1970; Schmidtchen, 1991), supplemented by the creative concept of a family play therapy (Schaefer & Carey, 1994; Kemper, 1997). Beyond this, there are a number of innovative and well-evaluated manualised, preventive programmes (see below).

## GROUP PSYCHOTHERAPY

Again, Axline's (1947) original approach has been supplemented by concepts for working with groups (Ginott, 1961; Ehlers, 1981; Jenny, Goetschel, Käppler, Samson & Steinhausen, 2006; Landreth & Bratton, 2005; Landreth & Sweeney, 2001).

## 2. HANDLING THE INTERPERSONAL RELATIONSHIP

The classic client-centred concept for child therapy, developed by Virginia Axline (1947; Tausch & Tausch, 1956) is still of key importance. Although her book is already more than 60 years old, nearly everything it tells us is valid for the way we look at children today, including their need for space to unfold and the way adults should relate to them. Axline's fundamental principles – her respect for the child and their non-manipulated growth – remain relevant, especially regarding the ethics and the attitude of the adult person. The helping relationship that she outlines offers a lot of space for the child to develop freely. The child moves about in the playroom – he or she is free to choose and play *his or her* games. The therapist affirms, gives permission, refrains from judgemental comment by simply repeating, and in this way verbalising, the child's experience. Axline evokes the image of an accepting adult person sitting on a chair whilst observing very accurately what happens; a person who is present verbally and keeps a record on a notepad in the absence of electronic media. She only joins in the play or becomes more personally involved when the child explicitly invites her to do so. This therapy concept is based on the assumption of a change process in which congruence increases in a person through unconditional acceptance offered by the other person.

However, one client-centred therapy dimension missing from Axline's work is the explicitly focused 'here-and-now' relationship (Rogers, 1970; Carkhuff, 1969) between her and the child. The principle of non-directed self-development can be extended and applied in such a way that it will govern the immediate interactions; the negotiations about the way child and therapist play together. In the play sessions, the child often reproduces familiar relationship patterns as well as developing new ones. For this he or she uses different play media that go beyond language. In the interaction, the therapist uses the media the child chooses, thus offering verbal or non-verbal resonance by his or her own way of acting. While doing this, the therapist is empathic on the verbal level, is responsive, tunes in to the child's affects and, at times, mirrors what the child is doing – although not too *literally*. In both creativity and activity the therapist must try, as far as possible, not to 'go ahead' (Martin, 2000), as this could lessen unconditional empathy and inhibit the autonomy or self-direction of the child. Neither should the therapist remain too far behind the child as that could become boring and reduce the therapist's immediacy and presence.

For this form of relational engagement, Behr (2003, 2007a, 2007b) suggested the term 'interactive resonance'. Such a new construct seems to be useful here because already existing constructs like responsiveness, affect attunement, mirroring etc. only name partial aspects of play therapeutic interventions. Interactive resonance offers a more comprehensive and holistic description. Primarily, it represents an enhancement and a modification of the client-centred core condition: *empathy*. Interactive resonance, however, also has a lot to do with the *authenticity* of the therapist. In reaction to what the child does, the therapist acts and focuses on the relationship by showing him or herself as a person who is present and who gets personally involved in the relationship. Finke (1999) also explicated a similar approach within a person-centred relationship with the terms 'alter-ego relation' and 'interactive relationship approach'.

## 3. THE COMBINATION OR INTEGRATION OF PERSON-CENTRED, CHILD AND ADOLESCENT PSYCHOTHERAPY WITH OTHER MAJOR APPROACHES OR METHODS

The integration of additional approaches or methods often generates controversy amongst person-centred therapists about whether these are really necessary. The self-exploration process will occur anyway with a sufficient quality of contact offered by the therapist. Being process- or otherwise-directive means, to some therapists, not trusting in the actualising tendency. On the other hand, many therapists feel that certain ways of meeting young people's resources to express themselves fosters valuable steps forward without violating the paradigm of self-directed change. Obviously, these interventions require a conscientious therapist, operating clearly on a person-centred background and having high awareness for the source of change processes. A key question is: can person-centred psychotherapy maintain its identity if other interventions, based on another paradigm, are included?

### SYSTEMIC WORK WITH THE FAMILY

Although concepts for working with families have been developed within the person-centred approach (Anderson, 1989, 2001; Bott, 2001; Gaylin, 2001; McPherrin, 2005; Moon & Pildes, 2007; O'Leary, 1999; Raskin & van der Veen, 1970; Schmidtchen, 1991), it seems to fascinate therapists to meet the family under a systemic perspective and to perform a person-centred play therapy at the same time. One reason for this may be that both paradigms are grounded on a constructivist or non-linear position (Cornelius-White & Harbaugh, 2008; Cornelius-White & Kriz, 2008). Both approaches understand communication processes to be the decisive element for learning, development and mental well-being. Many intervention techniques of systemic origin seem to be creative and adequate to foster experiential processes which focus on interpersonal relations and on problem-solving strategies.

### INTEGRATING COGNITIVE BEHAVIOURAL INTERVENTIONS

Cognitive behavioural interventions offer the promise of a precise and quick approach to reducing symptoms. In many cases, this does seem to be helpful – although person-centred therapy works on a psycho-structural level at the same time. For example, in the case of school anxiety, a young client refuses to go to school; immediate action may have to be taken using behavioural techniques of desensitisation in order to reinstate school attendance. Problems of school absence could be abolished by this. Therapy on a psycho-structural level is also necessary in order to process incongruence and thus gain long-lasting effects. In other cases, therapists may hope that quick behavioural changes will foster new and constructive experiential processes within a basically person-centred therapy.

*FOSTERING EXPERIENTIAL PROCESSES OR SELF-EXPLORATION BY DIVERSE TECHNIQUES*

Diverse methods not primarily attributable to family systems, or cognitive behavioural paradigms are also integrated. Numerous eclectic collections of interventions, particularly from gestalt theory, offer innovative methods to accelerate and enhance the depth of experiences within play therapy and to meet the child's special constellation of problems (e.g. Blom, 2006; Geldard & Geldard, 2002, 2006; Norton & Norton, 2002). Other examples of the integration of diverse methods into person-centred work are: metaphorical stories (Goetze, 2001b); arts therapy (Groddeek, 1997); mototherapy (Kormann & Saur, 1997); hypnotherapy (Schmidtchen, 1996; Mrochen, Holtz & Trenkle, 2001); and medications (Sweeney & Ross, 2001). Additionally, valuable ideas are discussed in works by Schmidtchen (2001b), Weinberger (2005), and West (1996).

## 4. TRAINING PARENTS TO BE PERSON-CENTRED CO-THERAPISTS

Guerney (1964), and later the team of Landreth and colleagues (Bratton, Landreth, Kellam & Blackard, 2006; Landreth & Bratton, 2005), developed and evaluated (Bratton, Ray, Rhine & Jones, 2005) the unique and most promising concept of filial therapy (known more recently as 'child–parent relationship therapy'). In small groups, parents are taught (and supervised by recording) to reserve a 30-minute weekly time and space in their home to exclusively play with one child, often the most problematic one. They are trained to perform basic play therapy techniques and establish a person-centred relationship with their child. Outcome studies support the effectiveness of these interventions to a high degree.

The training of parents in a more preventive sense was also conceptualised under the terms 'relationship enhancement' (Ginsberg, 1997; Guerney, 1995; Guerney & Guerney, 1989) and 'parent effectiveness training' (Gordon, 1970); again, in outcome studies for both approaches, high effectiveness could be proved (see below).

# ELABORATED FIELDS OF WORK BEYOND PSYCHOTHERAPY

The basic transition from the person-centred paradigm developed by Axline (1947) and Baruch (1949), has spread to a considerable variety of applications and adjusted concepts. The following five fields can be distinguished:

- *Identifying effective teacher behaviour:* A major transition in educational and learning processes within schools has developed under the titles of person-centred (Rogers, 1969, 1983; Rogers & Freiberg, 1994) or learner-centred (APA, 1997; Cornelius-White & Harbaugh, in press; McCombs & Whisler, 1997; McCombs & Miller, 2006) education. Much empirical research has been performed in this area and, among many valuable projects, notable work has been done by Aspy and Roebuck (Aspy, 1972; Aspy & Roebuck, 1977) and by Anne-Marie and Reinhard Tausch (1998). A recent meta-analysis assessing the effects of person-centred teacher behaviour within 119 research projects and published in English and German was carried out by Cornelius-White (2007a) and showed that teachers who demonstrate Rogerian conditions – particularly empathy – and develop positive, facilitative teacher–student relationships, have beneficial effects on young people's emotional and social development as well as their performance in school. Student classroom participation, self-initiated learning and critical thinking are uniquely associated with learner-centred instruction as compared with more traditional, teacher-directed approaches (Cornelius-White, 2007; Cornelius-White & Harbaugh, in press).

- *Individual teacher training:* In a logical continuation from these findings, trainings have been established to enhance teachers' capacity to have person-centred relationships with young people. Again, amongst the many approaches, effective training programmes have been developed by Aspy and Roebuck (1974), relationship enhancement for a diversity of people and problems by Guerney (1977, 1982), by Gordon (1974), and more recently, McCombs & Miller (2006) and Cornelius-White & Harbaugh, in press. With his books and training programmes, Gordon translated person-centred ideas into very simple and comprehensible principles. These training programmes within the educational domain are among the best-evaluated training paradigms and have been meta-analysed (Müller, Hager & Heise, 2001).

- *General school programmes:* Further progress can be seen in the development of special programmes to enhance personal, educational and relational processes with strong reference to person-centred theory. Rogers himself conducted the Immaculate Heart System reforms (Kugelmann, 2005). Recently, special skills programmes for young people have been designed, for example, to enhance values (Kirschenbaum, 1994); emotional competencies (Bieg & Behr, 2005; Haynes & Avery, 1979); to work on certain problems, especially classroom management (Cornelius-White & Harbaugh, in press; Freiberg, 2007); and violence (Fröhlich-Gildhoff, 2006a, 2006b).

- *Special education:* Concepts and applications have also been developed in the domain of special education (Roebuck, Buhler & Aspy, 1976; Kremer, 1981; Goetze & Bretschneider, 1981; Pixa-Kettner, Ahrbeck, Scheibel & Tausch, 1978; Sywulak, 1984; Krause, 2002). However, this mainly applies to German language areas – in the English language world these concepts seem to be integrated under other headings.

- *Relationship enhancement:* At least three important and complex concepts can be identified concerning the parent–child relationship building: the relationship enhancement programmes from Guerney (1977, 1982); the books and trainings from Gordon, designed for family problems (1970); and the concept of filial or parent–child relationship therapy (Guerney, 1964; Goetze, 2001a; Landreth & Bratton, 2005). These humanistic approaches are amongst the best-articulated and researched paradigms for fostering child development, offering sophisticated interventions that touch the basic causes and structures of children's disorders and at the same time are structured, controlled and well evaluated.

# RESEARCH

Research fields within the person-centred orientation are:

- Psychotherapy outcome studies
- Psychotherapy process studies
- Psychotherapist intervention research
- Parent counselling research
- Evaluation of parent training programmes
- Evaluation of teacher training programmes
- Teacher behaviour studies
- Outcome studies in school or educational settings
- Programme evaluation in prevention or education

Here, we will only highlight some outstanding major syntheses of outcome research in the fields of child and adolescent psychotherapy and education. There are also several smaller meta-analyses, such as Cooper's (this volume) meta-analysis of five secondary-school counselling studies of person-centred therapy with adolescents in the UK, that combine subsets of relevant studies (e.g. parenting, family therapy) not discussed here.

Worldwide, eight major meta-analyses of the outcome of child and adolescent psychotherapy have been identified: Casey & Berman (1985), Weisz et al. (1987), Kazdin et al. (1990), Weisz et al. (1995), Ray et al. (2001), LeBlanc & Ritchie (2001), Beelman & Schneider (2003), and Bratton et al. (2005). The meta-analyses of Ray et al. (2001) and Bratton et al. (2005) are written by the same group of authors and have a large overlap in the studies analysed and methods used.

Seven of the major meta-analyses give differentiated scores for effect sizes on the level of major approaches. Table 2 (p. 23) reports these scores together with some basic information about the studies. It would not be appropriate to calculate an average effect size for each approach, as the method of generating the effect size score was similar to Cohen's $d$ but not identical. Only three studies highlight outcome research with parents or family as the angle of therapeutic efforts. The study of Beelman and Schneider (2003) reports a mean effect size score of .37 for four parent or family-oriented psychotherapy outcome studies stemming from different approaches. From comparison of 30 studies with parental involvement in each session compared to another 64 studies, Ray et al. (2001) found that 'Parental involvement was a significant predictor of play therapy outcomes ($p = .008$)' (p. 91). They also found an effect size of 1.06 from 27 filial therapy studies. The study of Bratton et al. (2005) reports a mean effect size score of 1.15 for 22 humanistic filial therapy outcome studies.

The table (p. 23) provides evidence of the clear effectiveness of both person-centred and cognitive behavioural approaches. The scores for behavioural psychotherapy are higher in the three oldest meta-analyses; one reason for this is the confound of measurement method and therapeutic rationale: scores generated via empirical quantitative measurement fit better with manifest behavioural therapeutic aims than with aims focusing on psycho-structural development. These older meta-analyses contain few studies of person-centred approaches and do not include many of the most recent, most scientific studies on humanistic play therapies, particularly parent–child relationship therapy that has proven to have the highest of efficacies. All of the meta-analyses are subject to researcher allegiance effects which have been shown to account for many of the differences in findings (e.g. Elliott, Greenberg & Lietaer, 2004), with the older ones generally having more allegiance to behavioural approaches and the newer ones to humanistic approaches.

In the field of education, a meta-analysis has been performed by Cornelius-White (2007a) including 1450 findings from 119 studies showing relevant correlations between person-centred teacher variables and student behaviour. The overall correlation for person-centred teacher variables with student cognitive outcomes was $r = .31$ (equivalent to $d = .65$); higher for critical/creative thinking $r = .45$, math achievement $r = .36$, verbal achievement $r = .34$; lower for science $r = .17$ and social science $r = .13$. The overall score for affective or behavioural student outcomes was $r = .35$ (equivalent to $d = .75$), higher for participation $r = .55$ and student satisfaction $r = .44$; lower for positive motivation $r = .32$, social skills $r = .32$, reducing disruptive behaviour $r = .25$, and reducing work avoidance motivation $r = .06$.

Thus, an array of empirical research supports the person-centred rationale in fostering all facets of growth within the helping relationship with young people.

## ASSOCIATIONS AND TRAINING FACILITIES

These associations (see p. 24) organise training as well as being politically involved; most organise conferences, edit or cooperate with professional journals, communicate with legal and/or health-care institutions and organise and/or oversee educational and training programmes. In the English language world, some even run book stores and sell therapy materials, offering an eclectic, instead of integrative, person-centred training.

## CONCLUSION

On the whole, the person-centred approach with children, adolescents, parents and families is well developed, with elaborated branches of diverse sub-concepts and institutions, and with research validation. At the same time, the global status of the approaches within government and insurance bodies is somewhat threatened, as developments (especially in Germany, the Netherlands, the UK and the USA) show. Although there is a rich variety of elaborated special concepts and although there are openings for combining person-centred work with other methods, the theoretical basis of facilitative relationships remains. The approach itself mainly competes with cognitive behavioural and psychodynamic paradigms which present a similar variety of sub-concepts. While, at research level, the person-centred approach in the domain of child and adolescent psychotherapy is well supported, there is much to do within the politics of health care and education where the situation is quite complicated. Therefore, coping with discrimination and accreditation problems is a matter of current concern in a number of countries.

## REFERENCES

American Psychological Association (1997) *Learner-Centered Psychological Principles.* Washington, DC: Author.

American Psychiatric Association (2000) *Diagnostic and Statistical Manual of Mental Disorders-IV-TR* (4th edn, text revision). Washington, DC: American Psychiatric Association.

Anderson, H (2001) Postmodern collaborative and person-centred therapies: What would Carl Rogers say? *Journal of Family Therapy, 23,* 339–60.

Anderson, WA (1989) Family therapy in the client-centered tradition. *Person-Centered Review, 4,* 295–307.

Aspy, DN (1972) *Toward a Technology for Humanizing Education.* Champaign, IL: Research Press.

Aspy, DN & Roebuck, FN (1974) From humane ideas to humane technology and back again many times. *Education, 95* (2), 163–71.

Aspy, DN & Roebuck, FN (1977) *Kids Don't Learn from People They Don't Like.* Amherst, MA: HRD Press.

Axline, VM (1947) *Play Therapy. The inner dynamics of childhood.* Boston: Houghton Mifflin.

Baruch, D (1949) *New Ways in Discipline.* New York: McGraw-Hill.

Beelmann, A & Schneider, N (2003) Wirksamkeit von Psychotherapie bei Kindern und Jugendlichen. Eine Übersicht und Meta-Analyse zum Bestand und zu Ergebnissen der deutschsprachigen Effektivitätsforschung [Outcome of psychotherapy with children and adolescents. A meta-analysis of German language outcome research]. *Zeitschrift für Klinische Psychologie und Psychotherapie, 32* (2), 129–43.

Behr, M (2003) Interactive resonance in work with children and adolescents – A theory-based concept of interpersonal relationship through play and the use of toys. *Person-Centered and Experiential Psychotherapies, 2* (2), 89–103.

Behr, M (2006) Beziehungszentrierter Erstkontakt in der heilpädagogischen und psychotherapeutischen Arbeit mit Kindern, Jugendlichen und Familien [Relationship-centred initial contact with children, adolescents and families in special education and psychotherapy settings]. *Person, 11* (2), 108–17.

Behr, M (2007a) Gesprächspsychotherapie mit Kindern und Jugendlichen – Spieltherapeutische Konzepte und Praxis eines personzentriert-interaktionellen Vorgehens [Person-centred psychotherapy with children and adolescents – Play-therapy concepts and practice of a person-centred interactional work]. In J Kriz & T Slunecko (Hrsg) *Gesprächspsychotherapie – Die therapeutische Vielfalt der personzentrierten Ansatzes* (pp. 151–64). Wien: Facultas wuv UTB.

Behr, M (2007b) Interactieve speltherapie en orthopedagogie – over 'interactieve resonantie' als theoriegebonden concept voor de communicatie via spelen en speelgoed [Interactive play therapy and special education – about interactive resonance as a theory-based concept for communication through play and the use of toys]. *Tijdschrift Clientgerichte Psychotherapie 45* (2), 20–34.

Behr, M, Ruprecht, T, Aubele, S, Sonnentag, G & Jakob, N (2004) Diagnostik von Empathie-Fähigkeiten bei Kindern und Jugendlichen – Zusammenhänge mit emotionalen Störungen und prosozialem Verhalten [Diagnosis of empathy skills of children and adolescents – correlations with emotional disorders and prosocial behaviour]. In W Bos, EM Lankes, K Schwippert & N Plaßmeier (Hrsg) *Heterogenität* (pp. 1–12). Münster: Waxmann.

Bieg, S & Behr, M (2005) *Mich und Dich verstehen – Gefühle erkennen, Andere verstehen, Angst bewältigen. Emotionale Sensitivität für 7 bis 12 jährige – Ein manualisiertes und evaluiertes Programm für Schule und Pädagogik* [Understanding Me and You – Being aware of emotions, understanding others, coping with fear. Emotional sensitivity for 7 to 12-year-olds: A manualized and evaluated programme for school and education]. Göttingen: Hogrefe.

Blom, R (2006) *The Handbook of Gestalt Play Therapy: Practical guidelines for child therapists.* London: Jessica Kingsley.

Bott, D (2001) Client-centred therapy and family therapy: A review and commentary. *Journal of Family Therapy, 23,* 361–77.

Bratton, SC, Ray, D, Rhine, T & Jones, L (2005) The efficacy of play therapy with children: A meta-analytic review of treatment outcomes. *Professional Psychology: Research and Practice, 36* (4), 376–90.

Bratton, SC, Landreth, G, Kellam, T & Blackard, S (2006) *Child Parent Relationship Therapy (CPRT) Treatment Manual: A 10-session filial therapy model for training parents.* New York: Routledge.

Carkhuff, R (1969) *Helping and Human Relations. Vol.I. Selection and training.* New York: Holt, Rinehart and Winston.

Carkhuff, R (1969). *Helping and Human Relations. Vol.II. Practice and research.* New York: Holt, Rinehart and Winston.

Casey, RJ & Bermann, JS (1985) The outcome of psychotherapy with children. *Psychological Bulletin, 98,* 388–400.

Cornelius-White, JHD (2007a) Learner-centered teacher–student relationships are effective: A meta-analysis. *Review of Educational Research, 77* (1), 1–31.

Cornelius-White, JHD (2007b) Leading a good life: The evolving paradigm from the PCE 2006 keynote addresses. *Person-Centered and Experiential Psychotherapies, 6* (1), 61–71.

Cornelius-White, JHD & Harbaugh, AP (2008) Learner-centered instruction: Building relationships for student success. Thousandoak, CA: Sage.

Cornelius-White, JHD & Kriz, J (2008) The Formative Tendency: Person-centred systems theory, interdependence and human potential. In B Levitt (Ed) *Reflections on Human Potential: Bridging the person-centered approach and positive psychology* (pp. 116–30). Ross-on-Wye: PCCS Books.

Crane, J (2001) The parents' part in the play-therapy process. In GL Landreth (Ed) *Innovations in Play Therapy: Issues, process, and special populations* (pp. 83–95). Philadelphia, PA: Brunner-Routledge.

Ehlers, B (1981) Die personenzentrierte Gruppentherapie mit Kindern [Person-centered group psychotherapy with children]. In H Goetze (Hrsg) *Personenzentrierte Spieltherapie* (pp. 44–63). Göttingen: Hogrefe.

Ellinwood, C (1959/2005) Some observations from work with parents in a child therapy program. *The Person-Centered Journal, 12,* 33–49.

Elliott, R, Greenberg, LS & Lietaer, G (2004) Research on experiential psychotherapies. In MJ Lambert (Ed) *Bergin and Garfield's Handbook of Psychotherapy and Behavior Change* (5th edn) (pp. 493–540). New York: Wiley.

Fehringer, C (2006) Ja, so ist die Jugend heute, schrecklich sind die jungen Leute. (W Busch) Personzentrierte Psychotherapie mit Jugendlichen [Yes, such is youth today; these young people are dreadful. Person-centred psychotherapy with adolescents]. *Person, 11* (2), 176–86.

Finke, J (1999) *Beziehung und Intervention* [Relationship and Intervention]. Stuttgart: Thieme.

Freiberg, J (2007) A Person-Centered Approach to Classroom Management: How and why it makes a difference. Paper presented at the Annual American Educational Research Association conference, Chicago, IL.

Fröhlich-Gildhoff, K (2003) Bezugspersonenarbeit im Rahmen der personzentrierten Psychotherapie mit Jugendlichen [Working with parents within person-centred psychotherapy with adolescents]. In C Boeck-Singelmann, B Ehlers, T Hensel, F Kemper & C Monden-Engelhardt (Hrsg) *Personzentrierte Psychotherapie mit Kindern und Jugendlichen, Bd. 3: Störungsspezifische Falldarstellungen* (pp. 293–326). Göttingen: Hogrefe.

Fröhlich-Gildhoff, K (2006a) *Gewalt begegnen – Konzepte und Projekte zur Prävention und Intervention.* [Surrender Violence – Concepts and projects for prevention and Intervention]. Stuttgart: Kohlhammer.

Fröhlich-Gildhoff, K (2006b) *Freiburger Anti-Gewalt-Training (FAGT) – Konzept, Manual, Evaluation* [Freiburg Anti-Violence Training – Concept, manual, evaluation]. Stuttgart: Kohlhammer.

Gallo-Lopez, L & Schaefer, CE (Eds) (2005) *Play Therapy with Adolescents.* Lanham, MD: Rowman & Littlefield.

Gaylin, N (2001) *Family, Self and Psychotherapy: A person-centered perspective.* Ross-on-Wye: PCCS Books.

Geldard, K & Geldard, D (2002) *Counselling Children – A practical introduction* (2nd edn). London: Sage.

Geldard, K & Geldard, D (2006) *Counselling Adolescents* (2nd edn). London: Sage.

Ginott, H (1961) *Group Psychotherapy with Children: The theory and practice of play therapy.* New York: McGraw-Hill.

Ginsberg, BG (1997) *Relationship Enhancement Family Therapy.* New York: John Wiley and Sons.

Goetze, H (2001a) Filialtherapie. *Sonderpädagogik, 31* (2), 94–101.

Goetze, H (2001b) Metaphorical stories. In H Kaduson & C Schaefer (Eds) *101 More Favourite Play Therapy Techniques* (pp. 29–36). Northvale, NJ: Jason Aronson.

Goetze, H (2002) *Handbuch der personenzentrierten Spieltherapie* [Handbook of Person-Centred Play Therapy]. Göttingen: Hogrefe.

Goetze, H & Bretschneider, C (1981) Personenzentrierte Spieltherapie in der Sonderschule [Person-centred play therapy in special-education schools]. In H Goetze (Hrsg) *Personenzentrierte Spieltherapie* (pp. 131–48). Göttingen: Hogrefe.

Gordon, T (1970) *Parent Effectiveness Training.* New York: Wyden.

Gordon, T (1974) *T.E.T. Teacher Effectiveness Training.* New York: Wyden.

Groddeck, N (1997) Klientenzentrierte Kunsttherapie mit Kindern und Jugendlichen [Client-centred art therapy with children and adolescents]. In C Boeck-Singelmann, B Ehlers, T Hensel, F Kemper & C Monden-Engelhardt (Hrsg) *Personzentrierte Psychotherapie mit Kindern und Jugendlichen, Bd. 2: Anwendung und Praxis* (pp. 269–312). Göttingen: Hogrefe.

Guerney, BG, Jr (1964) Filial therapy: Description and rationale. *Journal of Consulting Psychology, 28* (4), 303–10.

Guerney BG, Jr (1977) *Relationship Enhancement: Skill-training programs for therapy, problem prevention, and enrichment.* San Francisco: Jossey-Bass.

Guerney, BG, Jr (1982) Relationship enhancement. In EK Marshall & PD Kurtz (Eds) *Interpersonal Helping Skills* (pp. 482–518). San Francisco: Jossey-Bass.

Guerney, L (1995) *Parenting: A skills training manual* (5th edn). North Bethesda, MD: IDEALS.

Guerney, L & Guerney, BG, Jr (1989) Child relationship enhancement family therapy and parent education. *Person-Centered Review, 4* (3), 344–57.

Haynes, LA & Avery, AW (1979) Training adolescents in self-disclosure and empathy skills. *Journal of Counseling Psychology, 26* (6), 526–30.

Hinz, A & Behr, M (2002) Biografische Rekonstruktionen und Reflexionen – Zum 100. Geburtstag von Carl Rogers [Biographic Reconstructions and Reflexions – 100 years of Carl Rogers]. *Gesprächspsychotherapie und Personzentrierte Beratung, 33* (3), 197–210.

Holzer, A (2006) Jugendliche in der Personzentrierten Psychotherapie. Eine Reflexion der Praxis. [Adolescents in person-centered psychotherapy. A reflexion of practice]. *Person, 11* (2), 164–75.

Jenny, B, Goetschel, P, Käppler, C, Samson, B, Steinhausen, H-C (2006) Personzentrierte Gruppentherapie mit Kindern: Konzept, Vorgehen und Evaluation [Person-centred group therapy with children: Concept, method and evaluation]. *Person, 11* (2), 93–107.

Jürgens-Jahnert, S (1997) Therapieeinleitung und Diagnostik in der personzentrierten Psychotherapie mit Kindern und Jugendlichen: einige theoretische Überlegungen und praktische Anregungen [Therapy initiation and diagnosis in person-centred psychotherapy with children and adolescents: Some theoretical considerations and practical suggestions]. In C Boeck-Singelmann, B Ehlers, T Hensel, F Kemper & C Monden-Engelhardt (Hrsg) *Personzentrierte Psychotherapie mit Kindern und Jugendlichen, Bd. 2: Anwendung und Praxis* (pp. 225–52). Göttingen: Hogrefe.

Kazdin, AE, Bass, D, Ayres, WA & Rodgers, A (1990) Empirical and clinical focus of child and adolescent psychotherapy research. *Journal of Consulting and Clinical Psychology, 58,* 729–40.

Kemper, F (1997) Personzentrierte Familienspieltherapie – am Beispiel einer Familie mit einem zähneknirschenden Knaben [Person-centred family play therapy – Exemplified by a family with a boy who grinds his teeth]. In C Boeck-Singelmann, B Ehlers, T Hensel, F Kemper & C Monden-Engelhardt (Hrsg) *Personzentrierte Psychotherapie mit Kindern und Jugendlichen, Bd. 2: Anwendung und Praxis* (pp. 71–134). Göttingen: Hogrefe.

Killough-McGuire, D & McGuire, D (2001) *Linking Parents to Play Therapy – A practical guide with applications, interventions, and case studies.* Philadelphia, PA: Brunner-Routledge.

Kirschenbaum, H (1979) *On Becoming Carl Rogers.* New York: Delacorte.

Kirschenbaum, H (1994) *100 Ways to Enhance Values and Morality in Schools and Youth Settings.* Boston: Allyn and Bacon.

Kirschenbaum, H (2007) *The Life and Work of Carl Rogers.* Ross-on-Wye: PCCS Books.

Kormann, G & Saur, B (1997) Personzentrierte Mototherapie mit verhaltensauffälligen Kindern [Person-centred mototherapy with the problem child]. In C Boeck-Singelmann, B Ehlers, T Hensel, F Kemper & C Monden-Engelhardt (Hrsg) *Personzentrierte Psychotherapie mit Kindern und Jugendlichen, Bd. 2: Anwendung und Praxis* (pp. 313–30). Göttingen: Hogrefe.

Kraft, A & Landreth, G (1998) *Parents as Therapeutic Partners.* Northvale, N.J: Jason Aronson.

Krause, MP (2002) *Gesprächspsychotherapie und Beratung mit Eltern behinderter Kinder* [Person-Centred Psychotherapy with Parents of Disabled Children]. München: Reinhard.

Kremer, JW (1981) Erfahrungen in der personenzentrierten Spieltherapie mit körperbehinderten Kindern [Experiences in person-centred play therapy with disabled children]. In H Goetze (Hrsg) *Personenzentrierte Spieltherapie* (pp. 109–30). Göttingen: Hogrefe.

Kriz, J (2007) Actualizing tendency: The link between person-centered and experiential psychotherapy and interdisciplinary systems theory. *Person-Centered and Experiential Psychotherapies, 6* (1), 30–44.

Kugelmann, R (2005) An encounter between psychology and religion: Humanistic psychology and the Immaculate Heart of Mary nuns. *Journal of the History of the Behavioral Sciences, 41*(4), 347–65.

Landreth, GL (Ed) (2001) *Innovations in Play Therapy: Issues, process, and special populations.* Philadelphia, PA: Brunner-Routledge.

Landreth, GL (2002) *Play Therapy: The art of the relationship* (2nd edn). New York: Brunner-Routledge.

Landreth, GL & Sweeney, DS (2001) Child-centered group play therapy. In GL Landreth (Ed) *Innovations in Play Therapy* (pp. 181–202). New York: Brunner-Routledge.

Landreth, GL & Bratton, S (2005) *Child Parent Relationship Therapy (CPRT): A 10-session filial therapy model.* New York: Routledge.

LeBlanc, M & Ritchie, M (2001) A meta-analysis of play therapy outcomes. *Counselling Psychology Quarterly, 14* (2), 149–63.

Levant, RF (1978) Family therapy: A client-centered perspective. *Journal of Marital and Family Therapy, 4* (2), 35–42.

Martin, DG (2000) *Counseling and Therapy Skills* (2nd edn). Prospect Heights, IL: Waveland Press.

McCombs, BL & Whisler, JS (1997) *The Learner-Centered Classroom and School.* San Francisco: Jossey-Bass.

McCombs, BL & Miller J (2006) *Learner-Centered Classroom Practices and Assessments.* Thousand Oaks, CA: Corwin.

McPherrin, J (2005) Client-centered family and couple therapy: A retrospective and a practitioner's guide. In B Levitt (Ed) *Embracing Non-directivity: Reassessing person-centered theory and practice in the 21ˢᵗ century* (pp. 303–13). Ross-on-Wye: PCCS Books.

Monden-Engelhardt, C (1997) Zur personzentrierten Psychotherapie mit Jugendlichen [Person-centered psychotherapy with adolescents]. In C Boeck-Singelmann, B Ehlers, T Hensel, F Kemper & C Monden-Engelhardt (Hrsg) *Personzentrierte Psychotherapie mit Kindern und Jugendlichen, Bd. 2: Anwendung und Praxis* (pp. 9–70). Göttingen: Hogrefe.

Moon, K & Pildes, S (2007) 'Automatic for the People': The practice of client-centered couple and family therapy. Manuscript submitted for publication.

Moustakas, C (1959) *Psychotherapy with Children: The living relationship.* New York: Ballantine Books.

Mrochen, S, Holtz, KL & Trenkle, B (2001) *Die Pupille des Bettnässers - Hypnotherapeutische Arbeit mit Kindern und Jugendlichen* (5. Auflage) [The Pupil of Enuresis: Hypnotherapeutic work with children and adolescents]. Heidelberg: Auer.

Müller, CT, Hager, W & Heise, E (2001) Zur Effektivität des Gordon-Eltern-Trainings (PET) – eine Meta-Evaluation [Effectiveness of the PET – A meta-evaluation]. *Gruppendynamik und Organisationsberatung, Zeitschrift für angewandte Sozialpsychologie, 3,* 339–64.

Norton, CC & Norton, BE (2002) *Reaching Children Through Play Therapy: An experiential approach* (2nd edn). Denver, CO: The Publishing Cooperative.

O'Leary, C (1999) *Counselling Couples and Families – A person-centred approach.* London: Sage.

Perry, LH & Landreth, GL (2001) Diagnostic assessment of children's play-therapy behavior. In GL Landreth (Ed) *Innovations in Play Therapy* (pp. 155–78). New York: Brunner-Routledge.

Pixa-Kettner, U, Ahrbeck, B, Scheibel, B & Tausch, AM (1978). Personenzentrierte Gruppen- und Einzelgespräche mit psychisch beeinträchtigten Hauptschülern aus 5/6. Klassen [Person-centred, group and individual counselling with low-achieving problem students]. *Zeitschrift für Klinische Psychologie, 7,* 28–40.

Raskin, NJ & van der Veen, F (1970) Client-centered family therapy: Some clinical and research perspectives. In JE Hart & TM Tomlinson (Eds) *New Directions in Client-Centered Therapy* (pp. 387–406). Boston: Houghton Mifflin.

Ray, D, Bratton, S, Rhine, T & Jones, L (2001) The effectiveness of play therapy: Responding to the critics. *International Journal of Play Therapy, 10* (1), 85–108.

Roebuck, FN, Buhler, JH & Aspy, DN (1976) A comparison of high and low levels of humane teaching/learning conditions on the subsequent achievement of students identified as having learning difficulties (Final Report No. PLD-6816-76-rc). Washington, DC: National Consortium for Humanizing Education, National Institute of Mental Health, US Department of Health, Education, and Welfare.

Rogers, CR (1939) *The Clinical Treatment of the Problem Child.* Boston: Houghton Mifflin.

Rogers, CR (1957) The necessary and sufficient conditions of therapeutic personality change. *Journal of Consulting Psychology, 21,* 95–103.

Rogers, CR (1959) A theory of therapy, personality and interpersonal relationships, as developed in the client-centered framework. In S Koch (Ed) *Psychology: The study of a science, Vol. III Formulations of the person and the social context* (pp. 184–256). New York: McGraw-Hill.

Rogers, CR (1963) The concept of the fully-functioning person. *Psychotherapy: Theory, Research and Practice, 1,* 17–26.

Rogers, CR (1969) *Freedom to Learn.* Columbus, OH: Charles Merrill.

Rogers, CR (1970) *On Encounter Groups.* New York: Harper and Row.

Rogers, CR (1983) *Freedom to Learn for the 80s.* Columbus, OH: Charles Merrill.

Rogers, CR, Cornelius-White, JHD & Cornelius-White, CF (2005) Reminiscing and predicting: Rogers' 'Beyond Words' speech and commentary. *Journal of Humanistic Psychology, 45,* 383–96.

Rogers, CR & Freiberg, J (1994) *Freedom to Learn* (3rd edn). New York: Charles Merrill.

Schaefer CE & LJ Carey (Eds) (1994) *Family Play Therapy,* Northvale, NJ: Jason Aronson, Inc.

Schmidtchen, S (1982) Diagnostik in der Kinderpsychotherapie [Diagnosis in child psychotherapy]. In ME Zielke (Hrsg) *Diagnostik in der Psychotherapie* (pp. 127–45). Stuttgart: Kohlhammer.

Schmidtchen, S (1991) *Klientenzentrierte Spiel- und Familientherapie* (3. Aufl) [Client-Centered Play- and Family therapy]. Weinheim: PVU.

Schmidtchen, S (1995) Klientenzentrierte Ätiologie und Diagnostik von psychischen Erkrankungen im Kindesalter [Client-centered etiology and diagnosis of mental illness in children]. In S Schmidtchen, GW Speierer & H Linster (Hrsg) *Die Entwicklung der Person und ihre Störung, Bd. 2* (pp. 181–228).

Schmidtchen, S (1996) Die Spieltherapie als indirektes Hypnoseverfahren für Kinder und Erwachsene [Play therapy as indirect hypnotherapy for children and adults]. *Hypnose und Kognition. 13* (1–2), 51–66.

Schmidtchen, S (2001a) *Allgemeine Psychotherapie für Kinder, Jugendliche und Familien: ein Lehrbuch* [General Psychotherapy for Children, Adolescents and Families: A textbook]. Stuttgart: Kohlhammer.

Schmidtchen, S (2001b) Effektivitätsverbesserung durch prozessleitende Hilfen – Neue Wege in der klientenzentrierten Psychotherapie für Kinder, Jugendliche und Familien [Effectiveness enhancement via process-directive interventions – New ways in client-centred psychotherapy for children, adolescents and families]. In I Langer (Hrsg) *Menschlichkeit und Wissenschaft. Festschrift zum 80. Geburtstag von Reinhard Tausch* (pp. 291–324). Köln: GWG-Verlag.

Schmidtchen, S (2003) Plädoyer für eine eigenständige Jugendlichentherapie [Plea for a special psychotherapy for adolescents]. In H-P Michels & M Borg-Laufs (Hrsg) *Schwierige Zeiten. Beiträge zur Psychotherapie mit Jugendlichen* (pp. 27–49). Tübingen: DGVT Deutsche Gesellschaft für Verhaltenstherapie.

Schmidtchen, S, von Ondarza, G & Dahme, B (1974) Factor analytic research of behavioral disorders of children. *Praxis der Kinderpsychologie und Kinderpsychiatrie, 23* (7), 270–76.

Sweeney, DS & Ross, JT (2001) What the play therapist needs to know about medication. In GL Landreth (Ed) *Innovations in Play Therapy* (pp. 51–63). New York: Brunner-Routledge.

Sywulak, AE (1984) Creating a whole atmosphere in a group home for retarded adolescents. *Academic Psychology Bulletin Vol. 6,* November, (pp. 325–7).

Tausch, R & Tausch, A-M (1956) *Kinderpsychotherapie im nicht-direktiven Verfahren* [Non-directive Child Psychotherapy]. Göttingen: Hogrefe.

Tausch, R & Tausch, A-M (1998) *Erziehungspsychologie* (10. Auflage) [Educational Psychology]. Göttingen: Hogrefe.

Thompson, C (2007) *Counseling Children* (7th edn). New York: Brooks/Cole.

Wagner, AC (1976) *Schülerzentrierter Unterricht.* [Student-Centred Instruction.] München: Urban und Schwarzberger.

Weinberger, S (2005) *Kindern spielend helfen* (2. Auflage)[Helping Children Through Play]. Weinheim: Beltz.

Weinberger, S & Papastefanou, C (2008) *Wege durchs Labyrinth: Personzentrierte Beratung und Psychotherapie mit Jugendlichen* [Ways Through the Labyrinth: Person-centred counselling and psychotherapy with adolescents]. Weinheim: Juventa.

Weisz, JR, Weiss, B, Alicke, MD & Klotz, ML (1987) Effectiveness of psychotherapy with children and adolescents: A meta-analysis for clinicians. *Journal of Consulting and Clinical Psychology, 55,* 542–9.

Weisz, JR, Weiss, B, Han, S, Granger, DA & Morton, T (1995). Effects of psychotherapy with children and adolescents: A meta-analysis of treatment outcome studies. *Psychological Bulletin, 117,* 450–68.

West, J (1996) *Child-Centred Play Therapy* (2nd edn). London: Arnold.

Wilson, K & Ryan, V (2006) *Play Therapy: A non-directive approach for children and adolescents* (2nd edn). St. Louis, MO: Elsevier Publishing.

World Health Organisation (1992) *The ICD-10 Classification of Mental and Behavioural Disorders.* Geneva: World Health Organization.

*Table 1*
Overview of selected disorder-specific concepts within the person-centred framework

---

**F3 Affective disorders/Depression**

Birmaher, B, Brent, DA, Klolko, D, Baugher, M, Bridge, J, Holder, D, et al. (2000) Clinical outcome after short-term psychotherapy for adolescents with major depressive disorders. *Archives of General Psychiatry, 57* (1), 29–36.

Ehlers, T (2002) Das Konzept einer globalen emotional bedingten Entwicklungsstörung und der personzentrierte Ansatz der Spieltherapie. In C Boeck-Singelmann, B Ehlers, T Hensel, F Kemper & C Monden-Engelhardt (Hrsg) *Personzentrierte Psychotherapie mit Kindern und Jugendlichen, Bd. 1: Grundlagen und Konzepte* (2. Auflage) (pp. 81–93). Göttingen: Hogrefe.

Hockel, C (2002) Das Spielerleben als Entwicklungsraum – mit einem Fall von Depression im Kindesalter. In C Boeck-Singelmann, B Ehlers, T Hensel, F Kemper & C Monden-Engelhardt (Hrsg) *Personzentrierte Psychotherapie mit Kindern und Jugendlichen, Bd. 1: Grundlagen und Konzepte* (2. Auflage) (pp. 211–35). Göttingen: Hogrefe.

Robinson, LA, Berman, JS & Neimeyer, RA (1990) Psychotherapy for the treatment of depression: A comprehensive review of controlled outcome research. *Psychological Bulletin, 108* (1), 30–49.

**F20 Schizophrenia**

Landreth, GL et al. (2005) *Therapy Interventions with Children's Problems: Case studies with DSM-IV-TR diagnoses* (2nd edn). Lanham, MD: Jason Aronson.

**F42 Obsessive compulsive disorders**

Hockel, C (2003) Angstbewältigung und ein Fall von Zwangserkrankung im Jugendalter. In C Boeck-Singelmann, B Ehlers, T Hensel, F Kemper & C Monden-Engelhardt (Eds) *Personzentrierte Psychotherapie mit Kindern und Jugendlichen, Bd. 3: Störungsspezifische Falldarstellungen* (pp. 203–36). Göttingen: Hogrefe.

**F43 Adjustment disorders**

Hollritt, D (2003) 'Am liebsten würde ich alles wieder gut machen': Personzentrierte Spieltherapie mit einem fünfjährigen Mädchen mit Anpassungsstörung nach Trennung der Eltern. In C Boeck-Singelmann, B Ehlers, T Hensel, F Kemper & C Monden-Engelhardt (Hrsg) *Personzentrierte Psychotherapie mit Kindern und Jugendlichen, Bd. 3: Störungsspezifische Falldarstellungen* (pp. 7–40). Göttingen: Hogrefe.

**F43 Adjustment disorders with somatic disorders**

Brandt, MA (2001) An investigation of the effectiveness of play therapy with young children. University of North Texas, *Dissertations Abstracts International, 61*, 7-A.

Kremer, JW (1981) Erfahrungen in der personenzentrierten Spieltherapie mit körperbehinderten Kindern. In H Goetze (Hrsg) *Personenzentrierte Spieltherapie* (pp. 109–30). Göttingen: Hogrefe.

Murphy Jones, E (2001) Play therapy for children with chronic illness. In GL Landreth (Ed) *Innovations in Play Therapy* (pp. 271–88). New York: Brunner-Routledge.

Sabrowski, S & Grützner, W (2003) Personzentrierte Psychotherapie bei einem Kind mit Hutchinson-Gilford Progerie. In C Boeck-Singelmann, B Ehlers, T Hensel, F Kemper & C Monden-Engelhardt (Hrsg) *Personzentrierte Psychotherapie mit Kindern und Jugendlichen, Bd. 3: Störungsspezifische Falldarstellungen* (pp. 105–32). Göttingen: Hogrefe.

Smith, NR (2002) A comparative analysis of intensive filial therapy with intensive play therapy and intensive sibling group play therapy, with child witnesses of domestic violence. University of

North Texas, *Dissertations Abstracts International. 62*, 7-A.

VanFleet, R (2000) Short-term play therapy for families with chronic illness. In HG Kaduson & CE Schaefer (Eds) *Short-Term Play Therapy for Children*, (pp. 175–193). New York: Guilford.

Wolff, G (1981) Personenzentrierte psychologische Betreuung lebensbedrohlich erkrankter Kinder und ihrer Familien. In H Goetze (Hrsg) *Personenzentrierte Spieltherapie* (pp. 95–108). Göttingen: Hogrefe.

### F44 Dissociative disorders

Corboz, RJ (1980) Die stationäre Behandlung neurotischer Störungen im Kindesalter. Ergebnisse von 100 Katamnesen. *Zeitschrift für Kinder- und Jugendpsychiatrie, 8*, 377–94.

Klein, JW, Landreth, GL (2001) Play therapy with dissociative identity disorder clients with child alters. In GL Landreth (Ed) *Innovations in Play Therapy* (pp. 323–33). New York: Brunner-Routledge.

Landreth, GL et al. (2005*) Therapy Interventions with Children's Problems: Case studies with DSM-IV-TR diagnoses* (2nd edn). Lanham, MD: Jason Aronson.

### F50 Eating disorders

Petersen, H (2003) Psychogener Appetitverlust. In C Boeck-Singelmann, B Ehlers, T Hensel, F Kemper & C Monden-Engelhardt (Hrsg) *Personzentrierte Psychotherapie mit Kindern und Jugendlichen, Bd. 3: Störungsspezifische Falldarstellungen* (pp. 257–92). Göttingen: Hogrefe.

Schmitt, GM (1980) Klientenzentrierte Gruppenpsychotherapie in der Behandlung der Pubertätsmagersucht. *Praxis der Kinderpsychologie und Kinderpsychiatrie, 29* (7), 247–51.

Schmitt, GM, Wendt, R & Jochmus, I (1981) Stationäre Behandlung magersüchtiger Jugendlicher mit vorwiegend klientenzentrierter Einzel- und Gruppentherapie. In R Meermann (Hg) *Anorexia nervosa. Ursache und Behandlung* (pp. 158–69). Stuttgart: Enke.

Schmitt, GM & Wendt, R (1982) Die stationäre Behandlung magersüchtiger Jugendlicher unter dem Gesichtspunkt der sozialen Reintegration. *Zeitschrift für Kinder–und Jugendpsychiatrie, 10* (1), 67–73.

### F6 Personality disorders

Mulherin, MA (2001) The Masterson approach to play therapy: A parallel process between mother and child. *American Journal of Psychotherapy, 55*, 251–72.

### F7 Intelligence disorders

Ginsberg, BG (1984) Beyond behavior modification: Client-centered play therapy with the retarded. *American Psychology Bulletin, 6*, November, 321–24.

Goetze, H (1982) Personenzentrierte Psychologie und Spieltherapie mit verhaltensgestörten und lernbehinderten Kindern. In J Benecken (Hrsg) *Kinderspieltherapie Fallstudien* (pp. 107–26). Stuttgart: Kohlhammer.

Guerney, L (1979) Play therapy with learning disabled children. *Journal of Clinical Child Psychology, 8*, 242–44.

Guerney, L (1982) Play therapy with the learning disabled. In C Schaefer & K O'Connor (Eds) *Handbook of Play Therapy* (pp. 419–35). New York: J Wiley & Sons.

Irblich, D (2003) 'Bau mir ein Haus!' Falldarstellung einer personzentrierten Psychotherapie mit einem geistig behinderten Jungen. In C Boeck-Singelmann, B Ehlers, T Hensel, F Kemper & C Monden-Engelhardt (Hrsg) *Personzentrierte Psychotherapie mit Kindern und Jugendlichen, Bd. 3: Störungsspezifische Falldarstellungen* (pp. 163–201). Göttingen: Hogrefe.

Landreth, GL et al. (2005) *Therapy Interventions with Children's Problems: Case Studies with DSM-IV-TR Diagnoses (*2nd edn). Lanham, MD: Jason Aronson.

## F80 Language disorders (+98.5, 98.6)

Benecken, J (1982) Spezielle Aspekte klientenzentrierter Kinderspieltherapie bei stotternden Kindern. In J Benecken (Hrsg) *Kinderspieltherapie Fallstudien* (pp. 74–81). Stuttgart: Kohlhammer.

Braun, H-O (1982) Verlauf und Ergebnisse einer klientenzentrierten Spieltherapie mit einem stotternden Jungen. In J Benecken (Hrsg) *Kinderspieltherapie Fallstudien* (pp. 94–106). Stuttgart: Kohlhammer.

Ems, A (2003) Gefangen in der eigenen 'Sprachlosigkeit'. Personzentrierte Psychotherapie bei der 'Sprechstörung' Stottern. In C Boeck-Singelmann, B Ehlers, T Hensel, F Kemper & C Monden-Engelhardt (Hrsg) *Personzentrierte Psychotherapie mit Kindern und Jugendlichen, Bd. 3: Störungsspezifische Falldarstellungen* (pp. 41–77). Göttingen: Hogrefe.

Kemper, F (1982) Klientenzentrierte Kinderspieltherapie bei sprach- und sprechgestörten Kindern. In J Benecken (Hrsg) *Kinderspieltherapie Fallstudien* (pp. 38–73). Stuttgart: Kohlhammer.

Landreth, GL et al. (2005) *Therapy Interventions with Children's Problems: Case studies with DSM-IV-TR diagnoses* (2nd edn). Lanham, MD: Jason Aronson.

Seifert, F (1982) Verlauf und Ergebnisse einer klientenzentrierten Spieltherapie mit einem stotternden Mädchen. In J Benecken (Hrsg.) *Kinderspieltherapie Fallstudien* (pp. 82–93). Stuttgart: Kohlhammer.

Wakaba, YY (1983) Group play therapy for Japanese children who stutter. *Journal of Fluency disorders 8,* 93–118.

## F81 Developmental disabilities of school performance

Landreth, GL et al. (2005) *Therapy Interventions with Children's Problems: Case studies with DSM-IV-TR Diagnoses* (2nd edn). Lanham, MD: Jason Aronson.

Schmidtchen, S, Pelz, F & Dietz, V (1973) Development and first outcome evaluation of a multifactorial training program for children with reading-writing disabilities. *Praxis der Kinderpsychologie und Kinderpsychiatrie, 22* (7), 257–62.

## F84 Autism

Mittledorf, W, Hendricks, S, Landreth, GL (2001) Play therapy with autistic children. In GL Landreth (Ed) *Innovations in Play Therapy* (pp. 257–69). New York: Brunner-Routledge.

Landreth, GL et al. (2005) *Therapy Interventions with Children's Problems: Case studies with DSM-IV-TR diagnoses* (2nd edn). Lanham: Jason Aronson.

## F90 Hyperkinesis

Blinn, EL (2000) Efficacy of play therapy on problem behaviours of a child with attention deficit hyperactivity disorder. *Dissertation Abstracts International: Section B: The Sciences and Engineering, Vol. 61* (1-B), 522.

Göbel, S (1982) Spezielle Aspekte klientenzentrierter Spieltherapie bei verhaltensgestörten Kindern mit minimaler zerebraler Dysfunktion. In J Benecken (Hrsg) *Kinderspieltherapie Fallstudien.* (pp. 127–48). Stuttgart: Kohlhammer.

Landreth, GL et al. (2005) *Therapy Interventions with Children's Problems: Case Studies with DSM-IV-TR Diagnoses* (2nd edn) Lanham, MD: Jason Aronson.

Saile, H (1996) Metaanalyse zur Effektivität psychologischer Behandlung hyperaktiver Kinder. *Zeitschrift für Klinische Psychologie, 25* (3), 190–207.

Yeager, D (2000) Play therapy with the ADHD child. *17th Annual Association for Play Therapy International Conference* [Brochure]. Association for Play Therapy, Fresno, CA (Address: 2050 N. Winery Ave., Suite 101, Fresno, CA 93703).

## F91 Conduct disorders

Just, H (1982) Kindzentrierte Spieltherapie mit aggressiven Kindern. In J Benecken (Hrsg) *Kinderspieltherapie Fallstudien* (pp. 149–79). Stuttgart: Kohlhammer.

Landreth, GL et al. (2005) *Therapy Interventions with Children's Problems: Case studies with DSM-IV-TR diagnoses* (2nd edn). Lanham, MD: Jason Aronson.

Peterson Johnson, S, Clark, P (2001) Play therapy with aggressive acting-out children. In GL Landreth (Ed) *Innovations in Play Therapy* (pp. 239–55). New York: Brunner-Routledge.

Reisel, B (2002) Wenn die Erfahrung zum Feind wird. Zum Verständnis kindlicher Verhaltensauffälligkeit aus personzentrierter Sicht. In Iseli, Keil, Korbei, Nemeskeri et al. (Hrsg) *Identität, Begegnung, Kooperation. Person/Klientenzentrierte Psychotherapie und Beratung an der Jahrhundertwende* (pp. 408–24). Köln: GwG-Verlag

Schmidtchen, S (2003) Behandlung der Störung des Sozialverhaltens durch eine klientenzentrierte Psychotherapie für Kinder, Jugendliche und Familien. *Gesprächspsychotherapie und Personzentrierte Beratung, 34* (4), 213–20.

## F93 Emotional disorders (Anxiety disorders)

Milos, ME, Reiss, S (1982) Effects of three play conditions on separation anxiety in young children. *Journal of Consulting and Clinical Psychology, 50* (3), 389–95.

Post, P (1999) Impact of child-centered play therapy on the self-esteem, locus of control, and anxiety of at-risk 4th, 5th, and 6th grade students. *International Journal of Play Therapy, 8* (2), 1–18.

Landreth, GL et al. (2005) *Therapy Interventions with Children's Problems: Case studies with DSM-IV-TR Diagnoses* (2nd edn). Lanham, MD: Jason Aronson.

Trostle, SL (1988) The effects of child-centered group play session on social and emotional growth of three-to-six-year-old bilingual Puerto Rican children. *Journal of Research in Childhood Eudcation, 3* (2), 93–106.

## F94 Disorders of social functioning (mutism, attachment disorders)

Axline, V (1964) *Dibs: In search of self.* New York: Ballantine.

Ehlers, B (2002) Störungskonzept und personzentrierte Behandlung des elektiven Mutismus. In C Boeck-Singelmann, B Ehlers, T Hensel, F Kemper & C Monden-Engelhardt (Hrsg) *Personzentrierte Psychotherapie mit Kindern und Jugendlichen, Bd. 1: Grundlagen und Konzepte* (2. Auflage) (pp. 317–37). Göttingen: Hogrefe.

Fröhlich-Gildhoff, K & Hanne, K (2002) Frühe Beziehungsstörungen bei Kindern und Jugendlichen. In C Boeck-Singelmann, B Ehlers, T Hensel, F Kemper & C Monden-Engelhardt (Hrsg) *Personzentrierte Psychotherapie mit Kindern und Jugendlichen, Bd. 1: Grundlagen und Konzepte* (2. Auflage) (pp. 369–89). Göttingen: Hogrefe.

Landreth, GL (2005) *Therapy Interventions with Children's Problems: Case studies with DSM-IV-TR diagnoses* (2nd edn). Lanham, MD: Jason Aronson.

Post, P (2001) Play therapy with selective mute children. In GL Landreth (Ed) *Innovations in Play Therapy* (pp. 303–22). New York: Brunner-Routledge.

## F98.0 Urinary incontinence

Jürgens-Jahnert, S (2002) Ätiologie und Behandlung der kindlichen Enuresis aus personzentrierter Sicht. In C Boeck-Singelmann, B Ehlers, T Hensel, F Kemper & C Monden-Engelhardt (Hrsg) *Personzentrierte Psychotherapie mit Kindern und Jugendlichen, Bd. 1: Grundlagen und Konzepte* (2. Auflage) (pp. 339–67). Göttingen: Hogrefe.

Landreth, GL et al. (2005) *Therapy Interventions with Children's Problems: Case studies with DSM-IV-TR diagnoses* (2nd edn). Lanham, MD: Jason Aronson.

**F98.1 Fecal incontinence**

Landreth, GL et al. (2005) *Therapy Interventions with Children's Problems: Case studies with DSM-IV-TR diagnoses* (2nd edn). Lanham, MD: Jason Aronson.

Reisel, B, Wakolbinger, C (2006) Kinder und Jugendliche. In J Eckert, EM Biermann-Ratjen & D Höger, D (Hrsg) G*esprächspsychotherapie. Lehrbuch für die Praxis* (pp. 295–332). Heidelberg: Springer.

**Traumatisation, violence, abuse**

Ater, MK (2001) Play therapy behaviors of sexually abused children. In GL Landreth (Ed) *Innovations in Play Therapy* (pp. 119–29). New York: Brunner-Routledge.

Döring, E (2004) Personzentrierte Psychotherapie mit Kindern und Jugendlichen: Was hilft Spielen mit traumatiiserten Kindern und Jugendlichen? *Gesprächspsychotherapie und Personzentrierte Beratung, 3,* 193–98.

Homeyer, LE (2001) Identifying sexually abused children in play therapy. In GL Landreth (Ed) *Innovations in Play Therapy* (pp. 131–54). New York: Brunner-Routledge.

Johnson, PA & Stockdale, DF (1975) Effects of puppet therapy on palmar sweating of hospitalized children. *The John Hopkins Medical Journal, 137,* 1–5.

Landreth, GL et al. (2005) *Therapy Interventions with Children's Problems: Case studies with DSM-IV-TR diagnoses* (2nd edn). Lanham, MD: Jason Aronson.

Rae, WA, Worchel, FF, Upchurch, J, Sanner, JH & Daniel, CA (1989) The psychosocial impact of play on hospitalized children. *Journal of Pediatric Psychology, 14* (4), 617–27.

Riedel, K (1997) Personzentrierte Kindertherapie bei sexueller Mißhandlung. In C Boeck-Singelmann, B Ehlers, T Hensel, F Kemper & C Monden-Engelhardt (Hrsg) *Personzentrierte Psychotherapie mit Kindern und Jugendlichen, Bd. 2: Anwendung und Praxis* (pp. 159–80). Göttingen: Hogrefe.

Shen, Y (2002) Short-term group play therapy with Chinese earthquake victims: Effects on anxiety, depression and adjustment. *International Journal of Play Therapy, 11* (1), 43–63.

VanFleet, R, Lilly, J & Kaduson, H (1999) Play therapy for children exposed to violence: Individual, family, and community interventions. *International Journal of Play Therapy, 8* (1), 27–42.

Webb, P (2001) Play therapy with traumatized children: A crisis response. In GL Landreth (Ed) *Innovations in Play Therapy* (pp. 289–302). New York: Brunner-Routledge.

White, J, Draper, K, Pittard Jones, N (2001) Play therapy behaviors of physically abused children. In GL Landreth (Ed) *Innovations in Play Therapy* (pp. 99–118). New York: Brunner-Routledge.

Wittmann, AJ (2006) Personzentrierte Spielthdrapie nach sexuellem Missbrauch – Eine Kasuistik zurVerdeutlichung zentraler Spiel- und Symbolisierungsprozesse. *Person, 11* (2), 142–50.

Zion, TA (1999) Effects of individual client-centered play therapy on sexually abused children's mood, self-concept, and social competence. *Dissertation Abstract International: Section B, 60* (4-B), 18–76.

**Special populations**

Chau, IY & Landreth, GL (1997) Filial therapy with Chinese parents: Effects on parental empathic interactions, parental acceptance of child and parental stress. *International Journal of Play Therapy, 6* (2), 75–92.

Constantino, G, Malagady, RG & Rogler, LH (1986) Cuento therapy: A culturally sensitive modality for Puerto Rican children. *Journal of Consulting and Clinical Psychology, 54* (5), 639–45.

Gil, E & Dreqes, AA (2005) *Cultural Issues in Play Therapy.* New York: Guilford Press.

Glover, GJ (2001) Cultural considerations in play therapy. In GL Landreth (Ed) *Innovations in Play Therapy* (pp. 31–41). New York: Brunner-Routledge.

Kao, S-C & Landreth, GL (2001) Play therapy with Chinese children: Needed modifications. In GL Landreth (Ed) *Innovations in Play Therapy* (pp. 43–49). New York: Brunner-Routledge.

Ledyard Haynes, P (2001) Play therapy with the elderly. In GL Landreth (Ed) *Innovations in Play Therapy* (pp. 335–47). New York: Brunner-Routledge.

Lee, M-K & Landreth, GL (2003) Filial therapy with immigrant Korean parents in the United States. *International Journal of Play Therapy, 12* (2) 67–85.

Wakaba, YY (1983) Group play therapy for Japanese children who stutter. *Journal of Fluency Disorders, 8,* 93–118.

Waterland, JC (1970) Actions instead of words: Play therapy for the young child. *Elementary School Guidance and Counseling Journal, 4,* 180–97.

Yuen, T, Landreth, G & Baggerly, J (2002) Filial therapy with immigrant Chinese families. *International Journal of Play Therapy, 11* (2), 63–90.

*Table 2*

Effect sizes (Cohen's *d* or similar) of child and adolescent psychotherapy in 8 meta-analyses broken down by major approaches

| | Casey & Berman (1985) | Weisz et al. (1987) | Kadzin et al. (1990) | Weisz et al. (1995) | Ray et al. (2001) | LeBlanc & Ritchie (2001) | Beelman & Schneider (2003) | Bratton et al. (2005) |
|---|---|---|---|---|---|---|---|---|
| No. of studies | 75 | 108 | 223 | 150 | 94 | 42 | 47 | 93 |
| Years | 1952–1983 | 1958–1984 | 1970–1988 | 1967–1993 | 1953–2000 | no info | 1952–1997 | 1953–2000 |
| *Effect size psychodynamic approaches* | | | | | | | | |
| Effect size | .21 | .01 | no info | .31 | no info | no info | – | no info |
| No. of studies | 5 | 3 | 5 | 9 | | | 0 | |
| *Effect size person-centred approaches* | | | | | | | | |
| Effect size | .49 | .56 | no info | .15 | .93 | no info | .55 | .92 |
| No. of studies | 20 | 20 | 10 | 6 | 74 | | 7 | 73 |
| *Effect size behavioural approaches* | | | | | | | | |
| Effect size | .91 | .88 | no info | .76 | .73 | no info | .55 | .71 |
| No. of studies | 37 | 126 | | 197 | 12 | | 33 | 12 |

*Table 3*

Major associations representing person-centered, child and adolescent psychotherapy (in alphabetical order)

| | |
|---|---|
| The Academy of Play and Child Psychotherapy | www.apac.org.uk |
| AFP-ACP Association Française de Psychothérapie dans l'Approche Centrée sur la Personne | www.afp-acp.com |
| Association for Play Therapy | www.a4pt.org |
| British Association of Play Therapists | www.bapt.info/ |
| Canadian Association for Child and Play Therapy | www.cacpt.com |
| Center for Play Therapy | www.coe.unt.edu/cpt |
| Fachverband Personzentrierte Kinder- und Jugendlichenpsychotherapie | www.ptkj.de |
| Faculteit voor Mens en Samenleving, Turnhout, Belgium | www.aula.com/fms |
| GwG - Gesellschaft für wissenschaftliche Gesprächspsychotherapie | www.gwg-ev.org |
| Institut für Gesprächspsychotherapie und personzentrierte Beratung Stuttgart | www.gespraechspsychotherapie.net |
| International Society for Child and Play Therapy | www.playtherapy.org |
| IPS – Institut für personzentrierte Studien Wien | www.ips-online.at |
| National Institute of Relationship Enhancement® (NIRE) | www.nire.org |
| ÖGwG - Österreichische Gesellschaft für wissenschaftliche Gesprächspsychotherapie | www.psychotherapie.at/oegwg |
| PTUK - The United Kingdom Society for Play and Creative Arts Therapies | www.playtherapy.org.uk |
| Sektion Forum der APG, Wien | www.apg-forum.at |
| SGGT - Schweizerische Gesellschaft für Personzentrierte Psychotherapie und Beratung. | www.sggt-spcp.ch |
| Vrp - Vereinigung Rogerianische Psychotherapie, Wien | www.vrp.at |

# CHAPTER 2

# EFFECTIVE FACTORS IN CHILD AND ADOLESCENT THERAPY

## CONSIDERATIONS FOR A META-CONCEPT

### KLAUS FRÖHLICH-GILDHOFF

## INTRODUCTION

This article reflects firstly on important new concepts in psychotherapy research, especially aspects of the therapeutic relationship and Grawe (1994, 1998, 2004; Grawe, Donati & Bernauer, 1994) and colleagues' concept of 'effective factors'. The article then shares initial results of a qualitative research project that tries to identify effective factors in child and adolescent psychotherapy following the theoretical concept of an integrative 'common factors' or 'general' adult psychotherapy by Grawe and colleagues. The project has no experimental, condition-varying design; the data comprises videotaped, real therapy processes, which are systematically deconstructed with content-analysis methods. These methods are a link between the different analyses of therapy practice and theoretical fundamentals that lead to aspects of a meta-conception of psychotherapy.

In the next sections, the questions and the design of the research practice project are introduced. The results focus on three aspects: the therapeutic relationship; therapeutic interventions; and the therapeutic effective factors in child and adolescent psychotherapy. The conclusion summarises the relevant issues under the perspective: 'What works in therapy?'

## SUMMARY OF GRAWE'S CONCEPTS IN PSYCHOTHERAPY RESEARCH

In every therapeutic situation, the therapist has to act – or not. The basis – the 'ground' of all kinds of interventions or 'acting' – is the therapeutic relationship (shown as the 'star' in Figure 1). On this basis, different interventions are realised. 'The findings of process-outcome research ... favor a complex but comprehensive view of therapy. Effective psychotherapy is clearly more than a set of technical procedures, but it is also more than a warm, supportive relationship' (Orlinsky, Roennestad & Willutzki, 2004: 363). Grawe clustered the methods and types of therapeutic interventions by meta-analysis of empirical psychotherapy studies and found four central 'effective factors'. The 'Grawe concept' has been the most discussed theory in Germany in the last ten years and is influential worldwide, so it is described in the second part of this chapter.

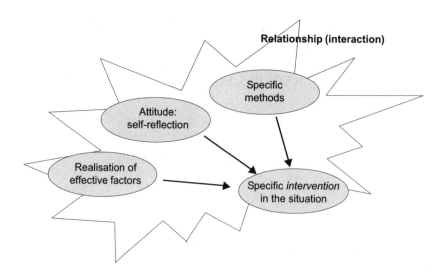

*Figure 1.* The therapeutic relationship as base and background for all kinds of intervention.

## THE THERAPEUTIC RELATIONSHIP

Many studies show that the quality of the therapeutic relationship has the most important influence on the outcomes of therapy (Orlinsky, Grawe & Parks, 1994; Grawe, Donati & Bernauer, 1994; Grawe & Fliegel, 2005) – there is 'no doubt, that relationship quality is one of the stronger correlations of outcome' (Beutler et al., 2004: 282). On the other hand, a complex mix with therapist and client variables influences the therapeutic process and its results: 'the effects of therapist traits on outcome cannot be adequately judged without inspecting aspects of patient functioning and the correspondence between patient and therapist qualities' (ibid.: 291). Many variables influence this relationship (see Figure 2).

Two people, with specific biographies, expectations and motivations, meet in a relationship together in an actual situation and setting. The relationship itself can be observed from two perspectives. First, there is the person-to-person relation in the real situation; then, every partner in the interaction imports (partly subconsciously) experiences and expectations from his past into the actual contact. He or she transfers these 'old' experiences and emotions into the 'new' situation which then structures his or her perception and processing of the interaction.

Gaston (1990) described 'four core components' (Lambert & Ogles, 2004: 174) of the therapeutic alliance: '(1) the patient's affective relationship to the therapist; (2) the patient's capacity to purposefully work in therapy; (3) the therapist's empathic understanding and involvement; and (4) the patient–therapist agreement on the goals and tasks of therapy' (ibid.).

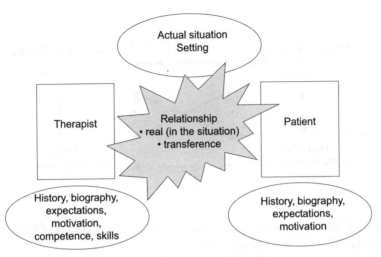

*Figure 2.* Influence variables on the therapeutic relationship.

Basic essentials, important for the success of the therapeutic relationship, are:

1. A 'fit' between therapist and client:

• There are no sure empirical results to identify this factor; sometimes, especially in the first sessions, aspects of a common culture or agreement in gender are important to help client retention but do not appear to help outcome (Beutler et al., 2004: 231). It seems to be more important that there is a 'sympathy', a fit, or shared values between the persons, especially in the first phase of the therapeutic process (ibid.: 277).

Orlinsky and Howard (1987) defined four dimensions of the 'fit' in the therapeutic relationship that show the complexity of the process (see Figure 3). The dimensions are a fit between:

(a) the therapeutic concept or strategy and the problems or 'disorder' of the patient

(b) the therapist (personality, experience, competence) and the client's problem or disorder

(c) the patient (personality, resources, motivation) and the therapeutic strategy

(d) the personhood of the therapist and the patient

All in all, the model clarifies the necessity for an idiosyncratic and disorder-specific adaptation of the therapeutic strategy and the necessity of the person-to-person encounter.

2. On the side of the *therapist* there are further important factors:

• The realisation of basic skills/attitudes (e.g. unconditional positive regard, empathy and congruence) and the structure (e.g. setting, time, boundaries) of the therapeutic relationship: the therapeutic relationship should be 'characterized by trust, warmth,

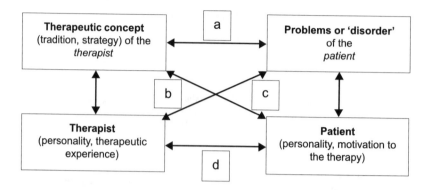

*Figure 3.* Dimension of fit in the psychotherapeutic situation (modified from a model by Orlinsky & Howard, 1987).

understanding, acceptance, kindness, and human wisdom' (Lambert & Ogles, 2004: 181).

- The ability and possibility to arrange new 'corrective emotional experiences' in the therapeutic relationship (e.g. Cremerius, 1979). This could be realised in the long-term of the therapeutic process and by 'treatments that specifically attempt to magnify and increase emotional experience' (Beutler et al., 2004: 263).

- Empirically, further markers of a good therapeutic relationship can be found, including so called 'therapist factors':

    - efficacy or perceived competence (Huf, 1992)
    - high degree of presence and attention; 'friendly behaviour' or a 'positive' interpersonal style (Beutler et al., 2004)
    - active engagement, interest and warmth (Grawe et al., 1994)
    - respect and positive regard (Rogers, 1959)
    - empathy and sensitivity (see Ainsworth et al., 1978)
    - communication on the same level (Grawe, Regli, Smith & Dick, 1999: 212)
    - relational holding (Grawe, 1998: 537)
    - specific co-regulation of affects (e.g. Papousek et al., 2004)

3. The *patient's* most important factors are:

- motivation and willingness to change
- participation in the treatment (Clarkin & Levy, 2004)

In psychotherapy research, there are inconsistent results on the effects of other client variables such as age, socio-economic status or other pre-treatment factors. 'Single variables do not operate alone ... the client variables are in a dynamic and ever-changing context of therapist variables and behaviour.' (Clarkin & Levy, 2004: 215)

Once again, the central results of psychotherapy effect and outcome research show that therapy is an interactive and co-constructive process, not conditioned and not possible to explain by isolated therapist or client variables (overview in Lambert, 2004). Therapists' attitudes and procedures have to fit the person and situation of the patient: 'the influence of any therapy procedure is dependent on patient factors' (Beutler et al., 2004: 249). For example, the impact of the realisation of the therapist variable 'therapist directiveness vs. patient self-direction' for the therapy outcome depends on the patient's moderator variable 'resistance'. The 'data suggest consistent evidence, that the effects of therapist directiveness are moderated by the level of patient resistance traits' (Beutler et al., 2004: 249). A second example concerns the question of whether a stronger 'insight-oriented' or a more 'symptom-focused' model is more effective. The analysis of different studies shows that patients who are self-reflective, introverted, and/or introspective tend to benefit from insight-orientated procedures, whereas patients who are impulsive, aggressive and under-controlled are responsive to symptom-focused procedures' (Beutler et al., 2004: 262). 'Such findings ... suggest that interpersonally compatible styles among therapists and clients may be indicative of whether or not psychotherapy will proceed in a positive direction' (Beutler et al., 2004: 240).

These results lead us to different observations and analyses of process variables which are relevant in this interactive and co-constructive action.


## GRAWE'S EFFECTIVE FACTORS

Grawe and colleagues (Grawe et al., 1994; Grawe, 1998, 2004) identified, on the basis of meta-analyses of more than 2000 adult psychotherapy effectiveness and comparison studies, four central 'effective factors' which, independent from the different psychotherapy 'schools' and in addition to the therapeutic relationship, are highly responsible for the therapeutic success.

These factors are:

1. *Activation of resources:* It is important to activate (recognise and support) the patient's strength and power, interests, motivations, competencies, talents and attributes.

2. *Support in problem-coping:* This means realistically and practically working towards solutions with the patient (problem analysis, goal analysis, searching for solution approaches, testing of solutions). If the patient has some experience of success, their expectation of self-efficacy will be increased and, thus, their self-esteem.

3. *Clarification:* This means supporting the patient's self-reflecting processes; clearing of intrapsychic conflicts and incongruities, and supporting the patient to achieve a greater awareness of their own situation.

4. *Process activation:* This is the activation of intrapsychic patterns for the purpose of organising 'corrective emotional experiences' or ways of finding new experiences and initiatives.

Grawe et al. (1994) established that these four factors must be realised in individualised ways that depend on the status of the therapeutic process, leading to the concept of a 'common' or 'general' psychological therapy (Grawe, 2004).

## ASSOCIATIONS WITH THE PERSON-CENTRED APPROACH

The concept of positive regard and unconditional acceptance connects closely to the perception and activation of the patient's resources. The focus of the therapeutic process is not primarily the symptom or the disorder but the 'whole' person with all his or her strengths and weaknesses. Valuing the person facilitates the client's actualisation through the mobilisation of resources (Hubble, Duncan & Miller, 1999; Duncan, Miller & Sparks, 2004).

Specific support in coping with problems or problem-solving is often not thought to be at the centre of 'classical' person-centred interventions. However, Bohart (2004), Bohart and Byock (2005), Martin (2000), and others working within the person-centred approach (e.g. Cornelius-White & Harbaugh, in press), have shown that person-centred therapy appears to work by providing a unique space that clients can utilise to solve problems. Unconditional regard opens a person's awareness of additional emotional and cognitive information with which to create new solutions and patterns of behaviour. Also, depending on the person and the status of the therapy process (i.e. the client might express a wish to work through a specific dilemma or request help in brainstorming options), therapists and clients can work collaboratively to find concrete solutions to individual problems without fundamentally altering the democratic, empathic nature of the work (Cornelius-White & Harbaugh, in press).

The support of self-clarification and self-awareness is a central issue in person-centred psychotherapy; this support is not reduced to a 'cognitive dialogue' – it includes the development of self-perception and self-understanding of clients' own emotional and relational schemes. And, in the therapeutic relationship, there is a focus on the 'organisation' of correcting emotional experiences. Specific interventions, based on the focusing concept, aim to reinforce the process activation, evoking and reworking inner psychic and relational patterns (e.g. Gendlin, 1996).

# QUESTIONS FOR FURTHER RESEARCH

The research of the Grawe group only concentrated on analysing the process and outcome research of adult psychotherapy. There are some important differences between adult and child psychotherapy, so it is useful to ask if it is possible to transfer the Grawe concept to psychotherapy with children and adolescents. The following presentation of a practice research project tries to answer three related questions:

1. Assuming the therapeutic relationship is also the central factor in child and adolescent psychotherapy, are there specific conditions or exceptional aspects that could be observed in the relationship between therapist and child/adolescent clients?

2. Is it possible to cluster the (therapeutic) interventions in the situation to operationalise therapeutic action for a better understanding of the interaction?

3. Is it possible to identify the 'effective factors' in psychotherapeutic play therapy?

## METHODS AND DESIGN

In the practice research project, a group of between eight and ten scientists and therapists[1] have analysed child and adolescent therapy sessions. The group have been meeting twice a year since 2001 in one- or two-day workshops in which videotapes of therapy processes have been analysed. In the first phase of the project, the members tried to identify the Grawe effective factors in child and adolescent therapies. A first step was the operationalisation of the factors for child therapy (Fröhlich-Gildhoff, Hufnagel & Jürgens-Jahnert, 2004). In the second phase, the therapeutic relationship was observed systematically and the concept of 'optimal reference' was revealed.

The researchers have already analysed more than 1500 therapy sessions with children and adolescents. The therapy sessions have been arranged by ten experienced therapists (with a minimum of more than ten years' experience after the training examination) with a person-centred or psychodynamic background and further training in cognitive-behaviour or systemic therapy. The videotapes cover 57 therapy processes (the range of the total number of sessions per therapy is 25–100); all the sessions have been recorded and the therapy processes documented by standardised minutes. This has been the basis for the discrimination of beginning, middle and end-phase of the therapy. The age range of the clients is 5–16 years.

The exploration and analysis is based on a combination of qualitative and quantitative methods (see Figure 4).

As a first step, the videotapes of the therapy sessions are analysed in a very open, hermeneutic way. The main goal is the creation of hypotheses and conclusions about possible coherences.

In the second step, the researchers compare and reflect upon these hypotheses with theoretical constructions. For example, they make comparisons between the Grawe construct of 'activation of resources' and the concrete acting in the therapy situation between therapist and child. This leads to a first form of operationalisation of this construct, specific for play therapy situations.

In the third step, the videotapes are analysed systematically in the form of a 'content analysis' (e.g. Mayring, 2000). The several dimensions and categories – for example, the four 'effective factors' – are now precisely described so that it is possible to measure the

---

1. With special thanks to the continuing members of the project group: Stephan Jürgens-Jahnert, Hildegard Steinhauser, Gerhard Hufnagel, Hans-Georg Derx, Katharina Heinen, Klaus Horstkötter, Wolfgang Siedenbiedel and Jutta Hoßfeld.

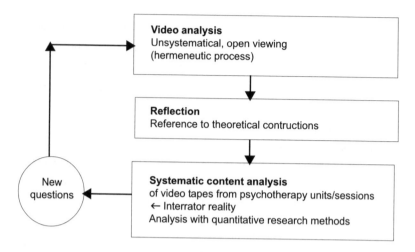

*Figure 4.* Methods and process of the practice research project.

frequency or intensity of their appearance in a therapeutic session. The sessions are rated by the team of experienced psychotherapists. In this phase, it is important to control the inter-rater reliability, therefore different sessions (videotaped) are rated by the whole team until there is an agreement about the assessment of a specific scene or situation. In this way, the team finds clear and consistent rules for the assessment (rating) process. A specific standardised rating leads to the possibility of a quantitative statistical analysis. For example, the team is looking for significant correlations between the appearance of the factor 'activation of resources' and the activity of the child, or making comparisons between the appearance of the different effective factors in different phases of the therapy process.

Finally, the results of the third step generate new questions, and the research process starts again, forming a loop of observation, reflection analysis and the exploration of new questions.

This methodical procedure is orientated on the quality criteria of qualitative research (e.g. Mayring, 2000; Hill & Lambert, 2004). The research group tries to establish reliability by finding a broad 'consensus among the judges' (Hill & Lambert, 2004: 104). The categories and the rating scales are discussed with independent groups at workshops or congresses. In experimental settings, these 'outside' groups also rate parts of the video material – so the research team receives feedback, offering additional reliability and validity. Validity should also be controlled by open embedding in theoretical systems and triangulation with other methods (e.g. standardised measures of therapy outcome).

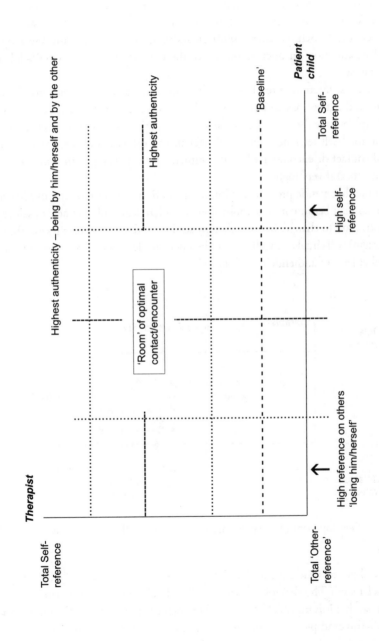

*Figure 5.* Dimensions of reference in the therapeutic process.

# RESULTS

### RELATIONSHIP

There are only initial results on specific factors of a helpful, containing and supportive therapeutic relationship in person-centred child and adolescent therapy (e.g. Weinberger, 2001; Behr, 2003; Schmidtchen, 2002). In addition to these results, the research team focused its attention on micro-processes in the interaction between child/adolescent and therapist.

The most interesting result is that the dimension of 'optimal reference' between therapist and patient has an important influence on the therapeutic process. It is also possible to describe the reference of therapist and patient as a continuum between the poles of 'total self-reference' and 'total reference to others'. And there is a 'room' of optimal contact or encounter when the authenticity (the being with him/herself and with the other) is very high.

In the therapeutic process, it is important to find ways of reaching this 'room' of optimal contact because in this 'room' there is a high degree of openness to self-regard and motivation to change. In every therapy session, and in the whole process, therapist (and patient) will circulate together with their personal levels of reference to come nearer to a higher level of authenticity in contact.

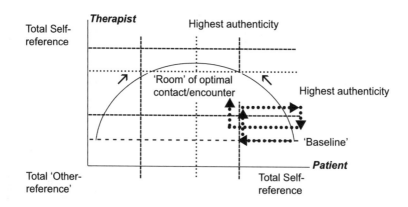

*Figure 6.* Development of interactional reference in the therapy process.

The initial point is the patient's level of reference and the degree of 'self-reference' vs. 'other-reference'. The therapist starts on a 'baseline'. This leads the patient to more security, so that it is possible for the child to open their own rigid self-concepts and to realise (in this example) a little bit more reference to the interaction partner (in this case, the therapist). In the next step, the therapist can try to realise more self-reference ... if that step is too large, the process stops and must start again on a lower level (the arrows in Figure 6 try to clear this movement). There is no simple or direct way in the development of the relationship, especially in the mutual reference to the (secure) 'room of optimal contact/encounter', but it is a common, co-constructive searching process between the two people involved.

## ADAPTING INTERVENTIONS APPROPRIATELY

At any time, there are a lot of possibilities of therapeutic interventions. Although the therapy as a whole is a co-constructive process, the therapist has to decide if and in what way he or she should act in the situation, and if and how he or she should 'answer' or respond to the child's expressions or actions.

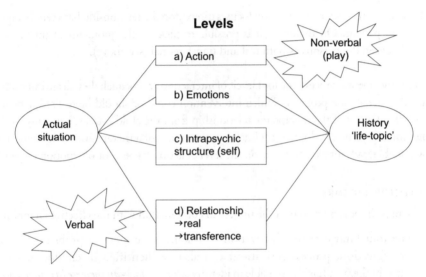

*Figure 7.* Possibilities and levels of intervention in the therapeutic situation.

Interventions can be realised in a verbal or non-verbal way: it is possible to 'comment' on situations, the acting or the interaction with words (or semi-verbal signals) or to 'answer' in play directly. The difficulty is that children demonstrate their issues and questions indirectly in play; the therapist has to understand the conflicts and 'life topics'. Therefore, to empathically understand, it is necessary to 'translate' the symbols the child shows in play, to understand them and to 're-translate' them in (play) re-action.

Generally, it is possible to make a difference between four levels of intervention that are embedded in the actual situation ('here and now') and the patient's history/biography and 'life topics':

1. Level of 'action': This means the verbal and non-verbal answers to the child's action. These could be verbal descriptions of the action, or forms of 'playing together'. The most important function of interventions on this level is that the child gains the experience of being seen by an adult (relevant) person; the child gets attention, can

experience positive regard and its action – and the whole person as well – is 'mirrored' by another person.

2. Level of emotion: Interventions on this level are characterised by the precise recording, understanding and verbalising of the child's emotions – this means the 'classic' verbalising of emotional experiences.

3. Interventions can also pick up the child's central 'life topics', issues or conflicts. With these kinds of interventions the therapist tries to 'reach' unconscious parts of the inner psychic structure (self-concept), to bring them nearer to awareness or consciousness; the aim is a better understanding of the symbolic (inter)action and finding a way for the open representation of the (unconscious, pre-symbolised) conflicts and incongruities.

4. The fourth level of intervention focuses directly on the relationship between therapist and patient. On this level, it is possible to pick up the moments of interaction between the persons as both real and transferential (see above).

In the therapeutic process, the four levels of interaction are coequal: they all are important for the therapeutic progress. Which intervention could or should be realised depends on the intensity of the therapeutic relationship from the child's status, especially his or her inner psychic development. Usually, in the course of a therapeutic session (and the whole therapy), interventions are on the level of action (type a) or of emotion (type b).

EFFECTIVE FACTORS

The most important results of the project in combination with the effective factors are:

• The four Grawe factors (activation of resources, support in problem-solving, clarification, process activation) can also be identified in child/adolescent psychotherapy. It is also possible to identify *a fifth factor – an increase in competences.* In all child therapy (much more than in psychotherapy with adults) there occurs real learning in cognitive, motoric, self-regulating or emotional abilities/skills, meaning that an extending of competences can be identified.

• A good realisation of the five effective factors is connected with a better therapy outcome. There are significantly high correlations between the frequency and intensity of the appearance of the factors and measurements of the therapy outcome.

• The realisation of these factors is connected with the phases of the therapeutic process: initially, there are more 'activating of resources', later, 'help in problem coping' and 'clarification' are realised.

• The realisation depends on:

    • the specific situation, problems and conflicts of the children/adolescents,

    • the status of the development of the children/adolescents,

    • the experience of the therapist (Fröhlich-Gildhoff, et al., 2004; Fröhlich-Gildhoff, 2007).

# CONCLUSION

The practice research project answers the research questions as follows:

1. The relevant elements and conditions of a supportive relationship in adult therapy can also be identified in child/adolescent therapy; the project focuses on a new perspective: the dynamic of reference between child-patient and therapist.
2. The therapeutic interventions could be clustered on four levels – these levels must be operationalised more precisely in further research.
3. The effective factors – identified by the Grawe group – are relevant in child/adolescent therapy too, and an additional fifth factor – the increase of competences – is important.

In summary, the following questions should be answered:

- 'What works in psychotherapy?'
- 'What leads to a high possibility of success on outcome measures?'

The reflection of the psychotherapy effectiveness studies and the results of the practice research project show four important elements:

1. the 'fit' between therapist and patient
2. reflective, relational work (e.g. the arrangement of 'corrective emotional experiences' in the therapeutic relationship)
3. the 'juggling' with the effective factors – depending on the patient's status of development and on the status of the therapeutic process
4. the activation of impulses for a change or modification of the self-concept (Stern, 1998)

These elements are compatible with the person-centred concept – at the centre of the process is the therapeutic relationship, the person-to-person interaction. The helpful variables of encounter and support are completed by the concept of effective factors – providing an empirically based orientation for (successful) interventions.

# REFERENCES

Ainsworth, M, Blehar, MC, Waters, ER & Wall, S (1978) *Patterns of Attachment. A psychological study of the strange situation.* Hillsdale, NY: Erlbaum.

Behr, M (2003) Interactive resonance in work with children and adolescents: A theory-based concept of interpersonal relationship through play and the use of toys. *Person-Centered and Experiental Psychotherapies, 2* (2), 89–103.

Beutler, LE, Malik, M, Alimohamed, S, Harwood, TM, Talebi, H, Noble, S & Wong, E (2004) Therapist variables. In MJ Lambert *Bergin and Garfield's Handbook of Psychotherapy and Behavior Change* (5th edn) (pp. 227–306). New York: Wiley.

Bohart, AC (2004) How do clients make empathy work? *Person-Centered and Experiential Psychotherapies, 3* (2), 102–16.

Bohart, AC & Byock, G (2005) Experiencing Carl Rogers from the client's point of view: A vicarious enthnographic investigation. Extraction and perception of meaning. *The Humanistic Psychologist, 33* (3), 187–212.

Clarkin, JF & Levy, KN (2004) The influence of client variables on psychotherapy. In MJ Lambert *Bergin and Garfield's Handbook of Psychotherapy and Behavior Change* (5th edn) (pp. 194–226). New York: Wiley.

Cornelius-White, JHD & Harbaugh, AP (in press) *Learner-Centered Instruction: Building relationships for student success.* Thousand Oaks, CA: Sage

Cremerius, J (1979) Gibt es *zwei* psychoanalytische Techniken? [Are there *two* psychoanalytic techniques?] *Psyche, 32* (7), 577–99.

Duncan, BL, Miller, SD & Sparks, J (2004) *The Heroic Client: A revolutionary way to improve effectiveness through client-directed, outcome-informed therapy.* San Francisco: Jossey-Bass.

Fröhlich-Gildhoff, K (2007) Wirkfaktoren in der Kinder- und Jugendpsychotherapie – Darstellung eines langfristigen Forschungsprojekts [Effective factors in psychotherapy with children and adolescents – methods and results of a practice research project]. In J Hein & K-O Hentze (Eds) *Das Unbehagen an der (Psychotherapie-)Kultur* (pp. 219–31). Bonn: Dt. Psychologen Verlag.

Fröhlich-Gildhoff, K, Hufnagel, G & Jürgens-Jahnert, S (2004) Auf dem Weg zu einer Allgemeinen Kinder- und Jugendlichenpsychotherapie – die Praxis ist weiter als die Therapieschulen [Toward a general psychotherapy with children and adolescents: Moving beyond traditions to better practice]. In H-P Michels & R Dittrich (Eds) *Auf dem Weg zu einer allgemeinen Kinder- und Jugendlichenpsychotherapie. Eine diskursive Annäherung* [Toward a general psychotherapy with children and adolescents: A discursive approach] (pp. 161–94). Tübingen: DGVT-Verlag.

Gaston, L (1990) The concept of the alliance and its role in psychotherapy: Theoretical and empirical considerations. *Psychotherapy, 27,* 143–53.

Gendlin, ET (1996) *Focusing-Orientated Psychotherapy: A manual of the experiential method.* New York: Guilford Press.

Grawe, K (1994) Psychotherapie ohne Grenzen – von den Therapieschulen zur Allgemeinen Psychotherapie [Psychotherapy without borders: From therapeutic schools to general psychotherapy]. *Verhaltenstherapie und Psychosoziale Praxis, 26* (3), 357–70.

Grawe, K (1998) *Psychologische Therapie* [Psychological Therapy]. Göttingen/Bern/Toronto/Seattle: Hogrefe.

Grawe, K (2004) *Psychological Therapy.* Seattle/Toronto: Hogrefe.

Grawe, K, Donati, R & Bernauer, F (1994) *Psychotherapie im Wandel. Von der Konfession zur Profession* [Psychotherapy in Change: From confession to profession]. Göttingen/Bern/Toronto/Seattle: Hogrefe.

Grawe, K & Fliegel, S (2005) 'Ich glaube nicht, dass eine Richtung einen Wahrheitsanspruch stellen kann'. Klaus Grawe im Gespräch mit Steffen Fliegel ['I don't believe that one psychotherapy theory can proclaim the truth', Klaus Grawe in discussion with Steffen Fliegel]. In *Verhaltenstherapie und Psychosoziale Praxis, 37* (3), 690–703. (First published in *Psychotherapie im Dialog,* Heft 2/2005).

Grawe, K, Regli, D, Smith, E & Dick, A (1999) Wirkfaktorenanalyse – ein Spektroskop für die Psychotherapie [Effective factors analysis: A new view on psychotherapy] In *Verhaltenstherapie und psychosoziale Praxis, 2,* 201–25.

Hill, CE & Lambert, MJ (2004) Methodological issues in studying psychotherapy processes and outcomes. In MJ Lambert, *Bergin and Garfield's Handbook of Psychotherapy and Behavior change* (5th edn) (pp. 84–136). New York: Wiley.

Hubble, ML, Duncan, BA & Miller, SD (1999) *The Heart and Soul of Change: What works in therapy.* Washington, DC: American Psychological Association.

Huf, A (1992) *Psychotherapeutische Wirkfaktoren* [Psychotherapeutic Effective Factors]. Weinheim: Psychologie Verlags Union.

Lambert, MJ (2004) *Bergin and Garfield's Handbook of Psychotherapy and Behavior Change.* (5th edn). New York: Wiley.

Lambert, MJ & Ogles, BM (2004) The efficacy and effectiveness of psychotherapy. In MJ Lambert *Bergin and Garfield's Handbook of Psychotherapy and Behavior Change* (5th edn) (pp. 139–93). New York: Wiley.

Martin, DG (2000) *Counseling and Therapy Skills* (2nd edn). Prospect Heights, IL: Waveland Press.

Mayring, P (2000) Qualitative Inhaltsanalyse [Qualitative content analysis]. *Forum Qualitative Sozialforschung* (online journal). *1* (2).

Orlinsky, DE, Grawe, K & Parks, B (1994) Process and outcome in psychotherapy. In AE Bergin & SL Garfield (Eds) *Handbook of Psychotherapy and Behavior Change* (pp. 270–376). New York: Wiley.

Orlinsky, DE & Howard, KI (1987) A generic model of psychotherapy. *Journal of Integrative Eclectic Psychotherapy, 6,* 6–27.

Orlinsky, DE, Roennestad, MH & Willutzki, U (2004) Fifty years of psychotherapy process-outcome research: Continuity and change. In MJ Lambert *Bergin and Garfield's Handbook of Psychotherapy and Behavior Change* (5th edn) (pp. 307–90). New York: Wiley.

Papousek, M, Schieche, M & Wurmser, H (Hrsg) (2004) *Regulationsstörungen der frühen Kindheit. Frühe Risiken und Hilfen im Entwicklungskontext der Eltern- und Kindbeziehung* [Regulation Disorders in Early Childhood. Early risks and support in the developmental context of the relationship between the child and its parents]. Bern/Göttingen: Huber.

Rogers, CR (1959) A theory of therapy, personality, and interpersonal relationships, as developed in the client-centered framework. In S Koch (Ed) *Psychology: A study of a science. Vol. III: Formulations of the person and the social context* (pp. 184–256). New York: McGraw-Hill.

Schmidtchen, S (2002) Neue Forschungsergebnisse zu Prozessen und Effekten der klientenzentrierten Kinderspieltherapie [New empirical results on the process and outcome of client-centred play therapy]. In C Boeck-Singelmann, B Ehlers, T Hensel, F Kemper & C Monden-Engelhardt (Eds) *Personzentrierte Psychotherapie mit Kindern und Jugendlichen* [Person-Centred Psychotherapy with Children and Adolescents]. *Band 1: Grundlagen und Konzepte* (2nd edn). (pp. 153–94). Göttingen/Bern/Toronto/Seattle: Hogrefe.

Stern, DN (1998) 'Now Moments', implizites Wissen und Vitalitätskonturen als neue Basis für psychotherapeutische Modellbildungen ['Now moments', implicit knowledge and vitality as a new basis for the building of psychotherapeutic models]. In S Trautmann-Voigt & B Voigt (Eds) *Bewegung ins Unbewußte, Beiträge zur Säuglingsforschung und analytischen KörperPsychotherapie* [Movement in the Unconsciouness. Contributions for infant research and analytic body psychotherapy] (pp. 82–96). Frankfurt: Brandes und Apsel.

Weinberger, S (2001) *Kindern spielend helfen. Eine personzentrierte Lern- und Praxisanleitung* [Helping Children by Play: A person-centred guide for training and practice]. Weinheim: Beltz.

# CHAPTER 3

# WHAT HAPPENS IN CHILD-CENTRED PLAY THERAPY?

## ELSE DÖRING

## PLAY AND RELATIONSHIPS IN PERSON-CENTRED CHILD PSYCHOTHERAPY

Relationships and play are important elements for person-centred therapists working with children. Play places the focus on the children and their coping, learning, and development. Relationships open up an interactive space, in which someone supports the development of the child by accompanying the child in a supporting way.

As opposed to adults, who express their problems mainly through speaking, play is 'the language of the child'. Children show themselves through play; it has a special function in the development of a child and cannot be replaced by attempts to train the child. In order to understand a child, it is useful to know as much about the significance of play as possible. Theories of play can help in the decoding and understanding of children's communication and experience. At the same time, attachment theory broadens our understanding and building of the therapeutic relationship with the child.

## PLAY

### THE IMPORTANCE OF PLAY IN EVOLUTION

Play has a preminent role in the evolution of human beings. Play is a genetic behavioural programme, activated by intrinsic motivation, and early forms of play can even be found in animals. The unfolding and differentiation of the play process have connections to the ways in which human beings adapt to their environment, which are determined by their physical ability, their level of fitness, and their environment. New elements of play can be found in more evolved species, including humans. They are in touch with the differentiation, behavioural adaptation, learning processes, and integration of experience.

This behavioural programme does not only exist in children, but is also reflected in a corresponding behavioural programme in the attached adult who 'knows' how to support the child appropriately in play. Children use a great deal of energy in play, and show great excitement when having to face unknown situations in play. Children have a need to gather enough information about the outside world to trust in the environment, to explore the outside world and to experience the pleasure and curiosity gained from new experiences. Play constitutes an important step in the development of human beings towards symbolic thinking (Papousek, 2003).

Through the ability of symbolic thinking, human beings have increased their chances of survival and it increases adaptation to the world. Symbolic thinking is the basis of human culture; it makes the communication of knowledge and experience possible despite the limitations of space and time. For the human being, the ability to use symbols opens up new mental fields of activity, and new forms of experience integration, such as fantasy activity, mental games, planning ahead, and the capability for problem-solving.

A newborn baby can interact with his or her physical and interpersonal environment from the very beginning. In the first year of life, babies use their first symbols in gesture and language. Play is spontaneous, self-initiated learning; it enables a child to acquire new abilities, problem-solving strategies and skills for coping with emotional conflicts.

In evolutionary terms play has two functions: it teaches us how to deal with new and unknown situations through fear reduction and it lessens boredom through engagement in novel situations.

Play and language are separate developmental functions; a deficit in one area does not automatically impact the other. Fantasy play – which develops on the base of symbolic thinking – is a mental activity independent of language. Behavioural patterns in play development are strong and probably biologically determined (Bornstein, 2003).

Play is innate; it has an evolutionarily important place in the development of human beings and also in the development of the individual child. So strong is the role of play that Bornstein (2003) asserts without it, a child cannot develop.

PIAGET, PLAY AND THE DEVELOPMENT OF THINKING

The relationship between cognitive development and play was the focus of several play theorists. Piaget (1969) was interested in children's play in order to understand better the cognitive development of children. His work shows how a child develops thinking by playing. Babies and infants interact with an object and thereby practise sensory motor behaviour; he refers to this as sensory motor play. The next stage he identified is exploration play: when children begin to categorise and to understand the relationship between two objects. This is where pretend play develops – an absent object is only present in the imagination – pretend play is characterised by fictional action and re-interpretation of reality.

Piaget names three main principles of the play scheme:

• play develops in a structured order, from one stage to the next
• activity is the basis of constructing knowledge
• play is integral in development

With the help of play, the cognitive stage of a child's development can be determined independently of language and the development of the child can be supported (Bornstein, 2003).

## OERTER'S PSYCHOLOGY OF PLAY

In order to understand better the phenomenon of play, it is useful to integrate the different strands of development functions. In *Psychologie des Spiels*, Oerter (1993) looks at the phenomenon of play from a unified, theoretical perspective and thereby expands an understanding of play; he integrates into his theory the cognitive perspective, as well as the communicative and the emotional aspects. He describes play as an intermediary space between inner and outer reality. His analysis is empirically based on his observation of many play processes by children over a long period of time.

The main theme of play is the existence of the self in the world. The main intention of play is the interaction of the child's self with his or her environment.

Play is important for:

- the development of the self
- regulation of emotions
- social relationships
- learning about the outer world
- coping with reality

### DEVELOPMENT OF THE SELF

Through play, the development of the self occurs. Children, noticing their activities and their impact on the environment, can increase their self-esteem. In play, children interact with the outside world through four different play processes: reification, internalisation, objectification, and subjectification.

- Through *reification*, children create something in play and thereby influence the environment. This could be something material like a picture, a construction, or something abstract like role play. Reification enables children to discover their impact on the environment and to thereby gain power and control over the world.

- *Internalisation* means that as children acquire something as a personal belonging, they are active in internalising the object. Hence, it then becomes part of the self. Knowledge about an object can be described as a process of internalisation.

- *Objectification* means that the play is oriented towards reality. Children adapt to their environment. Consequently, children discover that the world exists independently of themselves.

- *Subjectification* describes a process through which children re-shape reality according to their own desires and needs. Thereby, children try to become familiar with the outside world.

Through these processes, children create a working model of the relationship between themselves and the world. By interacting with the environment in play, children learn how to influence the environment, thus gaining knowledge about the functioning of the world and thereby broadening and strengthening their selves.

## REGULATION OF EMOTIONS

Play is important for children in dealing with their emotions because it helps in coping with their feelings and in changing bad feelings to good ones. Intrinsic motivation and flow experience[1] are integral in play processes. Play enables children to create a new reality, in which needs and desires can be instantly realised. By playing, the children create security and safety for themselves.

## SOCIAL RELATIONSHIPS

As active agents in the world, children develop an understanding of themselves and others within play – here, a step occurs, from self-reference to partner-reference. In role play, children first imitate roles, then they undertake these roles, and then they face a virtual partner in order to understand him better. By undertaking different roles, children can construct an early understanding of social identity. 'Therefore, through the medium of play, children grasp parts of images of humanity' (Oerter, 1993: 50, translation by ED).

## LEARNING ABOUT THE OUTER WORLD

When interacting with objects in play, children build a set of terms of reference with the world. Within play, children develop the capability to plan ahead more intensively. When playing, children can stabilise their experiences through repetition.

## COPING WITH REALITY

Play is a vital activity in order for a child to process reality. Children can cope with reality in the following ways: they reproduce reality, they change reality, and they escape from reality.

Processing problems in play follows certain rules. First, children express the problem either in play stories or in acting out as a drama. Next, they try to solve the problem by playing. Later, they represent the solution to the problem in play. Finally, the problem and the solution tend to disappear.

General themes of development are:

- power and control [2]
- self and identity [3]
- coping processes [4]

Themes of relationships are:

- desire for friendship
- competition between siblings and friends
- loss of attachment and insecurity in attachment

---

1. Csikszentmihalyi created this term to describe the experience of happiness.
2. Children try to shape the reality corresponding to their ideas, thus they achieve the positive feelings of efficacy with objects and reality.
3. This developmental theme includes the sub-themes of separation and autonomy, of construction of identity through attachment to an object and the development of gender roles.
4. Children process in play unsolved conflicts, traumatic experiences and problems.

General themes of play are:

- solving of current conflicts
- processing of reality in extreme situations
- play of survival

Oerter describes the three ways in which children communicate their themes in the play process. Children put their themes in a story with a beginning and an end; Oerter calls this a narrative transformation. Children express their emotional states by spatial relations (i.e. security is symbolised in an attachment figure). Children materialise their themes by creating objects or sculptures and constructing buildings.

Play is development and coping simultaneously. In order to understand the meaning of play, its structure, themes, development and rules help in understanding the child. However, children don't play alone. They always need a person who supports and stimulates their activities, even if only in their imagination or as an internal representation of a real person. Ideally, this person should be an attached person, who provides the appropriate setting for the child's play activities. The quality of the attachment has an impact on the play activities of the child. How to provide an appropriate relationship to support unsettled children is of great interest to child therapists. Attachment theory gives us an answer to these questions.

## INSIGHTS INTO ATTACHMENT THEORY FOR THE THERAPEUTIC RELATIONSHIP

### BASIC LEARNING STEPS IN ATTACHMENT

Attachment theory can be described as an all-encompassing concept for the development of human personality as a consequence of social experiences (see Bowlby, 1975). An attachment is a specific relationship to a person, the central attachment figure, often the mother, parent, or primary caregiver, who provides the child with a feeling of security and helps the child to make important steps in learning to cope with their environment or with other people. The attachment figure is therefore a supporter of the child's personality development. Many studies have shown how important this attachment system is for psychological, physiological, and social learning, development and adjustment. Basic steps of learning in the first years, supported by the attachment figures are as follows:

- growth of neurons through the attachment (Siegel, 2006: 84)

- the understanding of the child's own emotions and their regulation (Fonagy et al., 2004)[5]

---

5. The process of understanding through the attachment figure works like this: the mother first reflects the experience of the baby and following this, changes the reflection in such a way that calming elements are integrated, thereby she differentiates between her own and the baby's experiences.

- development of empathy, theory of mind (Fonagy et al., 2004) [6]
- development of an internal working model – a 'virtual other' person or relationship (Siegel, 2006)[7]
- development of a self as differentiated from the non-self (Crittenden, 2000)
- development of predictability of what happens in the environment (Crittenden, 2005)
- experience of self-efficacy (Crittenden, 2005)

A secure attachment is supported by a reliable and caring attachment figure, which also provides an open and coherent communication close to reality. From this secure base the child is able to explore, and learn about, the environment. This means that the attachment relationship is important in a number of ways. Through the relationship, children learn about themselves, their feelings, the world, how predictable the world is, and what kind of impact they can have on the world. They also learn about the possibility of self-regulation and how to establish relationships with different people by developing an idea of the 'virtual other,' an inner model of a relationship.

## WHEN THE ATTACHMENT FIGURE REACTS INADEQUATELY

Attachment theory emphasises the importance of the reaction of the attachment figure in a predictable, as well as contingent way. This process is described as a mutual process, in which both sides have to adjust to each other and in which it is important that the attachment figure reacts flexibly, according to the needs of the child. If the mother adjusts her reaction to the emotional state of the baby, the baby learns that its feelings are understandable. In this attachment relationship, the baby learns to see the relationship between its own behaviour and the subsequent consequences. Responsive attachment figures, who react in sufficient time, can communicate to the baby that there are predictable relationships between events and that its behaviour causes a certain reaction from the mother. Mothers of babies attached in an insecure-avoiding way do not realise the needs of the baby and thus do not react when it cries. They communicate to the baby that it has no influence on its environment; events are not predictable, and negative feelings cannot be calmed. The baby suppresses its negative expression of affect and does not learn anything about its feelings. Mothers of babies attached in an insecure-ambivalent way do not react to the crying baby predictably. Sometimes they react as a caring mother; sometimes they reinforce the negative affect. The emotional arousal of the baby disturbs both the mother and the baby. Therefore, neither is able to regulate their feelings anymore. These babies are full of rapidly increasing negative feelings. The child does not learn anything about the regulation of emotions and about coping strategies. These erroneous working models of relationships are maintained throughout adult life and they continue

---

6. I.e. to understand how another person thinks and feels.
7. I.e. an idea about how one's self works, how the attachment figure works and how she reacts, these learning processes play an important role in the development of social competences.

to influence the idea of one's own self and the self-environment relationship. However, a reorganisation is possible within a therapeutic context.

## PSYCHOTHERAPEUTIC IMPLICATIONS

An attachment relationship with a therapist develops a new adaptive and flexible 'internal working model' (Grossmann & Grossmann, 2004: 61). In psychotherapy, it is necessary to create a secure environment so that the child can begin to explore current and past experiences. In a therapeutic process, both therapist and patient enter into a resonance of mental states. Hence, it is of crucial importance that the therapist also reacts to the non-verbal signals of the client. The therapist, therefore, needs to understand the experiences of the client and to reflect their expressions, thus intrapersonal experience forms the structures and functions of the brain. The therapist needs to work towards integration and growth (Siegel, 2006).

Crittenden argues that the work of a therapist should be to correct any false development of the self: the self should be reorganised. Clients need to develop fitting strategies in the therapeutic process that they couldn't learn in the attachment with their parents, and to integrate different representations of their self. To initiate this process, it is necessary that the therapist shows their own self and cares about the needs of the client, as would an attachment figure. Thus the therapist has to set limits on destructive clients and to react appropriately to the needs of clients who have learned to suppress their feelings. The therapist has to keep a balance between self-perception, flexibility and adjustment. Besides knowing therapeutic techniques, therapists have to know how to use themselves as tools.

## CONCLUSION FOR PLAY THERAPY

This paper has acknowledged that play theories and attachment theories are connected. But while attachment theory describes what kind of foundation children need in order to be able to develop and to learn, play theories represent how this development takes place. To help children in therapy, knowledge from both theories is useful.

### PERSON-CENTRED ASSUMPTIONS ABOUT RELATIONSHIPS AND PLAY

Axline (1976) emphasises the therapist's special relationship to the child. In terms of play, she mentions that play can be a medium for the self-performance of the child, as the child can express its 'feelings and conflicts' in play (p. 14).

Goetze (2002) proposes that play presents an opportunity for the child symbolically to play out its experiences. Play represents the natural way of communication: 'in therapy, the play offers the possibility for the child to give a new order to its experiences, to organise them and thereby bring them to consciousness' (Goetze 2002: 24, translation by ED). Goetze says that, in terms of the relationship, the child is offered a secure basis on which he or she can explore the scope of play in a realistic way, in order to explore the world in a symbolic sense and counterbalance the negative experiences of relationships.

Behr (2003) broadens the possibilities of intervention in play therapy by adding the term 'interactive resonance'. He explicitly refers to attachment theory and refers to the adjustment of emotion. He places emphasis on the non-verbal contingent reactions of the therapist that do not necessarily have to be communicated through language.

## INTEGRATION

Because play and relationships are the key elements for play therapists as I have shown above, there are two levels which are important for the therapist's attitude and their interventions. The first level concerns relationships. Child therapists have to create the special supporting and nurturing relationship that attachment theory talks about. Only through a grounded relationship are therapeutic play activities possible. On the second level – the play level – child therapists have to deal with the child's play activity.

## RELATIONSHIP INTERVENTION

The person-centred principles of Axline are relevant on a level of interaction. They give the therapist an indication as to how to build a helpful relationship. Attachment theory can provide a theoretical background about how to shape relationships in person-centred play therapy. To summarise Axline's principles, in terms of attachment theory, we can also say that the therapist should establish a secure base for the child.

In addition to the Axline principles, I propose the following essentials for building a therapeutic relationship. The therapist should:

- establish a secure basis for the child so that it can explore their environment.
- react in a predictable way, so that children can develop contingencies and reduce their fear and stress.
- adjust his state of arousal to that of the child, so that the child can learn about, and understand, their feelings.
- show a calming behaviour towards a highly emotional child, so that the child learns to regulate their emotions.
- identify the needs of the child and flexibly react to them.
- help children identify and learn about emotions.
- help children develop cognitive strategies.
- help children develop a structure.
- reflect the non-verbal behaviour of the child in an appropriate way, so that the child learns about their behaviour and reactions.
- by validating the different mental states of the child, help the child to develop a concept of themselves.
- enable the child to learn and differentiate between the self and non-self, by showing his own identity and by setting limits.

- react in an authentic, open and honest way, in order to offer the child an appropriate and honest reaction to their personality and to thereby support the child's personality development.

## CASE ILLUSTRATION

George, a four-year-old boy, was neglected by his mother, and as his father had died, nobody cared for him. I met him in a children's hospital where I worked as a therapist. When I saw him for the first time his facial expression was frozen, and he could speak only a few words. He was full of fear and stress, he observed his environment accurately but showed no reaction. He was interested in toys, but was initially afraid to touch them. He did not react to me as a person and during the play therapy sessions, he sat alone, too afraid to even look at me. I showed interest in his person by giving him non-verbal positive reactions and by verbalising his activities. Thus, we established contact.

Later he was able to look at me and even enjoyed coming to the play therapy session. When George felt safe enough he began to carefully explore the playroom. I let him decide what he wanted to play with, paying positive attention to all of his activities. He found a little red toy car he became familiar with. I shared with him his good feelings towards the car and gave him ideas of what he could do with this red car. Our contact improved again through this. The more he felt safe and secure, the more George began to explore the whole playroom. His confidence in the world around him increased as well as his efforts and his motivation to learn about the world inside and outside the playroom.

After four months, before he went into a foster family, he had made a great deal of progress in his development. He had learned many words, was interested in many play activities, expressed his needs, and began to use the word 'I', which showed his awareness of himself. In terms of play development, he was now on the level of role play. Building a relationship was the first step towards, and a requirement for, George's further development. Without this, George would not be able to perceive the world around him nor want to explore it.

## PLAY INTERVENTIONS

Interventions on a play level:

- provide a space for playing
- enable the play to begin
- activate the child in their exploration of the environment
- help the child to express themselves in play
- help the child to gain new experiences in play
- understand the themes of the child and support his or her expression
- help the child to express their scenes in play stories
- be a good actor for the play scenes of the child
- understand the child's play scenarios

- react in the right way to support their coping process
- facilitate the coping process
- help the child to get over stagnation in the play process

## CASE ILLUSTRATION

Karen, an eight-year-old girl, was brought to play therapy by her mother because of the traumatic experience she and her whole family had with her father. Her father hit her, as well as hitting her mother and her brothers. Karen witnessed her father attacking her mother with a chain saw when the mother wanted to leave home. When Karen was five years old, the mother succeeded in leaving the father and taking the children with her. She found a new partner and decided to move herself and her children in with him in a different city. Since then, Karen has not seen her father. Karen suffered from sudden fits of anxiety, she had problems going to asleep, she struggled to make friends, she had problems saying 'No', and she would go out with anyone without even knowing them.

After having built up a good relationship with me as a therapist, Karen began playing the same play scene with animal toys in every session. She always took the same animals: there was a group of adult animals, 'the good ones', four little animals belonging to 'the good ones', and four adult animals, 'the bad ones'. I was ordered to play the bad ones. The bad animals tried to catch the four little animals because they wanted to eat them. But this was not easy as the good adult animals watched over the little ones. They made a circle around them. Every session, the bad ones made new plans to catch the little animals. Every time, they were very close to catching them, but, at the last minute, the little ones were saved by their elders. Every session, she instructed me to improve my attempts. After a long period of time, the play scene started to change. The little animals began to defend themselves, with the good adult animals not having to intervene until later. There was a little brown horse that she liked very much which then took on an important role. This horse showed more and more self-assertiveness and succeeded in defending itself more and more. The play ended when the little horse became more afraid of the bad animals and had learned to protect itself. In the end, the little horse is proud of being so good. At this point, Karen stopped playing with these animals and never played with them again. During this period of playing, she had many issues at home with her mother, and was not accepting her mother's rules. By the end of this play cycle, her relationship with her mother had improved and she began doing what her mother said again.

Karen's main themes were self and identity, and, at the same time, the processing of reality in extreme situations. She put her experience into a play story and manifested in the story how much her development had been in danger. During play, she began to notice her own power and built up her sense of self and achieved more self-confidence.

My input was to give her a place to play out this story, to support her, by understanding how important this play was for her, to encourage her to continue, and to be a good play partner. My input has been to play the bad characters in a way in which Karen could react in her own way. She always gave me instructions. I tried to follow these instructions as best I could.

49

## CONCLUSION

A lot of important principles of child-centred play therapy have been supported, or proven, by attachment theory and play theories. Attachment theory assists the therapist to know how to build a good relationship with the child. It also indicates to the therapist how to react to children verbally and non-verbally to support their development. Attachment theory broadens our understanding of how therapeutic relationships should be and differentiates and clarifies intervention and goals in child psychotherapy. Attachment patterns can help in placing the therapist's focus on erroneous steps of self-development in order to change them.

Play theories:

- tell the therapist how they can foster the development of the self in children and how they can influence developmental problems.

- tell the therapist how to identify the stage of development in children through observing them playing.

- inform how the therapist can support children to get power and control over their environment and experience self-efficacy.

- help the therapist decode the themes children represent in play to understand them better.

The goal is not interpretation or explanation but comprehension of latent and manifest content.

Finally, for the therapist, play theories illuminate the task of supporting children's coping mechanisms for present stress and past traumatic experiences through play. Play is a special medium which nature has given to human beings to facilitate their actualising tendency (Rogers, 1959). It helps the child to process and develop their experiences of their life. In practice, child-centred play therapists have always known this.

## REFERENCES

Ainsworth, MDS, Blehar, MC, Waters, E & Wall S (1978) *Patterns of Attachment. A psychological study of the strange situation.* Hillsdale, NJ: Erlbaum.

Axline, VM (1976) *Kinder-Spieltherapie im nicht-direktiven Verfahren* [Play therapy. The inner dynamics of childhood]. München: Ernst Reinhardt Verlag.

Behr, M (2003) Interactive resonance in work with children and adolescents – A therapy-based concept of interpersonal relationship through play and the use of toys. *Person-Centered and Experiential Psychotherapies, 2* (2), 89-103.

Bornstein, MH (2003) Symbolspiel in der frühen Kindheit. [Play with Symbols in early Childhood]. In M Papousek, A von Gontard, (Eds) *Spiel und Kreativität in der frühen Kindheit* [Play and Creativity in Early Childhood]. Stuttgart: Pfeiffer bei Klett-Cotta.

Bowlby, J (1975) *Bindung* [Attachment and Loss, Vol.1: Attachment]. München: Kindler Verlag.

Crittenden, PM (2000) Molding clay. Retrieved 25 February, 2007, from http://www.patcrittenden.com/images/Molding%20Clay.pdf

Crittenden, PM (2005) Attachment theory, psychopathology, and psychotherapy: The Dynamic-Maturational Approach. Retrieved 25 February, 2007, from http://www.patcrittenden.com/images/Attachment-theory-2005.pdf

Fonagy, P, Gergely, G, Jurist, EL & Target, M (2004) *Affektregulierung, Mentalisierung und die Entwicklung des Selbst* [Affect Regulation, Mentalization, and the Development of the Self]. Stuttgart: Klett Cotta.

Goetze, H (2002) *Handbuch der personenzentrierten Spieltherapie* [Handbook of Person-Centred Play Therapy]. Göttingen: Hogrefe-Verlag.

Grossmann, K & Grossmann, KE (2004) *Bindungen-das Gefüge psychischer Sicherheit.* [Attachment-the Structure of Mental Security]. Stuttgart: Klett-Cotta.

Oerter, R (1993) *Psychologie des Spiels* [Psychology of Play]. München: Quintessenz.

Papousek, M (2003) Spiel in der Wiege der Menschheit [ Play in the Cradle of Mankind]. In M. Papousek, A. von Gontard, (eds) *Spiel und Kreativität in der frühen Kindheit.* Stuttgart: Pfeiffer bei Klett-Cotta.

Piaget, J (1969) *Nachahmung, Spiel und Traum.* [Play, Dreams and Imitation in Childhood]. Stuttgart: Klett-Cotta.

Rogers, CR (1959) A theory of therapy, personality and interpersonal relationships, as developed in the client-centred framework. In S Koch (Ed) *Psychology: A study of a science. Vol. 3: Formulations of the person and the social context* pp. 184–256. New York: McGraw-Hill.

Siegel, DJ (1999) *The Developing Mind.* New York NY: The Guilford Press.

Siegel, DJ (2006) *Wie wir WERDEN die wir SIND* [How We Become Who We Are]. Paderborn: Jungfermann.

# CHAPTER 4

# SEXUALLY ABUSED CHILDREN AND ADOLESCENTS

## A PERSON-CENTRED PLAY THERAPY PROTOCOL

DOROTHEA HÜSSON

## INTRODUCTION

During the last three decades, a wide range of literature has been created addressing sexual violence against young people from diverse perspectives. Comprehensive textbooks in the German language area include Hirsch (1987), Steinhage (1989) and Enders (1990). At the same time, concepts for therapy of traumatic experiences have gained a new importance within psychosocial and therapeutic work (e.g. the enormous spread of Eye Movement Desensitisation and Reprocessing (EMDR) methods). As play therapists genuinely deal with violated feelings of children, these new views and concepts have offered the challenge of rethinking earlier concepts, under the special perspective of working with these young clients. Conceptual considerations (Ater, 2001; Webb, 2001; Riedel, 1997; Weinberg, 2005) case studies (Wittmann, 2006) or diagnostic tools (Homeyer, 2001; Perry & Landreth, 2001) demonstrate the differentiation of person-centred methods in regard to the work with sexually abused young people.

## THEORETICAL BACKGROUND

To meet these new challenges in therapy practice, some of the basic concepts of humanistic play therapy practice have to be reconsidered. Today, the basic concept of Axline (1947) with its highly space-giving and nurturing methods has been supplemented by a more interactional approach (Behr, 2003). However, the principle of non-directiveness and self-regulation within the therapeutic process remains the basic rationale for all behaviour of the therapist within the person-centred paradigm. The challenging therapy practice with sexually violated children is supported by the general concepts but may be assisted by further developments. This article attempts to provide a play therapy protocol which addresses the special problems and therapeutic interventions within a person-centred play therapy process with sexually violated young people. It therefore advances the more space-giving paradigms of Axline (1947) or Ater (2001) and at the same time refrains from the more directive approach of Weinberg (2005). Instead, it seeks an interaction-focused work with process-directive elements which conceptualises an active and sometimes leading therapist on the basis of the authenticity concept. The therapist can address traumatic experiences but at the same time protect the client in a comprehensive way.

The following sections outline some typical situations during the therapy process and suggest possible interventions on the basis of a differentiated person-centred concept.

## EXPERIENCES OF SEXUALLY ABUSED CHILDREN

Sexually abused children are exposed to experiences which become negative forces that they bring into therapy:

- The offender usually commands the child to hold their tongue; sometimes the child is too inhibited by this prohibition to either talk about the abuse or to act it out on the play level.
- The child usually knows the offender and has a confidential relationship with him or her. The experience of this relationship leads many children to fear and distrust all relationships: they no longer know who or what to trust.
- The child experiences powerlessness, helplessness and a complete lack of control and is in danger of remaining in the role of the victim.
- The child is exposed to experiences which do not correspond with their childlike needs and which cannot be integrated into their self-image.

The child takes responsibility for the suffered trauma and feels guilt and shame.

## ADDRESSING THE ABUSE

In person-centred play therapy the therapist allows the child to develop and express his or her inner issues (congruence and incongruence). Throughout the play process the therapist offers the child his or her warm, empathic attitude in a pleasing play environment. Many children use this secure place to live out their experience on a play-symbolic level. So they become able to work their experiences out in the company of their therapist and to integrate the experience of violence in their life story. Self-healing processes become active, without any special influence from the therapist (Axline, 1947: 73–120; Behr, 1996: 41–54; Weinberger, 2001: 22–37; Riedel, 1997: 164).

It does seem that there is a need for a modified process when working with children who have experienced sexual violence: inner blockages and forced secrecy often inhibit the child to such a degree that the help of a therapist is essential.

### CASE ILLUSTRATION 1

Katja, now 11 years old, was abused by her grandfather when she was eight. She tells her mother about the incident who stops all contact with the grandfather to protect her child. After a while, Katja shows the distinctive symptoms of distress: she gets bad grades, stops connecting with friends, develops an argumentative relationship with her brother and begins to suffer from an eating disorder; she eats compulsively and has gained lot of weight. She has an appointment at a paediatric centre. The psychologist there recommends psychotherapy. Katja is allocated a person-centred therapist and uses the playroom, where she brings up many issues: school, friends, being a model, looking good – but not the alleged abuse. The therapist wonders, 'How do we deal with this? Is there a possibility that the issues are being brought up indirectly?'

In person-centred therapy, whilst counsellors usually try to avoid getting ahead of the child or suggesting a topic (Riedel, 1997: 165–8), the child will probably not be able to overcome these obstacles on their own. If the child cannot face the issue verbally or on the play level, the therapist can consider expressing the unexpressed in order to open the space of congruency for the child. This proposed expansion to the person-centred play model should be restricted to cases where the abuse is proved – it is not usable in cases of suspicion.

The topic of sexual abuse can be addressed in the following sense: 'Katja, your Mum told me that you have been touched in your vagina by your grandfather, and you did not like it. I have seen other children before who have experienced similar things. Other kids can sometimes get distressed, their sleep is disrupted or they have problems paying attention at school or with friends. Sometimes they think about it a lot. Are you feeling like this at all?'

By bringing up the topic, the therapist achieves the following:

- The secret of the concealed, the 'taboo', can be uncovered. Often, the child has been strictly warned not to talk about the abuse. This pressure to keep the secret is very strong – even after the abuse has been uncovered. By talking about it, the therapist gives *permission* to talk about it: children may need to be informed that it is allowable to talk about the issue of sexual abuse in therapy. If the therapist does not talk about the topic, the known scheme of secrecy could be continued.

- Throughout the process, the therapist must show that she or he is able to deal with the issue and is not afraid of confrontation. Parents are often very emotionally involved and have conveyed to their child that this issue is stressing and overwhelming them. By bringing it up, the therapist shows the strength to talk about it – so it's easier for the child to talk about it.

- Often, it can be feelings of shame that stop a child from talking about abuse: if the therapist takes the first step, approaching the subject will be easier for the child. The issue of shame can also be brought into the discussion if this appears appropriate and the child does not have the emotional vocabulary or feels too vulnerable to bring it up themself.

Children and adolescents in counselling may have had previous therapeutic experiences but, when the abuse is addressed, it can become clear that this has not previously been brought up; even though they would have appreciated it, shame and embarrassment have prevented the young people from introducing the subject themselves, so it has not been given any explicit space. It is an interesting fact that children reporting abuse to the police often feel relieved after the court hearing because they have finally had an opportunity to talk about it.

Sometimes the therapist develops more anxiety and fear than the child; the therapist's insecurity about how to name the issue without burdening the child progressively leads to the point of avoiding the issue. If, in the therapist's own personal history, emotionally charged experiences are now being reactivated by this contact with the child, there is an obvious additional reason why the topic doesn't get its space in therapy (Rogers, 1989: 73–83).

Approaching the child should not mean investigating, asking repeatedly or forcing the conversation towards the subject. The approach should resemble an invitation, and the child's reaction will make it easy to judge whether or not this is accepted. If the child is open to sharing their experiences and feelings, the therapist can work with them on these expressions in a person-centred way, but if the child refuses the invitation, the therapist should not push the issue. Sometimes, if the child avoids the topic on a verbal level, another action on a playful level can open a new way. Children, like everyone else, need time to approach particular issues – even though they might not have reacted so far, they could well bring the subject up in a subsequent session.

For children who have developed strong fears and feelings of threat, introducing relevant books can be helpful. But, again, this should be just an offer in the sense of 'Look, I have brought a book in which you may or may not be interested', or just placing a book in the playroom without any comment. Many children succeed in approaching their own experience through fictitious characters; they want to know what happens to the children in the story, and the therapist can reflect with them on how the character is feeling and what they choose to say or do. At this distance children can sometimes control their own shock and fear, they become able to deal with the subject (Weinberger, 2001: 159–66), but if the child declines this invitation as well, there should be no pressure to continue.

When working with children who have experienced sexual abuse, the following considerations are often helpful.

## TRANSPARENCY AND DIRECTNESS

The work with children and their parents should be as direct and transparent as possible. Sexual abuse happens in an atmosphere of secrecy so the therapy environment should convey absolute transparency: no secrets are necessary, and secrecy must not be introduced at any level. Whatever has happened or is happening in the family is an appropriate subject for discussion or play in therapy.

### CASE ILLUSTRATION 2

When the mother brings her child into therapy, she whispers quickly to the therapist that her 12-year-old daughter has been stealing money from her purse because money is being extorted from her by classmates. During the therapeutic setting, the child continues playing the same games as if nothing has happened. The therapist's waiting for the child to bring up the family stress brings her into incongruence and, at the same time, contributes to the family's scheme of secrecy. To avoid this, it is important for the therapist to communicate directly and transparently, to face the problem by addressing the child after having talked about her to her mother. The therapist says: 'Your mother has told me that the two of you have just argued because you have taken money from her to give to your classmates who are forcing you to give them money. I am guessing that this is uncomfortable for you.'

It is important not to be judgemental or moralistic but to offer the child a conversation which they can either respond to or decline. Correcting old behaviour schemes by transparency and directness on the part of the therapist can give back to the child safety in contact with people (Behr, 1996: 52).

The emotional charge and the shame of the sexual abuse, for both the child and the parents, is sometimes so unbearable that it becomes unspeakable – a taboo.

## CASE ILLUSTRATION 3

Miriam is six years old. Her mother is brutally beaten and abused by her partner. After the mother and children are rescued and given refuge at a house for abused women, Miriam starts therapy. Miriam always talks about her mother's partner as 'the asshole'. She explains to me that her mother has said, 'We won't call him by his name anymore; we'll just call him 'the asshole'. Whilst acknowledging the family's term for him, the therapist chooses to call the partner by his name.

By not saying the partner's name, he receives a special form of denigration but also power. By not speaking his name and instead substituting a curse, there might be increased fear in the family. But it is very effective to give a name to the unmentionable in order to remove the fear from it. This same theme is recognised in Harry Potter's story: Voldemort's name is spoken directly by Harry Potter, while most of the other characters in the book are too afraid to call him by a name that fuels their fear. The therapist gives permission to name the unmentionable in order to destroy the strategies of the offender.

## POST-TRAUMATIC PLAY

In play therapy, post-traumatic play is of specific interest. In many cases, it is a symbolic performance of fear – of being absolutely helpless. Within this play, a child can affect some emotional regulation. When the child repeats and reworks in post-traumatic play its own traumatic experiences, this can be considered as self-salvation and a healing process (Levine, 1998: 255).

The following guidelines support this process (ibid.: 256):

- The child says how fast and how intense the play should be.
- The therapist must be able to see the difference between fear and positive affection in the child.
- When the emotional stress becomes too heavy for the child, it can develop dissociations, losing contact with present reality and retreating to an inner world in order to avoid confronting fear. It can be helpful to bring the child back into reality and to stimulate in this way the actualising tendency intervening within reality reflection ('I see you here in this room), emotional reflection ('I see your face looking so sad') and body reflection (the therapist moves her body in symmetry with the child).

As long as the child is able to find an inner helper or saviour in the play, he or she can hope for another and better future; certainly, the results for the development of the child will be less destructive. Weinberg is convinced that the child must confront themselves with the trauma again, therefore, following the child, 'the therapist stages sadism, cruelty and fantasies of murder during the play. If the therapist allows the child to stage and experience all these cruel fantasies of violence, the play will open the possibility of symbolising these experiences and achieving a "catharsis"' (Weinberg, 2005: 210).

TIME OUT, SECURE PLACES AND 'HELPING' FIGURES

CASE ILLUSTRATION 4

Later in therapy, Miriam plays at 'killing'. She tries to 'kill' the therapist in different ways – with a sword, a machine-gun and a knife. She appears to be enjoying the game very much as evidenced by her smiling and enthusiastic engagement although she sometimes calls out for a break, saying 'Time out!' Depending on her feelings, she allows the therapist to come closer or she 'kills' him faster. This play shouldn't be interrupted, because Miriam is showing an actually developed self-actualising tendency. She becomes able to integrate her fear by facing it in a controlled way; to integrate her incongruence – her damaged self-image – into a new self-image; able to perceive and to express her own feelings. The therapist supports her, verbalising empathically her emotional experiences with unconditional positive regard; he does not try to mimic Miriam by being aggressive towards her, trying to scare her, or being alternately warm and cold with her. Now the way can open for her to overcome her fears; she plays like this for two hours then says, 'I'm not doing this anymore', before changing to other topics.

By offering the child this possibility for play, there's not a lot to do other than tolerate and follow the child, which in itself can be challenging. Often, children build hideaways during the play which are free from fear. So 'Time out!' means, for example: 'Here you (the perpetrator) can't attack me anymore,' or, 'I'm invisible. You can't do anything to me and can't harm me in any way.' Within fearful playing situations, the child can create inwardly and environmentally secure places. If the child doesn't construct such a secure place in the playing room when there is fear in their fantasy roleplay, the therapist can invite the child to do so (Reddemann, 2003: 40; Weinberg, 2005: 174).

Most of the children know and have 'helper' figures; the therapist can ask for these helper figures and get to know them – that's better than installing new ones. On the playing level, the positively defined figures are the helper figures. For example, 'Oh, this is a good monster. He could help the knight', or, 'Oh, here comes a friend who's going to beat the bad guy.' More familiar little helpers could also be used: stuffed animals or soft toys from home that the children use as 'helpers' when they need comfort (Reddemann, 2003: 41; Lackner, 2004: 83–5).

## CASE ILLUSTRATION 5

Peter couldn't sleep – but after giving him his toy elephant in a police uniform from the playroom he slept soundly through the whole night.

The development of the child in post-traumatic play can become more effective when the different levels of a child's experience – cognitions, sensual perceptions, feelings and body perceptions – are verbalised by the therapist. For example, the therapist could put the inner processes of people or play figures into words when the child stages a roleplay: 'Aha, he thought he could steal it and run away'; sensual perceptions: 'He felt so faint he couldn't speak '; or feelings: 'He felt so lonely'; and body perceptions: 'After that, he got bad stomach pains'.

## FACILITATING ESCAPE FROM TRAUMATIC PLAY

A problem can arise when the child is stuck in traumatic play during the therapy. The therapist might perceive, in his congruency, that the child's play is becoming tiring and boring for them – it seems repetitive and does not lead to any apparent conclusion. If the therapist feels frustrated or bored, or if he or she intuits that the child has arrived at an impasse where the processes of experiential digestion do not continue, the therapist can offer the child a proposition that might be accepted and integrated into its play. In this case a child can benefit from additional support from the outside to find an urgent solution for their situation. The therapist can interfere in order to support the self-healing process.

Some severely traumatised children don't show obvious self-protecting reactions. Therapists can help create self-healing places when these self-righting tendencies are not apparent. Showing secure places or allowing or inviting time-outs is one way to help.

## THE THERAPIST IN THE ROLE OF THE AGGRESSOR

The therapist has to pay special attention in the playing process when the child encourages the therapist to play the role of the aggressor. The child says, for example: 'Beat me!' 'Torture me!' Weinberg insists that such a staging should be played out, but the therapist must be very careful to maintain the play character of the whole process within the child's awareness. The child must not shift into a trance-like state where he or she will fail to experience the difference between the therapist and offender (cf. Weinberg, 2005: 211).

Coming into incongruence the therapist feels it is impossible to continue the roleplay. Of course, they don't want to act aggressively towards the child, but they now face a dilemma: as a person-centred therapist, they want to offer the child the possibility of working on this issue in their own way. This inner dilemma can be solved by therapists simply speaking transparently and directly to set limits that involve an acknowledgement of the child's feeling or desire, a self-disclosing or congruent statement, and a relevant but open-ended alternative: 'You want me to kill you, but I am not comfortable killing you. You are not for killing. You can ask me to kill one of these toy animals' (Landreth & Bratton, 2005).

If the child picks up the idea and installs a helping figure, the process of the play continues in an uncomplicated way. Usually, the child becomes able to get out of the role of victim and to conquer the aggressor.

In addition, the therapist can express their own feelings whilst helping the child to escape the identification of victim. For example: 'Hey, stop that, please! When I see this big bear being so cruel I feel very angry with him.' The key for the self-actualisation of the child and for the construction of a reliable inner authority will be found in the congruency, the highly concentrated and careful self-perception of the therapist.

## THE THERAPIST IN THE ROLE OF THE VICTIM

The degree to which the therapist perceives, in the role of the 'victim', the feeling of helplessness, will correspond to the feeling of helplessness in the child – and to their sense of being at the mercy of a real threat. The therapist needs the emotional stability to become immersed affectively into the feelings of the victim at the level of play; keeping an alertness to how their own history and worldview might influence the roleplay in a way not consistent with the child's own feelings and experience.

### CASE ILLUSTRATION 6

The therapist is playing at being a little rabbit locked in a toilet and feeling terrified. In this role the therapist can verbalise what they perceive on the level of play, for example, by talking to themselves: 'Oh, now I'm sitting here behind this locked toilet door and I can't get out. What shall I do? I'm so afraid. Nobody is helping me and I feel so alone. Oh, if only I was tall and strong! But I'm so small and nobody protects me.'

The therapist can make a 'play stop' after realising their own feelings of being a helpless victim on the play level. Now they could say: 'Hey, we must have a break. Time out please! I can feel how horrible and cruel this is for the little rabbit. I'm wondering how anyone can possibly live with such a great fear. There's absolutely no help. That's really hard.'

This is not the place for recriminations or moral judgement: it's very important just to say it like it is and to be objective and accepting. For the therapist, this means being in touch with the child's feelings of helplessness and desperation and, in verbalising these emotional experiences, to stay in touch with them. It is the therapeutic challenge to bear these feelings and, at the same time, to carry out the defined therapeutic role (Weinberg, 2005: 214–19).

# SAFETY WITH BOUNDARIES

All children who have been victims of sexual violence and abuse have experienced a massive violation of boundaries. Many of these children have problems perceiving their own boundaries and keeping these with others (Goetze, 2002: 343). That's why this topic has a special meaning and place in therapy. The therapist should always be aware of keeping boundaries because they offer safety and orientation to the child (Axline, 1972: 126; Weinberg, 2005: 232–3).

Installation of boundaries can be realised:

- at the play level (for example, if the child wants to bring gallons of water into the playroom)
- when a too-close body contact occurs
- when the therapist's personal boundaries are violated during the play
- when the structural boundaries of the therapeutic setting are not kept (for example, when the child prolongs the therapy hours or is absent without having cancelled)

It is also interesting that more often than not in cases of sexual abuse, the family's own system has no recognition of boundaries – not even in the context of the sexual-abuse counselling that has just taken place. For example, there are mothers who keep talking after the therapy hour is over and the next child is waiting; they ignore the offer of an appointment and continue to talk to the therapist while their own child is next to them. This shows the importance of focusing on 'boundaries in the family' in therapeutic parents' appointments; very often it is helpful to address the parents' experience with boundaries and to offer space for this topic.

# FEELING GUILTY

Another challenge in therapy is the question of how to work with the topic of feeling guilty. This is a very common issue in therapy with adolescents and older children. Most of the time they say: 'It was my own fault. I have done something wrong. If I had done it right, it wouldn't have happened.' The rationale in this way of magic thinking is: 'If I had done it another way, if I had been different, I could have prevented the disaster.'

In therapy, there could be a big temptation to tell the child or the adolescent: 'Of course you couldn't do anything. It wasn't your fault. The adult was responsible for what happened. He must know what's OK and what isn't. But you couldn't have done anything different.'

But in most of the cases, although the children and the adolescents initially agree, they then say: 'I know you're right. But on the other hand, I could have run away.' This objection must be perceived and valued. For many children and adolescents, the 'taking away of guilt' means a shift into a feeling of absolute helplessness, powerlessness and loss of control; the belief that they could have somehow changed what has happened gives them more security and self-respect. This may be a trap for the counselling process. The counsellor attempts to remove stress from the child by conveying that feelings of guilt are superfluous, but for many children or adolescents these feelings of guilt seem less threatening than the confrontation in which they had no control at all. In cases like this, the classic empathic and accepting approach, in which no judgement is made, should prove especially helpful and constructive.

## WORKING WITH PARENTS

In order to improve the therapeutic process, intensive work with parents is particularly important. Parents too will be traumatised by their child's situation and this is an opportunity to explore any issues and worries – about how their own lives are going to be affected; the possibility of losing their partner; feelings of guilt and just the sheer horror of the situation – that could be preventing them from being supportive or helpful. To ensure that the therapist is not unconsciously drawn into manipulative family dynamics or prejudiced in relation to the child, this sort of therapy should be carried out by another colleague.

The parent sessions, in parallel with the child therapy, aim:

- to empower the parents in their task of responding to the child's emotions
- to show the parents how to react appropriately to the behaviour of the child (i.e. to their depression or aggression resulting from the abuse)
- to create clear boundaries
- to ensure safety and security for the child

It is important to have an agreement with the child about what information may be transferred to the parent session – the child must not suffer from a new abuse of confidence – and any information provided by the parents that might prove helpful to the child will be brought to the therapy process with the same sense of transparency. The most usual way of pursuing these aims is to arrange one-to-one counselling sessions between therapist and parents (e.g. once a month). It can also be useful to work with parents with the method of 'filial therapy'.

Landreth and Bratton (2005) offer a child-centred, humanistic approach to working with parents, strongly supported by gold-standard research, referred to as child–parent relationship therapy (e.g. filial therapy). Essentially, they suggest that therapists provide a 5–10 session manualised training showing how parents can provide 30-minute special playtimes with one child to improve many of the above concerns. Research has shown significant effects, beyond those of non-humanistic play therapy, for a variety of child-presenting issues.

## CONFIDENCE OF THE THERAPIST

It is important not to continue to see the child and the adolescent simply as a victim. Being a victim means feeling continually helpless, hurt and at someone else's mercy. However every human being has the resources to heal the wounds that life inflicts, the will to survive and to fight for a better life. If the therapist credits children and adolescents with this power and if she or he meets them in this attitude, then hope, joy of living and strength will develop and grow (Lackner, 2004: 98; Rogers, 1989: 45–52).

## CONCLUSION

Children and adolescents who have experienced sexual violence mostly come into therapy with behavioural symptoms which can be explained as a result of these experiences – distrust, intrusiveness, feelings of threat and loneliness. That's why in therapy they need a particularly high measure of safety (for example, by clear structures and trustworthiness), clarity in dealing with boundaries and a conscious dealing with physical closeness and distance. During therapy children benefit from total transparency and openness, the experience of an honest and trustworthy relationship (not attached to any conditions) and the sensitive dealing with emotional problems like guilt and ambivalence.

This makes it absolutely necessary to offer the client a person-centred relationship. On the level of the therapeutic relationship, no other concept is possible. Additional therapeutic interventions quite often appear to be useful, but they make no sense if they are not grounded on the qualities of the person-centred behaviour of the therapist.

Thus, a completion by trauma-therapeutic intervention is often necessary if the child or adolescent is stuck by their highly charged emotional experiences in traumatic play scenarios. In order to demonstrate to the child alternative ways of behaving – autonomously unreachable because of their traumatised condition – a time-limited, more directive procedure by the therapist can be necessary.

If the space of acting in the therapeutic play remains limited, the therapist should become active: in this situation of impasse the therapist can offer a next step within the child's play process and thus give a leading cue at a crucial moment. If, by the dynamic of the play process, the child or adolescent is confronted in a threatening way with their overwhelming feelings, they will need the security of structured therapeutic procedure to help them control these emotions.

The therapist can also be guided by their own experiential process. For example, they might become aware that they can't relate to the play – it's boring or tiring, or no dynamic arises. This could imply that the inner processing of the child has come to a standstill – perhaps in contrast to the therapist's own experience of, say, interest, curiosity, tension or concern, which has made them suppose that the emotional processes within the child were active. Thus, in severe and repetitive cases of boredom and tiredness, the therapist could use these personal emotional cues to progress to more active behaviour, with leading steps and/or thoughtful self-disclosure.

Supplementary, helpful interventions are imagination exercises, known in trauma therapy as 'the safe inner place', 'the helpful helper', 'safe' exercises (Reddemann, 2003: 45, 46, 51). In therapy, the child learns supporting strategies, helping them to stay calm and in control in challenging situations. Following the non-directive basics of the person-centred approach, the exercise should not be used in the sense of a technique (for example: 'Imagine an inner secure place …') but, more appropriately, developed with regard to the capacities and resources already known (for example: 'You told me you'd love to have a tree house. Perhaps you'd like to imagine such a tree house – the most secure place in the whole world …').

In many cases, it is helpful to explain to the children, the adolescents and their parents which emotions and symptoms have developed as reactions to their traumatic experiences. Many children and adolescents are enormously relieved when they understand that their reactions are explainable rather than crazy.

Thus, person-centred psychotherapy offers – by its core conditions, empathy, acceptance and congruence – many possibilities to process traumatic experiences. Supplementary methods can support this process in a very helpful way, but never without the basis of the person-centred relationship.

The person-centred relationship has a special significance with complex traumatised children and adolescents who have suffered from emotionally charged, painful and violating bonding experiences – often through people close to them. In these cases, mere 'techniques' are of no use: only trustworthy and continuing relationships can counteract persistent and damaging relationship patterns and establish new healing processes.

Normally in classical person-centred psychotherapy, the child determines the contents of play and the therapist follows the child with empathy, congruence and unconditional regard at the play level. Specific experiences suffered in sexual abuse can produce an inner impasse blocking the self-actualising tendency of the child. Sometimes, classical person-centred strategies will not lead to a resolution. The aim of this article has been to introduce for discussion a modified person-centred therapy in which the therapist develops helpful interventions in therapeutic play based on the person-centred concept of congruence.

## REFERENCES

Ater, MK (2001) Play therapy behaviors of sexually abused children. In GL Landreth (Ed) *Innovations in Play Therapy* (pp. 119–29). New York: Brunner-Routledge.

Axline, VM (1947) *Play Therapy: The inner dynamics of childhood.* Boston: Houghton Mifflin.

Behr, M (1996) Therapie als Erleben von Beziehung – Die Bedeutung der interaktionellen Theorie des Selbst für die Praxis einer personzentrierten Kinder - und Jugendlichenpsychotherapie [Therapy as experience of relationship: The importance of the interactional theory of the self for the practice of a person-centred therapy of children and adolescents]. In C Boeck-Singelmann, B Ehlers, T Hensel, F Kemper & C Monden-Engelhardt (Eds) *Personzentrierte*

*Psychotherapie mit Kindern und Jugendlichen,* [Person-Centred Psychotherapy with Children and Adolescents]. *Bd. 1: Grundlagen und Konzepte* [Vol. 1: Foundations and concepts]. (2. Auflage) (pp. 41–68). Göttingen: Hogrefe.

Behr, M (2003) Interactive resonance in work with children and adolescents: A theory-based concept of interpersonal relationship through play and the use of toys. *Person-Centered and Experiential Psychotherapies, 2* (2), 89–103.

Enders, U (1990) *Zart war ich, bitter war's. Handbuch gegen sexuellen Missbrauch* [I was Young, It was a Bitter Experience. Handbook against sexual abuse]. Köln: Kiepenheuer & Witsch.

Goetze, H (2002) *Handbuch der personenzentrierten Spieltherapie.* [Manual of Person-Centred Play Therapy.] Göttingen: Hogrefe.

Hirsch, M (1987) *Realer Inzest. Psychodynamik des sexuellen Missbrauchs in der Familie.* [Real Incest: Psychodynamism of sexual abuse in family]. Heidelberg: Springer.

Homeyer, LE (2001) Identifying sexually abused children in play therapy. In GL Landreth (Ed) *Innovations in Play Therapy* (pp. 131–54). New York: Brunner-Routledge.

Lackner, R (2004) *Wie Pippa wieder lachen lernte – Fachliche Hilfen für traumatisierte Kinder* [How Pippa Relearned Laughter: Special support for traumatised children]. Wien: Springer Verlag.

Landreth, GL & Bratton, SC (2005) *Child Parent Relationship Therapy (CPRT).* New York: Routledge.

Levine, PA (1998) *Trauma-Heilung. Das Erwachen des Tigers. Unsere Fähigkeit, traumatische Erfahrungen zu transformieren* [Trauma Healing. The awakening of the tiger. Our capacity for transforming traumatizing experiences]. Essen: Synthesis.

Perry, LH & Landreth, GL (2001) Diagnostic assessment of children's play therapy behavior. In GL Landreth (Ed) *Innovations in Play Therapy* (pp. 155–78). New York: Brunner-Routledge.

Reddemann, L (2003) *Imagination als heilsame Kraft* [Imagination as a Healing Power]. Stuttgart: Pfeiffer.

Riedel, K (1997) Personzentrierte Kindertherapie bei sexueller Misshandlung. [Person-centred therapy for children in cases of sexual abuse]. In C Boeck-Singelmann, B Ehlers, T Hensel, F Kemper & C Monden-Engelhardt (Eds) *Personzentrierte Psychotherapie mit Kindern und Jugendlichen, Bd. 2.: Anwendung und Praxis.* [Person-Centred Psychotherapy with Children and Adolescents Vol. 2 Application and practice] (pp. 159–80). Göttingen: Hogrefe.

Rogers, C (1989) *Entwicklung der Persönlichkeit* [On Becoming a Person: A therapist's view of psychotherapy]. Stuttgart: Klett Cotta.

Steinhage, R (1989) *Sexueller Missbrauch an Mädchen Ein Handbuch für Beratung und Therapie.* [Sexual Abuse of Girls: A manual for counselling and therapy]. Reinbek: Rowohlt.

Webb, P (2001) Play therapy with traumatized children: A crisis response. In GL Landreth (Ed) *Innovations in Play Therapy* (pp. 289–302). New York: Brunner-Routledge.

Weinberg, D (2005) *Traumatherapie mit Kindern* [Trauma Therapy with Children]. München: Pfeiffer.

Weinberger, S (2001) *Kindern spielend helfen. Eine personzentrierte Lern- und Praxisanleitung* [Helping Children in Play: A person-centred instruction for learning and practice]. Weinheim: Beltz.

Wittmann, AJ (2006) Personzentrierte Spieltherapie nach sexuellem Missbrauch – Eine Kasuistik zur Verdeutlichung zentraler Spiel- und Symbolisierungsprozesse [Person-centred play therapy after sexual abuse: Casuistic study to clarify central processes of play and symbolisation]. *Person, 11* (2), 142–50.

# CHAPTER 5

# FREEING CHILDREN TO TELL THEIR STORIES

## THE UTILISATION OF PERSON-CENTRED AND EXPERIENTIAL PSYCHOTHERAPY IN CHILD WELFARE INVESTIGATIONS

### FRANCES BERNARD KOMINKIEWICZ

## INTRODUCTION

At first glance, the Rogerian concept of emphasising perception and understanding over objective behaviours appears to be contraindicated as a psychotherapeutic technique in an investigative process. The investigative process is one that is meant to elicit the child's factual description of maltreatment in order to determine whether criminal charges should be filed against the alleged perpetrator and, if so, to prepare the court case. As a result, psychotherapy is not the primary purpose of the investigative process.

Although a major movement to assist children in therapeutically processing the child maltreatment experience is occurring in the United States, the child welfare system does not view this as the overarching function of the investigation. Training for child welfare investigators generally focuses upon eliciting information from children without prompting them to provide inaccurate information. Therefore, it would seem that the child's ability to verbalise about the maltreatment also serves as the first stage of the child's healing.

The legal investigative process emphasises questions directed at the child and assesses the child's responses to determine if and what type or types of maltreatment have occurred. However, if the child is not given the opportunity to unfold his or her story according to his or her worldview, much will remain in the psyche of the child that may assist in the investigative process. Allowing children to move at their own tempo will encourage them to discuss any issues which at the time may or may not seem relevant to the investigation. Not only does this process assist them in dealing with the abusive situation, but it also allows them to tell the situation in their own words, thus increasing the accuracy of the investigation. If the investigator does not provide children with the opportunity to verbalise in their own words, and attempts to clarify their statements using adult language, the investigation may be compromised.

The preceding aspect of the child maltreatment investigation encourages the investigator to refrain from interjecting language into the interview with the child and therefore contributes to an unbiased investigation. Although the investigator is not referred to as a psychotherapist during the investigative process, he or she may receive training in person-centred techniques to enhance forensic interviewing skills, including refraining from asking suggestive or leading questions and building rapport (Cronch, Viljoen & Hansen, 2006; Orbach, Lamb, Sternberg & Horowitz, 2006; Aldridge & Wood, 2000).

## THE ENVIRONMENT OF MALTREATED CHILDREN

Children may experience neglect, physical abuse, emotional abuse, verbal abuse, sexual abuse, or multiple types of abuses. They can experience all types of maltreatment simultaneously and, therefore, the form of maltreatment can affect the signs of maltreatment symptoms. Complicating the issue of child maltreatment is the difficulty of identifying maltreatment definitions globally, a task that has affected the overall statistical analysis of maltreatment types internationally. The various definitions of psychological maltreatment and child neglect in particular have contributed to the difficulty in comparing the rates of child maltreatment internationally (Barnett, Miller-Perrin & Perrin, 2005). The extent of international child maltreatment has not been accurately determined, since many countries have no mandatory reporting statutes or existing social processes to statistically maintain child maltreatment reports (Krug, Dahlberg, Mercy, Zwi & Lozano, 2002). Some researchers have hypothesised that the lack of evidence of child maltreatment can be interpreted as the *absence* of child maltreatment in these countries (Kashani & Allan, 1998). It seems more likely that child maltreatment has not yet been identified as a problem in particular countries (Barnett, Miller-Perrin & Perrin, 2005) and that there is more availability of child maltreatment data, including published research regarding child maltreatment, in Western countries (Al-Mahroos, Abdulla, Kamal & Al-Ansari, 2005).

Several studies and reports have found that child maltreatment exists globally. Finkelhor (1994) reviewed the international statistics of child sexual abuse from 21 studies, and found that child sexual abuse international rates in northern European countries, as well as Costa Rica, the Dominican Republic, Greece and Spain, were comparable to those in the North American research. Another study reported that two-thirds of parents in the Republic of Korea related that they whipped their children and 45 per cent disclosed that they beat, hit or kicked their children (Hahm & Guterman, 2001). Following a ban on parental corporal punishment of children by the German government in 2000, research found that close to 44 per cent of children surveyed in 1992 reported being slapped hard across the face compared to 14 per cent of children surveyed in 2002 (Bussman, 2004). In 2002, 4 per cent of those surveyed related that they had received severe physical punishment 'such as being beaten on the bottom with a stick or beaten to the point of bruising'; in 1992, the rates for these two forms of punishment were about eight to ten times greater (Bussman, 2004: 296).

Child maltreatment was found to be the second leading cause of death of children in the United States (Felzen Johnson, 2002). The US Administration for Families and

Children reported that during 2004, 62.4 per cent of child maltreatment victims experienced neglect, 17.5 per cent were physically abused, 9.7 per cent were sexually abused, 7.0 per cent were psychologically maltreated, and 2.1 per cent were medically neglected. In addition, 14.5 per cent of maltreated children experienced 'other' types of maltreatment such as 'abandonment', 'threats of harm to the child', or 'congenital drug addiction' (US Administration for Families and Children, 2004). The individual states in America are allowed to code as 'other' any form of maltreatment that cannot be categorised as physical abuse, neglect, medical neglect, sexual abuse, psychological maltreatment, or emotional maltreatment (ibid.).

The environment of the maltreated child involves the perpetrator of the maltreatment. The relationship of the maltreated child to the perpetrator is affected by the abuse and/or neglect and this process impacts the child's worldview. According to Finkelhor and Browne's (1985) traumagenic model, post-traumatic stress disorder (PTSD) symptoms manifested by maltreated children following the trauma of abuse are connected to changes occurring in the children's self-concept and worldview. Finkelhor and Browne propose that inappropriate sexual behaviour may also occur in sexually abused children. Maltreated children were also found to have emotional or behavioural problems at the clinically significant level (Burns et al., 2004). The application of person-centred concepts within the child welfare investigation allows the child to talk about experiences in his or her world that may have led to the inappropriate sexual behaviour and other clinical, emotional, and behavioural problems.

## THE CHILD ABUSE INVESTIGATIVE PROCESS

Several countries have developed required reporting procedures for alerting the authorities regarding child maltreatment cases. England and Wales are introducing, through Section 12 of the Children Act 2004, that professionals report any 'cause for concern' pertaining to a child's welfare, a procedure that appears to be more extensive than a mandatory system of child abuse reporting (Munro & Parton, 2007). Professionals in Sweden are required to report suspected child maltreatment and the public is also supported in reporting these cases (Cocozza, Gustafsson & Sydsjo, 2006). In the United States, child protection service offices are legally mandated to investigate child maltreatment cases reported, and professionals in all fifty United States are legally mandated to report child maltreatment (Alvarez, Kenny, Donohue & Carpin, 2004; Weinstein, Levine, Kogan, Harkavy-Freidman & Miller, 2001) in order to receive funding through the Child Abuse and Prevention Treatment Act (Westby, 2007).

Child abuse investigations in the United States are conducted primarily through a collaborative effort of child protective services (CPS) and child abuse law enforcement (LE). This joint process has been required by most states when investigating criminal cases of child abuse (Newman, Dannenfelser & Pendleton, 2005). According to Newman et al. (2005), the essential parts of a model child investigative programme include 'a multidisciplinary team for response to child abuse allegations; a designated legal entity responsible for program and fiscal operations; capacity for forensic interviews specialised medical evaluation; and specialised therapeutic services, such as victim support, advocacy, case review and monitoring' (p. 166). The role of clinical consultation and the application of the psychodynamic viewpoint in child welfare investigations have also been recommended (Bassett & Johnson, 2004).

Although child abuse investigative collaboration has been emphasised in the child welfare field since 1974, role conflicts and organisational dissimilarities may occur (Newman & Dannenfelser, 2005). Seven practices are considered the most progressive methods in child abuse criminal investigations: victim advocacy programmes; child forensic interviewers; videotaped interviews; trained forensic medical examiners; multidisciplinary team investigations; increased entry for victims into mental health treatment; and child advocacy centres (Jones, Cross, Walsh & Simone, 2005). Higher rates of law enforcement involvement, substantiation of child welfare cases, and medical examinations are found in those cases in which the child advocacy centre was involved in comparison to those cases based in child protective service agencies (Smith, Witte & Fricker-Elhai, 2006). While collaboration between law enforcement and child protective services has been found to improve the quality of child welfare investigations and assists families and children, resistance has occurred at times between these two investigative sources (Cross, Finkelhor & Ormrod, 2005) due to different training in child maltreatment investigations. If both law enforcement and child protective services received training in person-centred techniques, the enhanced collaborative relationship between these two investigative offices would further improve the accuracy of the investigation across the criminal justice system.

While many collaborative programmes operate in centres throughout the United States to investigate criminal cases, some centres are designed to primarily investigate child sexual-abuse cases. An example of a child abuse investigative programme focusing on child sexual abuse is the Child Abuse Services Investigation and Education Center (CASIE Center) in South Bend, Indiana. CASIE Center operates jointly with the local police departments and the justice system. A trained forensic interviewer, who may also have additional training as a social worker or counsellor, will meet with the alleged sexually abused child in a room with a two-way mirror. Investigators, including prosecutors, detectives, and police officers, may be present behind this mirror. The forensic investigator will have an earpiece allowing the investigators to communicate with the forensic interviewer without interrupting the interview process with the child.

The child-friendly physical environment allows the child to be interviewed throughout the investigative process with a minimum or absence of potential investigative trauma. Not only does this type of investigative process decrease the possibility of interviewer effect on the child's verbalisation of their stories, but he or she is also provided an opportunity to speak with a minimum amount of questioning. This serves as the beginning of the abused child's journey of self-disclosure in person-centred psychotherapy.

# UTILISATION OF PERSON-CENTRED PSYCHOTHERAPY WITH MALTREATED CHILDREN

Person-centred experiential approaches can be particularly helpful in working with children (Bratton, Ray, Rhine & Jones, 2005; Cornelius-White, 2007a). Although little research exists regarding the application of person-centred therapy with maltreated children, it has been found to be helpful in working with maltreated children and adolescents in multicultural residential, non-residential, and educational settings (Cornelius-White, 2007a; Freire, Koller, Piason & da Silva, 2005; Goodman, Morgan, Juriga & Brown, 2004). Moon (2001) found that person-centred therapy allowed children to enter into a relationship of acceptance and increased a child's ability to become more self-accepting and strive toward self-fulfillment.

Maltreated children can receive unconditional positive regard in a person-centred child welfare investigation as compared to an investigation that primarily focuses on the objective of obtaining information from the child for a criminal proceeding against the perpetrator and/or to remove a child from an abusive environment. Often, these children are unable to enter into a relationship of unconditional positive regard with any significant adult due to an abusive relationship with one adult or particular adults. The child welfare investigator continues to develop a relationship with the maltreated child that will lead to an increase in that child's self-concept throughout the investigative process. Through this application of person-centred techniques, maltreated children can find that a significant adult, the investigator, supports the child in their revision of the self and worldview.

To Rogers, self is equivalent to self-concept. Rogers (1959) discusses self-concept as the 'organized, consistent, conceptual gestalt composed of perceptions of the characteristics of the "I" or "me" and the perceptions of the relationships of the "I" or "me" to others and to various aspects of life, together with the values attached to these perceptions' (p. 200). A maltreated child has experienced relationships that have negatively affected the development of self and, therefore, self-concept. It is necessary that those who are working with the child in any capacity, including the child welfare investigator, interact with the child in a positive manner so that he or she is allowed to develop a positive self-concept. Through not commenting either verbally or non-verbally on what has occurred in the child's life, the investigator can encourage the development of positive self-esteem through these person-centred techniques.

The utilisation of person-centred techniques in child maltreatment investigations can also affect the child's long-term development. Since children have experienced environments that are harmful, their experiences will affect how they view themselves. The maltreated child's perceptions of his or her environment will have a major effect on how the world is viewed and thus impact his or her self-concept. Life presents to all individuals an environment full of experiences that can be both positive and negative to a child's developing self-esteem.

In the world of the maltreated child, a therapist can work with the child to determine how he or she has perceived this world. The child welfare investigator can have a role in helping that child to learn what happened in his or her world by allowing verbalisation of experiences without comment. The perception of the child's experiences will impact the development of his or her self-concept and it is therefore important to allow them to develop their own perception of what occurred between the perpetrator and themselves.

The concepts of person-centred therapy can be applied to maltreated children at various developmental stages. By utilising person-centred techniques during a child abuse investigation, the investigator assists the maltreated child in beginning the healing process necessary in developing a secure self-concept. Four therapist attributes are necessary to create an environment in which the maltreated child can develop positive growth. These four attributes can also be applied to a relationship with a client (Kirschenbaum & Henderson, 1989) and to the child welfare investigative relationship with a maltreated child; these attributes are: empathic understanding, genuineness, unconditional positive regard and the transcendental or spiritual characteristic.

EMPATHIC UNDERSTANDING

Key to working with maltreated children is the concept of empathic understanding. Children often learn cognitively through verbalisation and clarification facilitated by accurate empathy. Allowing children to verbalise their experience with others creates space for children to speak at their own pace when discussing alleged abusive situations. Providing this type of space for children helps them to more comfortably and freely share their feelings. Children who have experienced maltreatment earlier in their lives can also enter person-centred therapy at a later age and feel a high enough comfort level to disclose during the therapy session.

In the child welfare investigation, the objective is to have the child accurately relate what has transpired in his or her experience without leading them. Empathy not only helps the child to deal with the emotional issues of the abuse at their own pace but also allows the investigator to gain accurate information. If the child does not experience empathy from the investigator, they may find it difficult accurately to recall the abusive event – an anxiety-provoking experience. As Cornelius-White and Godfrey (2004) discuss, it is only 'through empathy and compassion [that] students can more likely liberate and accept themselves and others' (p. 174). If the child welfare investigator does not show empathy, the maltreated child may not feel free enough to verbalise the event.

The demonstration of empathy during the child welfare investigation increases the comfort level of the maltreated child and encourages him or her to speak without interruption. Therefore, the child welfare investigator will not need to ask the child closed-ended questions calling for a 'yes', 'no', or very short answer. Open-ended questions are most appropriate during an investigation since the investigator will be able to 'tap free-recall memory' (Orbach & Lamb, 2001: 323), and it is recommended that open-ended questions be utilised throughout the interview (Orbach & Lamb, 2000). Children will also continue to respond during the investigation if the investigator has commenced the interview with open-ended questions (Sternberg et al., 1997). Interviewing children by using open-ended questions – eliciting free narratives and enhancing the ability of children to tell their story according to their own experiences – is especially important since children's cognitive and language skills are not as well-developed as those of adults in these areas (Wright & Powell, 2006).

The demonstration of unconditional positive regard and empathy can exert a positive influence on the ability of the child welfare investigator to maintain free-narrative techniques throughout the investigation. Although child investigative interviewers are trained in interviewing skills, emphasising free-narrative accounts through the use of open-ended questions, they have frequently not utilised these procedures (ibid.). Child investigators provided three reasons to explain why they continued to ask specific questions, even after receiving training in using free-narrative techniques. These were: the different character of the open-ended communication method; the multifaceted variation between open-ended versus specific questions; and the exactness of the legal information considered necessary from children in these situations (ibid.).

Training in investigative interviewing techniques has been found to have a limited effect on interviewing methods, with child maltreatment investigators not changing their tendency to elicit information through closed-ended questions when building rapport, and specifically questioning children about their maltreatment experiences (Warren et al., 1999). No additional information was obtained from children after the completion of training in this study (ibid.). Child maltreatment forensic interviewers in England, Wales, the United States, Israel and Sweden, were found to infrequently use open-ended questions to gain information from the children, with almost 40 per cent of the information elicited using option-posing and suggestive prompts known to obtain less dependable information (Sternberg, Lamb, Davies & Westcott, 2001).

The person-centred technique of asking open-ended questions to elicit free narrative is therefore not used as extensively as it could be, even after training is provided. It should be noted that person-centred techniques are not always labeled as such in child maltreatment investigations, and research in this area requires an extensive review of the literature. Further monitoring of interview methods, interview skills practice, critical skill assessment and corrective evaluation are recommended to improve child maltreatment interviewing methods (Warren et al., 1999) and to increase the utilisation of person-centred techniques.

The influence of high-pressured investigative techniques by an investigator can lead to child suggestibility, negatively affecting the investigation by not allowing the child to accurately tell his or her own story (Finnila, Mahlberg, Santtila, Sandnabba & Niemi, 2003). Since general psychopathology can also influence memory and suggestibility in maltreated children (Eisen, Qin, Goodman & Davis, 2002), the empathic investigator will increase the probability of an accurate investigation by eliminating the use of leading words.

## GENUINENESS

Genuineness, also referred to as congruence or transparency, refers to the concept that the therapeutic child welfare investigator does not mislead maltreated children about

71

Unconditional positive regard encourages the investigator to look past the child's words into actions and meanings – not to lead the child into verbalisations or responses that are not in the repertoire of their experience, but rather to allow them to tell their story at the pace at which they are most comfortable – leading to a more precise outcome in the investigation.

A maltreated child entering an investigation is dealing with a traumatic experience in which an authority figure in his or her worldview has not followed either their own or societal expectations for unconditional positive regard. This worldview of the maltreated child affects the initiation of a relationship with another authority figure: the child welfare investigator. As therapists and investigators utilising person-centred concepts, 'the most important dimension of the person-centred approach for work with this clientele is the attention we pay to fostering the client's symbolisation while not inserting "suggestive" material of our own. This orientation is critical at a time when therapists are accused of inducing "false memories" of childhood abuse' (Warner, 2000: 170). Interview methods that assist the child and the investigator to establish an environment of unconditional positive regard will encourage the child to freely discuss their experience without the use of questioning that may be viewed by the court system as leading to 'false memories' of a child's maltreatment experience.

### THE TRANSCENDENTAL OR SPIRITUAL CHARACTERISTIC

Rogers also discussed the transcendental or spiritual characteristic as a group facilitator (Anderson, 2001; Kirschenbaum & Henderson, 1989; Rogers, 1980). According to Rogers:

> I find that when I am closest to my inner, intuitive self, when I am somehow in touch with the unknown in me ... then whatever I do seems to be full of healing. Then simply my *presence* is releasing and helpful to the other. There is nothing I can do to force this experience, but when I can relax and be close to the transcendental core of me, then I may behave in strange and impulsive ways in the relationship, ways which I cannot justify rationally, which have nothing to do with my thought processes. (Rogers, 1980: 129)

In an interview with Michele Baldwin (1987), Rogers described his 'own definition of spirituality. I would put it that the best of therapy sometimes leads to a dimension that is spiritual, rather than saying that the spiritual is having an impact on therapy. But it depends on your definition of spiritual' (p. 50).

The transcendental or spiritual characteristic as described by Rogers remains an area under discussion in person-centred therapy. Thorne (1992) describes this 'fourth condition': that of a 'mystical, spiritual dimension' (pp. 39, 40) that was not addressed in the posthumous article of Rogers and Sanford (1989). However, Thorne relates that Rogers did not develop this characteristic further because 'he was unable to study [this concept] empirically in the months before his death', and that 'I am persuaded, however, that had he lived, we might well have heard much more of the quality of "presence" of which he speaks in this passage and that both the theory and practice of person-centred therapy might have undergone important revision as a consequence' (Thorne, 1992: 40).

The development of this spiritual aspect in Rogers' later years is also discussed in an interview with Natalie Rogers, his daughter, as she related:

> We [the women around Rogers] also pushed and prodded him to open to the spiritual realm, which is ironic because he came from such a deeply religious background. As a 22-year-old, he rejected all religion and shifted his focus to psychology. So it was interesting to see him open up to new possibilities in his older years – that there may be some higher energy source, a God or a power that was greater than human power. I think that was quite remarkable. (Sommers-Flanagan, 2007: 123)

Others have viewed the existence of this 'spiritual realm' described by Natalie Rogers. The application of Rogers' person-centred therapy has been cited as useful to pastoral counselors, spiritual directors, and spiritual psychotherapists (West, 2004; Thorne, 2001; Culligan, 1980, 1983).

The spiritual or transcendental aspect, as utilised in child welfare investigations, can be approached from two perspectives. First, to encourage the child to explore his or her experiences, the investigator should view the child in the totality of their environment taking all their traits and environmental subsystems, including spirituality, into consideration. This will also allow the child to relate experiences to the investigator through a lens – the lens of spirituality – with which the child may feel comfortable. This approach reflects the statement of Robins and Tracy (2003): 'The overarching assumption of the person-centred approach is that personality traits should not be studied in isolation. Instead, personality researchers should focus on the total constellation of traits that define each person, and the way these traits work together as a dynamic, integrated system' (p. 111).

The second approach directly relates to the transcendence that arises from the relationship between the investigator and the maltreated child during the investigative process. This aspect of spirituality is more closely aligned to that discussed by Rogers. As Rogers (1980) describes the 'growth-promoting relationship' in working with clients, 'Our relationship transcends itself and becomes a part of something larger. Profound growth and healing are present' (p. 129). He continues by explaining that this 'kind of transcendent phenomenon has certainly been experienced sometimes in groups in which I have worked, changing the lives of those involved' (p. 129). This characteristic, present but not formally recognised in person-centred therapy (Sheerer interview, cited in Barrineau, 1990), can be useful in the investigative process through strengthening the relationship between investigator and child.

## CONSIDERATION FOR FUTURE RESEARCH

The area of child welfare is constantly developing, and the application of person-centred techniques to child maltreatment investigations should be addressed more fully in research. As we assess the accuracy of child welfare investigations, we must also advocate for investigations that focus on the training and education of child welfare investigators in the area of person-centred techniques. We must also assess the specific techniques and methods utilised in child maltreatment forensic interviewing, and determine if person-centred techniques need to be implemented or strengthened in the investigative process. Child welfare workers often have academic qualifications in areas other than social work or related fields (Kominkiewicz, 2004) and may lack formal training in person-centred techniques. The long-term implications of child welfare investigator education should be further studied to determine the effect of differences in education and training in developing working investigative relationships with maltreated children.

Additionally, the issue of the use of best practices in child welfare investigations should be further studied. Person-centred and experiential psychotherapy in child welfare investigations should include follow-up evaluations of the investigations post-training to determine the utilisation of free-narrative accounts and open-ended questions throughout the investigative process. Funding and policy issues regarding child maltreatment investigations and child welfare investigator training should be further explored so that the application of person-centred techniques can be implemented and accurately assessed.

## REFERENCES

Aldridge, M & Wood, J (1998) *Interviewing Children: A guide for child care and forensic practitioners.* Chichester: Wiley & Son.

Aldridge, M & Wood, J (2000) Interviewing child witnesses within memorandum guidelines: A survey of police officers in England and Wales. *Children & Society, 14* (3), 168–81.

Al-Mahroos, F, Abdulla, F, Kamal, S & Al-Ansari, A (2005) Child abuse: Bahrain's experience. *Child Abuse & Neglect, 29* (2), 187–93.

Alvarez, K, Kenny, M, Donohue, B & Carpin, K (2004) Why are professionals failing to initiate mandated reports of child maltreatment, and are there any empirically based training programs to assist professionals in the reporting process? *Aggression and Violent Behavior, 9* (5), 563–78.

Anderson, H (2001) Postmodern collaborative and person-centered therapies: What would Rogers say? *Journal of Family Therapy, 23* (4), 339–60.

Baldwin, M (1987) Interview with Carl Rogers on the use of self in therapy. In M Baldwin & V Satir (Eds) *The Use of Self in Therapy* (pp. 45–52). New York: Haworth Press.

Barnett, O, Miller-Perrin, C & Perrin, R (2005) *Family Violence across the Lifespan: An introduction.* (2nd edn). Thousand Oaks, CA: Sage.

Barrineau, P (1990) Chicago revisited: An interview with Elizabeth Sheerer. *Person-Centered Review, 5* (4), 416–24.

Bassett, J & Johnson, J (2004) The role of clinical consultation in child protection investigations. *Smith College Studies in Social Work, 74* (3), 489–504.

Bratton, S, Ray, D, Rhine, T & Jones, L (2005) The efficacy of play therapy with children: A meta-analytic review of treatment outcomes. *Professional Psychology: Research and Practice, 36* (4), 376–90.

Burns, B, Phillips, S, Wagner, H, Barth, R, Kolko, D, Campbell, Y & Landsverk, J (2004) Mental health need and access to mental health services by youths involved with child welfare: A national survey. *Journal of the American Academy of Child & Adolescent Psychiatry, 43* (8), 960–70.

Bussman, KD (2004). Evaluating the subtle impact of a ban on corporal punishment of children in Germany. *Child Abuse Review, 13* (5), 292–311.

Cocozza, M, Gustafsson, P & Sydsjo, G (2006) Child protection in Sweden: Are routine assessments reliable? *Acta Paediatricia, 95* (11), 1474–80.

Cornelius-White, JHD (2007a) Learner-centered teacher–student relationships are effective: A meta-analysis. *Review of Educational Research, 77* (1), 113–43.

Cornelius-White, JHD (2007b). *The Handbook of Person-Centered Psychotherapy and Counselling* (pp. 168–81). Basingstoke: Palgrave-Macmillan.

Cornelius-White, JHD & Godfrey, PC (2004) Pedagogical crossroads: Integrating feminist critical pedagogies and the person-centred approach to education. In G Proctor & MB Napier (Eds) *Encountering Feminism: Intersections between feminism and the person-centred approach* (pp. 166–78). Ross-on-Wye: PCCS Books.

Cronch, L, Viljoen, J & Hansen, D (2006) Forensic interviewing in child sexual abuse cases: Current techniques and future directions. *Aggression and Violent Behavior, 11* (3), 195–207.

Cross, T, Finkelhor, D & Ormrod, R (2005) Police involvement in child protection services investigations: Literature review and secondary data analysis. *Child Maltreatment, 10* (3), 224–44.

Culligan, K (1980) Toward a contemporary model of spiritual direction: A comparative study of Saint John of the Cross and Carl R Rogers. *Ephemerides Carmeliticae, 31* (1).

Culligan, K (1983) *Saint John of the Cross and Spiritual Direction: Vol. Twenty.* T Curran (Ed). Dublin, Ireland: Carmelite Centre of Spirituality.

Eisen, M, Qin, J, Goodman, G & Davis, S (2002) Memory and suggestibility in maltreated children: Age, stress, arousal, dissociation, and psychopathology. *Journal of Experimental Child Psychology, 83* (3), 167–213.

Felzen Johnson, C (2002) Child maltreatment, 2002: Recognition, reporting, and risk. *Pediatrics International, 44* (5), 554–60.

Finkelhor, D (1994) The international epidemiology of child sexual abuse. *Child Abuse & Neglect, 18* (5), 409–17.

Finkelhor, D & Browne, A (1985) The traumatic impact of child sexual abuse: A conceptualization. *American Journal of Orthopsychiatry, 55*, 530–41.

Finnila, K, Mahlberg, N, Santtila, P, Sandnabba, K & Niemi, P (2003) Validity of a test of children's suggestibility for predicting responses to two interview situations differing in their degree of suggestiveness. *Journal of Experimental Child Psychology, 85* (1), 32–51.

Freire, E, Koller, S, Piason, A & da Silva, R (2005) Person-centered therapy with impoverished, maltreated and neglected children and adolescents in Brazil. *Journal of Mental Health Counseling, 27* (3), 225–37.

Goodman, R, Morgan, A, Juriga, S & Brown, E (2004) Letting the story unfold: A case study of client-centered therapy for childhood traumatic grief. *Harvard Review of Psychiatry, 12* (4), 199–212.

Grafanaki, S (2001) What counselling research has taught us about the concept of congruence: Main discoveries and unresolved issues. In G Wyatt (Ed) *Rogers' Therapeutic Conditions: Evolution, theory, and practice. Vol. 1: Congruence* (pp. 18–35). Ross-on-Wye: PCCS Books.

Hahm, H & Guterman, N (2001) The emerging problem of physical child abuse in South Korea. *Child Maltreatment, 6* (2), 169–79.

Hartwig, J & Wilson, J (2002) Factors affecting children's disclosure of secrets during an investigatory interview. *Child Abuse Review, 11* (2), 77–93.

Jones, S (2005) Attachment style differences and similarities in evaluations of affective communication skills and person-centered comforting messages. *Western Journal of Communication, 69* (3), 233–49.

Jones, L, Cross, T, Walsh, W & Simone, M (2005) Criminal investigations of child abuse. *Trauma, Violence, and Abuse, 6* (3), 254–68.

Kashani, J & Allan, W (1998) *The Impact of Family Violence on Children and Adolescents.* Thousand Oaks, CA: Sage.

Kirschenbaum, H & Henderson, V (1989) *The Carl Rogers Reader.* Boston, MA: Houghton Mifflin.

Kominkiewicz, F (2004) The relationship of Child Protection Service caseworker discipline-specific education and definition of sibling abuse: An institutional hiring impact study. *Journal of Human Behavior in the Social Environment, 9* (1/2), 69–82.

Krug, E, Dahlberg, L, Mercy, J, Zwi, A & Lozano, R (Eds) (2002) *World Report on Violence and Health.* Geneva: World Health Organization.

Miller, M (Ed in Chief) (2006) Client-centered therapy. *Harvard Mental Health Letter, 22* (7), 1–3. Boston, MA: Harvard Health Publications.

Moon, K (2001) Nondirective client-centered therapy with children. *Person-Centered Journal, 8* (1), 43–52.

Munro, E & Parton, N (2007) How far is England in the process of introducing a mandatory reporting system? *Child Abuse Review, 16* (1), 5–16.

Newman, B & Dannenfelser, P (2005) Children's protective services and law enforcement: Fostering partnerships in investigations of child abuse. *Journal of Child Sexual Abuse, 14* (3), 97–111.

Newman, B, Dannenfelser, P & Pendleton, D (2005) Child abuse investigations: Reasons for using Child Advocacy Centers and suggestions for improvement. *Child and Adolescent Social Work Journal, 22* (2), 165–81.

Orbach, Y & Lamb, M (2000) Enhancing children's narratives in investigative interviews. *Child Abuse and Neglect, 24* (12), 1631–48.

Orbach, Y & Lamb, M (2001) The relationship between within-interview contraindications and eliciting interviewer utterances. *Child Abuse & Neglect, 25* (3), 323–33.

Orbach, Y, Lamb, M, Sternberg, K & Horowitz, D (2006) Dynamics of forensic interviews with suspected abuse victims who do not disclose abuse. *Child Abuse & Neglect, 30* (7), 753–69.

Poole, D & Lamb, M (1998) *Investigative Interviews of Children: A guide for helping professionals.* Washington, DC: American Psychological Association.

Robins, R & Tracy, J (2003) Setting an agenda for a person-centered approach to personality development. *Monographs of the Society for Research in Child Development, 68* (1), 110–22.

Rogers, CR (1959) A theory of therapy, personality and interpersonal relationships, as developed in the client-centered framework. In S Koch (Ed) *Psychology: A study of science. Vol. III: Formulations of the person and the social context* (pp. 184–256). New York: McGraw-Hill.

Rogers, CR (1980) *A Way of Being.* Boston, MA: Houghton Mifflin.

Rogers, CR & Sanford, R (1989) Client-centered psychotherapy. In HI Kaplan & BJ Sadock (Eds) *Comprehensive Textbook of Psychiatry, V* (pp. 1482–501). Baltimore, MD: Williams & Wilkins.

Santtila, P, Korkman, J & Sandnabba, K (2004) Effects of interview phase, repeated interviewing, presence of a support person, and anatomically detailed dolls on child sexual abuse interviews. *Psychology, Crime, & Law, 10* (1), 21–35.

Shapiro, J, Foster, C & Powell, T (1968) Facial and bodily cues of genuineness, empathy and warmth. *Journal of Clinical Psychology, 24* (2), 233–6.

Sherer, M & Rogers, R (1980) Effects of therapist's nonverbal behavior on rated skill and effectiveness. *Journal of Clinical Psychology, 36* (3), 696–700.

Smith, D, Witte, T & Fricker-Elhai, A (2006) Service outcomes in physical and sexual abuse cases: A comparison of child advocacy center-based and standard services. *Child Maltreatment, 11* (4), 354–60.

Sommers-Flanagan, J (2007) The development and evolution of person-centered expressive art therapy: A conversation with Natalie Rogers. *Journal of Counseling & Development, 85* (1), 120–5.

Sternberg, K, Lamb, M, Davies, G & Westcott, H (2001) The memorandum of good practice: Theory versus application. *Child Abuse & Neglect, 25* (5), 669–81.

Sternberg, K, Lamb, M, Hershkowitz, I, Yudilevitch, L, Orbach, Y, Esplin, P & Hovav, M (1997) Effects of introductory style on children's abilities to describe experiences of sexual abuse. *Child Abuse & Neglect, 21* (11), 1133–46.

Tepper, D & Haase, R (1978) Verbal and nonverbal communication of facilitative conditions. *Journal of Counseling Psychology, 25* (1), 35–44.

Thorne, B (1992) *Carl Rogers.* London: Sage.

Thorne, B (2001) The prophetic nature of pastoral counselling. *British Journal of Guidance & Counselling, 29* (4), 435–45.

US Administration for Families and Children (2004) (Ch 3) Victims, child maltreatment. Retrieved 22 June 2006, from the US Department of Health and Human Services, Washington, DC website: http://www.acf.hhs.gov/programs/cb/pubs/cm04/chapterthree.htm#types.

Warner, M (2000) Person-centred therapy at the difficult edge: A developmentally- based model of fragile and dissociated process. In D Mearns & B Thorne. *Person-Centered Therapy Today: New frontiers in theory and practice* (pp. 144–71). London: Sage.

Warren, A, Woodall, C, Thomas, M, Nunno, M, Keeney, J, Larson, S & Stadfeld, J (1999) Assessing the effectiveness of a training program of interviewing child witnesses. *Applied Developmental Science, 3* (2), 128–35.

Weinstein, B, Levine, M, Kogan, N, Harkavy-Freidman, J & Miller, J (2001) Therapist reporting of suspected child abuse and maltreatment: Factors associated with outcome. *American Journal of Psychotherapy, 55* (2), 219–33.

West, W (2004) Humanistic integrative spiritual psychotherapy with a Sufi convert. In PS Richards & A Bergin (Eds) *Casebook for a Spiritual Strategy in Counseling and Psychotherapy* (pp. 201–12). Washington, DC: American Psychological Association.

Westby, C (2007) Child maltreatment: A global issue. *Language, Speech, and Hearing Services in Schools, 38* (2), 140–8.

Wright, R & Powell, M (2006) Investigative interviewers' perceptions of their difficulty in adhering to open-ended questions with child witnesses. *International Journal of Police Science & Management, 8* (2), 316–25.

# FOCUSING TRAINING FOR ADOLESCENTS WITH LOW SELF-CONFIDENCE AND A NEGATIVE SELF-IMAGE

## ERWIN VLERICK

### INTRODUCTION

The training introduced here has grown out of my conviction and experiences over the last 15 years that offering some concrete life skills to adolescents is a very powerful way to stimulate their development. These trainings are mostly based on a cognitive-behavioural model and are of great value for many adolescents. However, those who know and use these skills, but are nevertheless restricted by their hesitations, their doubts, their sometimes overwhelming negative self-image or inner critic, seem to need more. This last group could probably gain more benefit from acquiring focusing skills. Focusing (Gendlin, 1981a, 1996), a specific way to handle one's own feelings, could help these young people who 'live in their heads' to reconnect with the wisdom of their bodies. I will describe my working model which has contributed to the development of this training format, follow with the description of the profile of the adolescents who participated in the focusing trainings, continue with an overview of the sessions, and conclude with some measured results.

### WORKING MODEL

Offering focusing training to adolescents is based on the following six premises:

#### 1. FOCUSING WITH CHILDREN OR ADOLESCENTS WORKS

This has been confirmed by various pilot projects, my own personal experiences in working with this target group, and research data. Several articles on this subject can be consulted on the website of the Focusing Institute www.focusing.org/chfc. The advantages of this method have been demonstrated on a cognitive (Zimring, 1983, 1985; Zimring & Katz, 1988) as well as a socio-emotional and therapeutic (Santen, 1988, 1990, 1999) level.

The first preparatory step before focusing is often 'clearing a space'. When offered adapted working methods children and adolescents are very good at this. It gives them the opportunity to relax temporarily, to concentrate better on their study tasks at hand and to develop less psychosomatic or relational complaints.

The other steps in the focusing process are also realisable with children and adolescents. Moreover they are quite capable of listening to each other in a focusing way as a kind of peer-to-peer counselling. This last element creates a new culture of interaction among adolescents, as they take both their own and the experiential processes of others into consideration. The felt sense as an inner reference gets a place in their interaction. Such a process of sensitive listening to oneself and to each other enhances the relational quality and leads to a better connection.

## 2. AN OFFER OF FOCUSING IS APPROPRIATELY ADAPTED TO THE CENTRAL DEVELOPMENT TASK OF ADOLESCENTS

Adolescents are in a phase of life characterised by many changes and the feeling of insecurity that goes with this. Their central development task in this phase is to form their own identity (Erikson, 1963, 1968). There is the process of autonomy in which they become independent from their parents whilst developing a personal style in their relations with significant others (Marcia, 1993; Berzonsky, 2003). By trying out different styles and making choices, they discover their own preferences, possibilities and limitations. The exploration of oneself and the search for a place in this world is an existential theme inherent to this age (Renders, 2005). Questions arise, such as, 'Who would I like to be?', 'Who am I according to myself?' and 'Who am I according to others?' All this means that youngsters often feel insecure, develop a negative self-image and hardly dare to be themselves in relationships. The contact with their basic self gets lost, and therefore they often incline towards a way of being that is adjusted to what others expect or appreciate, which leaves them with a feeling of dissatisfaction.

Focusing, or the development of a High Experiencing Manner, restores the relationship with oneself (Hendricks, 2001). It offers a direct entry to the continually self-organising 'self'. Not the 'self' seen as something static, but as an experiential, living 'self' who, through a continuous dialectic between the inner and outer world (between experience and conceptualising) and between the various self-images, leads to a new integrative experience. Dwelling upon one's experience in a focusing (i.e. dialoguing) way brings adolescents to a place where they feel more themselves; this contact with their experience brings about a sense of empowerment which feeds their self-confidence. The connectedness with themselves makes adolescents stand more assuredly, depend less on others or on constantly changing fashion trends and cultural influences, and from there, they are capable of making their own choices: of being true to themselves (which is what they really feel comfortable with). More importantly, focusing offers the adolescent a tool with which to contribute actively to this process; to become more of a 'person' and to develop an individual identity in relation to the surrounding world (Morikawa, 1997).

## 3. TODAY'S ADOLESCENTS NEED LIFE SKILLS AS THEY APPROACH ADULTHOOD AND AUTONOMY

By this, I mean good social, cognitive, rational or healthy thinking, as well as emotional skills. Skills give adolescents a feeling of empowerment and so reduce fear. 'Emotional skill' refers to the ability adolescents have to access, make use of, and regulate emotions to guide themselves toward appropriate actions to deal with situations (Elliott, Watson, Goldman & Greenberg, 2004).

Each individual uses emotional skills to develop his or her values; a process which remains relevant far beyond adolescence. In such a process, the person has to adjust emotionally and make a judgement about whatever outside influences he or she perceives. Focusing both offers a guideline to develop this emotional skill and gives adolescents a method to keep this dialoguing process – this specific relationship between yourself and the world – open for the future. The adolescent discovers that they themselves are an active 'agency' in this process of becoming conscious of their own experiences. Focusing teaches them that they themselves can make choices in the way they deal with their own experiences: sticking to them and further exploring them or, conversely, steering away from them by going onto a cognitive level only and giving explanations, or simply talking about something else. Rennie (2006) calls this the possibility of 'radical reflexivity' which provides the adolescent with a feeling of self-control and, more specifically, responsibility for his or her own emotional experience: not merely at the mercy of emotions but able to deal with them in a constructive and significant way.

## 4. BODY AND AFFECT ATTUNEMENT

Focusing demands an openness to one's own experiences; a specific attitude of giving space to emotions. In this sense, focusing has a link with *sensory awareness* (Tophoff, 2006). For, whilst focusing on the 'felt sense' of a specific problem or situation, one always needs to create moments of a similar free-floating attention: to let happen and allow what comes up in the body. Besides, it is a crucial element to let a felt sense form itself. Focusing is creating an openness for what is to be felt in the body – it is a recognition of this – and consequently to dialogue with this and to explore the encoded significance (felt sense). Here, experience comes before the narration, the putting into words. It is making contact with the body 'before the felt sense' (Depestele, 1995): making contact with the 'physically felt self' or the physically felt level of experience – the resonating body as sounding board and guideline.

In the proposed focusing training, the natural path from experiencing to symbolising is respected in the structure of the sessions. Movement exercises as a form of mindfulness are used to stimulate such an openness to the physically felt. I have selected these exercises from various movement and dancing lessons which I have followed, such as contact improvisation, dance-expression or body-weather. Adolescents are taught in a playful way to be attentive, alert and sensitive to their physical reaction from inside – as a kind of awakening to their bodily receptivity. They are indirectly invited to be open and uninhibited, mild, patient, non-judgemental, curious and friendly to themselves whilst moving in a kind of attitude of meditation-in-action (ibid.).

Which movements and attitudes does my body want to express or take in? Which direction in the room and how much intensity does it choose in its moving pattern? How does it feel for my body to find its own walking rhythm? How does my body want to react to a partner? The adolescents are invited to register consciously how the 'outside' (the room in which they move; the presence of others; the music; etc.) influences them 'inside', and then allow to arise from *that* certain moving phrases (Dosamantes-Alperson, 1986; Gendlin, 1981b; Noel & Noel, 1981). What we see is like a resonating body in action, an organism that captures impulses (whether they come from inside or outside the organism) and in a moment of silence processes this to an 'answer of movement'.

This process shows similarities with the affective attunement of a mother with her baby during early childhood imitation (Stern, 2000; Peters, 2003; Vliegen & Cluckers, 2001). A mother reads her child's feelings through its behaviour; she then reflects back to the child the same emotional qualities using her own personal intonation and body expression. Through this, the child understands that its mother's response has something to do with its own emotional experience and message. The child experiences a kind of intersubjective communication in which 'feelings can be shared and understood in a verbal and non-verbal way in a significant relationship' (Vliegen & Cluckers, 2001: 28). This primary capacity to verbally and non-verbally adjust oneself to oneself and to others is actualised again by offering movement exercises as a part of the focusing training. Thus, the foundation is laid for the focusing and sensitive listening attitude which the adolescents are expected to acquire during the training.

## 5. FOCUSING AS A WAY OF EXISTENTIAL CONNECTEDNESS IN 'BORDERLINE TIMES'

Most young people go through adolescence without too many problems with either themselves or their parents. On the whole, adolescents growing up in families with close and harmonious parent–child relationships have better mental health (Steinberg, 2001; Buist et al., 2004). Research into the well-being of adolescents between the ages of 14 and 25 in Belgium (Huysmans, 2007), indicates that 86 per cent consider themselves to have good qualities; 78 per cent consider themselves OK; 69 per cent are proud of who they are; 67 per cent look forward with optimism; and 78 per cent have no anticipation of being unemployed in the near future. Most of them feel themselves secure: 85 per cent claim to be unafraid of being home alone at night; 76 per cent dare to walk alone on the streets in the evening; and 80 per cent like living in their neighbourhood.

However, there is a group of adolescents in our Western society who can't cope with themselves or with the world surrounding them. In Belgium, we found that between one and two out of every ten adolescents have a low self-image, are depressive and think about committing suicide (Vettenburg et al., 2006: 248) – those adolescents, it seems, are reflecting the new values of this highly individualistic society. Elchardus and Heyvaert (1991), for instance, amongst groups of young adults in Belgium with bad working conditions, irregular hours and a low standard of education, found a deeply materialistic view of life and a general indifference towards any moral frame of reference. These are the 'flexible employees' who have become simply faceless workers and are living in conditions where there is no chance of autonomy, of looking forward to the future, or of finding security within their community .

We live in 'borderline times' (Rorty, cited in De Wachter, 2005) in which marginal phenomena, such as a psychiatric syndrome, are becoming mainstream and the norm of life bears a strong resemblance to behaviour shown by average borderline patients (ADHD-like behaviour, failing relationships, fear of failure, self-mutilation, depression, suicide, isolation and aimlessness, drug abuse and aggression). Rorty claims we are all 'borderline': our society seems to be dwelling in a constant youth culture in which there is an obsession with appearance, trends, computer games and visual culture; a society in which mobile communication dominates and the virtual internet world replaces the real (relational) world.

Could we be becoming even further alienated from ourselves – who we are and our connection with other people, the material and social environment, our culture and the complete natural cycle? (Deklerck, 2005). 'When the outside evolves so quickly and becomes so important it becomes increasingly difficult to find depth, to seek "grounding", to choose foundation and stability as starting points: the death of the person as a subject has set in' (De Wachter, 2005: 64). If everything is so fleeting and replaceable, what am I doing here in this world and why? Who am I and who would I like to be? And who loves me and holds me tight – just for a moment – when I cannot manage any longer? These are 'slow questions in a fast world' (Harry Kunneman, cited in Van Tilt, 2005). Crucially, they are also emotional questions. 'But slow questions are also vague questions; questions which can only be answered in – sometimes impatient – searching and in slow dialogue with oneself and with others; questions which can only be answered when they are embedded in a culture of interpersonal carefulness. Far away from any fast and efficient result commitments' (Van Tilt, 2005: 204).

Adolescents today need to have the opportunity for existential learning – as an addition to the instrumental learning they get in traditional education – through an authentic encounter with others within their environment. This already happens in early childhood, where the foundation is laid for safe attachment relationships. But in the adolescent years, in the so-called second individuation and separation phase, true contacts with others remain essential. Friendships and relationships with adults in which adolescents feel safe, understood and supported play an important part. Relational security is the fundament of life.

Today's adolescents sometimes struggle with an ever-increasing lack of such connectedness. School counsellors increasingly report that despite all the material wealth, pupils often do not succeed in building up significant relationships. Educational systems support this climate through numerous study options and modular teaching systems. Pupils are constantly confronted with parting and the pain this brings about. Some of them lack the skills or courage to engage in (new) relationships. They become emotionally isolated. They can't find anybody who understands them, a person who listens to them with real 'inter-human attention' (Gendlin, 2005). However, research in Belgium (Huysmans et al., 2007: 147–59) shows us that the situation is not that dramatic: about 80 per cent of adolescents between the ages of 14 and 25 were shown to have two or more friends; 49.2 per cent had a boy- or girlfriend at the time of questioning; 5.3 per cent had no friends at all; 15 per cent said they had only one friend; and about 20 per cent indicated that they had never had a boy- or girlfriend.

Life continually expects young people to come to terms with all kinds of feelings; to give these a meaning or a place; to integrate them psychically. If they succeed, they can further flourish – they can acquire 'food' for the future. This process of material, emotional and existential integration is like a 'mental composting' (Deklerck, 2005), which enables events – both pleasant and painful – to be 'digested', and gives people the ability to make further choices, develop their own life projects and reach self-fulfilment. Therefore, they should be invited to dwell on their own stream of experience through different working methods.

Connectedness can be realised from a conscious connecting with the deeper layers of the stream of life and experience. Focusing is a working method that could help to realise those psychic and existential purposes. In focusing training, the adolescents can taste the value of a good talk, more specifically of being able to share what really matters to them with someone who takes the trouble to fully understand them. This leads to connections – with themselves and with others – which, in turn, lead to further self-development.

## 6. THE GROUP AS AN AREA OF EXPERIENCE FOR THE SELF

Groups offer a range of developing factors which meet the specific needs inherent in adolescence. Research into the helping factors in groups (Dierick & Lietaer, 1990) name group cohesion, self-understanding, interpersonal learning in the here and now of the group, and internal experiencing, as the most important factors. Moreover, belonging to and feeling at home in a group seem to be extremely important. This is even more so for an adolescent.

My own experiences with groups of adolescents confirm this: adolescents who take part in social skills training name group cohesion as one of the main factors in their evaluation of a group. Horwitz (1984) also names three group functions which influence or change the self of a group member: mirroring, peer relationships (partnering) and a sense of belonging.

In his process of individuation and personality, the adolescent conforms to his peers; the peer group functions as the space in which to explore himself and others. At the same time, existential themes such as 'autonomy versus dependence' or 'binding and intimacy' play an important part in adolescent groups. Being someone *and* being appreciated for it – belonging – is a continuous field of tension. In a new group, most adolescents experience a sense of anxiety or even fear about who they will meet, how it will be, who the others will be and what their attitude will be towards them. In the interpersonal environment of the group, the adolescent is invited to think about his own feelings and ways of reacting and to compare these to the feelings, reactions and behaviour of the other members of the group. By mirroring themselves with each other like this the similarities and differences become clear. Being able to share recognition has a therapeutic and relativising effect. Discovering differences strengthens self-identity. By committing oneself in relationships with peers, self-awareness and self-esteem are enhanced, which in its turn counteracts a negative self-image. The group offers the adolescent a kind of 'corrective emotional experience' towards former negatively experienced social relations. Such observable process is strongly comparable with research findings about group therapy with adults (Dierick & Lietaer, 1990).

In a focusing training, through its task-oriented 'training character', the group becomes a safe place to get to know oneself and others. By first focusing on one's own felt sense and then gradually sharing it with others, by learning to use a supportive listening attitude, the feeling of mutual recognition and support grows. More group cohesion is developed and the group starts considering itself as a group with its own story, its own history. This is intensified by the fact that the focusing training views the felt sense of the participants as the main working resource. Focusing teaches that giving recognition to felt senses stimulates growth and leads to a more complete experience of the self. The most personal acquires a space, a place in which to make oneself explicit in the presence of others.

## DESCRIPTION OF THE INTERVENTION

The focusing training has the global goal of learning the focusing steps and skills and introducing a focusing way of handling the inner critic. The training has therefore a certain structure where two sessions are used to introduce the felt sense and the focusing steps and skills; two sessions are spent exploring and using the felt sense; and a further two sessions are spent describing and handling the inner critic. Each session lasts for two hours and is held weekly or fortnightly. Movement exercises are introduced as a regular part of each session. Table 1 shows an overview of the separate sessions.

All the participating adolescents are seeking to change their self-image. By active self-reflection and comparison with the experiences of their peers they come to see the obstacles in their lives and look for a handle.

## METHOD

### PARTICIPANTS

Participants in this study comprise 15 adolescents (10 girls and 5 boys) between the ages of 14 and 19. The mean age is 17.1, sd = 1.4. The adolescents who enrol for this training have a specific profile. This is partly a consequence of the way in which the focusing training is advertised: the advertisement is targeted at adolescents between 15 and 18 who are sensitive; master most social skills but often doubt themselves due to an active inner critic; have a negative self-image; and difficulty in making choices. So far, 18 adolescents between the ages of 14 and 19, divided into groups of six at a time, have taken part in the training.

The Self Perception Profile for Adolescents (SSPA/CBSA; Harter, 1988/Treffers et al., 2002) reveals that, on average, the participating adolescents have a very low score on

*Table 1*
Focusing training for adolescents (15–18 years) with low self-confidence or negative self-image

| Global purpose of the training | Learning the focusing steps and skills: |
|---|---|
| | • awareness of own feelings/felt sense |
| | • keeping the right distance |
| | • finding a handle for the felt sense |
| | • listening to and exploring felt senses |
| | • listening to each other in a focusing way |
| | • handling the critic |

| Session No. | Central theme | Bodywork | Excercises/group activity |
|---|---|---|---|
| 1 | Introducing the concept 'felt sense'. | Connecting the body by movement. | • Re-experiencing bodily impressions of the day: a guided group exercise.<br>• Group sharing with reflection turns.<br>• Some theory about the 'felt sense'.<br>• Exercise: connect and draw the felt sense of a personal object.<br>• Homework: have an own felt sense exercise and literature and FCL-A, CBCL-YRF, SPPA. |
| 2 | Focusing steps and skills. Peer-to-peer focusing. | Following the impulse of the body. Allowing movements connected to a personal object. | • Group sharing about homework with reflection of the members.<br>• Introducing the listening role.<br>• Information about focusing steps and skills.<br>• Modeling focusing session.<br>• Exercise: focusing/listening in pairs about a personal object.<br>• Group sharing, questions.<br>• Homework: have a personal focusing moment and literature. |
| 3 | Clearing a space. Exploring the felt sense (1). | Letting one's body choose the directions. | • Group exercise: clearing a space and group sharing/reflections.<br>• Exercise in pairs: exploring the felt sense and asking.<br>• Modeling focusing session.<br>• Group sharing/reflections, questions.<br>• Homework: focusing with someone and literature. |
| 4 | Exploring the felt sense (2) and asking. | Breathing is crucial. | • Group sharing/reflections about homework, what's OK, difficulties, steps and skills.<br>• Exercise: individual focusing about a life decision: sensing, breathing, |

| Session No. | Central theme | Bodywork | Excercises/group activity |
|---|---|---|---|
| 4 contd | | | moving, drawing, writing, exploring … the felt sense.<br>• Group sharing/reflections, questions.<br>• Homework: focusing with someone and literature. |
| 5 | Describing the critic. | Body-weather relaxation.<br>How the critic moves your body. | • Short group sharing/reflections about homework or free subject.<br>• Exercise: each member is invited to describe his critic: sensing, breathing, moving, drawing the impact, writing, exploring, asking.<br>• Group sharing/reflections, questions.<br>• Homework: observing your critic and literature about handling the critic. |
| 6 | Handling the critic in a focusing way. | Short free-relaxation time. | • Group sharing/reflections about homework or free subject.<br>• Overview of characteristics of the inner critic versus a focusing mode.<br>• Possibilities of handling the critic.<br>• Modeling focusing session.<br>• Exercise in pairs: handling your critic in a friendly way by being with and empathising about its function in your life, by using two chairs and a listening coach.<br>• Group sharing/reflections, questions. |
| Evaluation | | | • Focusing exercise about the whole training: What do you take with you? What do you need more of?<br>• Focusing checklist<br>• Satisfaction questionnaire<br>• CBCL/CBSA<br>• Refreshments |

the subscales 'social acceptance', 'close friendship' and 'feeling of self-esteem'. Next to a negative feeling of self-esteem, they seem to be less accepted by peers and to have fewer close friends. The Child Behaviour Checklist – Youth Self-Report (CBCL-YSR) (Achenbach, 1991; Verhulst, Van der Ende & Koot, 1997) has found that these adolescents have internalising problems and specifically score higher on the 'anxious–depressive' subscale (clinical and sub-clinical). Only a few of them also score higher on externalising problems (sub-clinical) compared to the internalising problems. This corresponds to the image of the active inner critic with many inhibitions (introvert, shy and quickly embarrassed), with brooding, daydreaming and loss of concentration, psychosomatic complaints and weariness as a result. Many of them have mood fluctuations, feel lonely, confused and worthless. The remarkable thing is that these adolescents feel they can stand up for themselves, and see themselves as stubborn, honest, pleasant and complaisant; they like to be with others and to have fun, they like jokes, trying out new things, and they are animal lovers. They show evidence of 'soft values'. They would hardly ever hurt others as, due to their sensitivity, they realise all too well what this would mean to them. On the other hand, this sensitivity also means that they easily feel hurt: so many of them have been victims of bullying in the past. This is not surprising. In recent research on bullying and personality, victims of bullying often tend to have low self-esteem; are anxious, sensitive and quiet; score higher on neuroticism; have a negative and diffident attitude towards others; score lower on extraversion and lower on friendliness and carefulness (Barelds, Luteijn & Vervaeke, 2004; Olweus, 1995).

It is clear that bullying has an enormous impact on the personality development of young people and more specifically on their self-image and interaction with others.

MEASURES

The CBCL-YSR is intended to assess self-reported problem behaviour from age 11 onwards. Adolescents rate the frequency of problematic behaviours on a 3-point Likert scale. Two basic syndromes can be derived: Internalising, with items referring to somatic complaints, social withdrawal, and anxiety/depression; and Externalising, including items indexing aggression, hyperactivity, and delinquency.

The SSPA/CBSA measures the competencies and global self-worth as seen by adolescents between 12 and 18 years. Adolescents rate items on a 4-point scale. Items are organised under seven scales, with Cronbach alphas of .70 and .80 respectively for the Flemish and the Dutch research groups. The scales are derived as: (a) scholastic competence; (b) social acceptance; (c) athletic competence; (d) physical appearance; (e) behavioural conduct; (f) close friendship, and (g) global self-worth.

The Focusing Checklist for Adolescents (FCA) (Vlerick, 2003) is a newly devised questionnaire which has not yet been standardised. Its purpose is to work out the extent to which adolescents master the focusing steps and skills. Adolescents rate the frequency of their focusing abilities on a 4-point scale. Items are organised under six scales, with Cronbach alphas indicating moderate to good internal consistency: (a) consciousness of one's body; (b) inviting a felt sense/receiving; (c) finding a handle; (d) resonating; (e) being with/questioning; and (f) clearing a space. Due to the small sample size it was not possible to conduct factor analysis to evaluate the structure of the questionnaire.

SATISFACTION QUESTIONNAIRE

In an ordinal scale with five possible replies (ranging from highly dissatisfied to highly satisfied) this list investigates the satisfaction from an organisational point of view (place, waiting time, information given in advance, cost), as well as being concerned with content (literature, acquired knowledge and skills, group aspect). Some open questions ask if the adolescent wants further help or have any suggestions for the training.

*Table 2*

Item examples and Cronbach alphas of the focusing checklist for adolescents (Vlerick, 2003)

| Scales | N items | Item example | Cronbach alpha[1] |
|---|---|---|---|
| Consciousness of one's body | 4 | I can feel my body without looking at it. | .73 |
| Inviting felt sense / Receiving | 9 | I am often sensitive to how I am feeling inside. | .72 |
| Finding a handle | 7 | I am looking to express a feeling in the best way. | .75 |
| Resonating | 4 | If I give a feeling a name, that name fits with what I am really feeling. | .75 |
| Being with / Questioning | 6 | As I stay close to a feeling, it becomes clear what the feeling needs. | .79 |
| Clearing a space | 5 | Each time I release a feeling, I breathe easier, feel calmer and have more energy. | .64 |

1. Alphas were averaged across the pre- and post-administrations

## PROCEDURE

Most adolescents are sent to my private practice by a student's counsellor, come spontaneously with their parents' support, or are sent after a temporary individual therapy. In a first exploratory talk, the actual difficulties, the development history and the kind of help which is expected are investigated. The content and targets of the training are explained, after which a decision to take part in the training is taken.

All the adolescents who took part in the training did the complete training as described. At the outset of the training, the adolescents fill in three questionnaires: the CBCL-YSR, the SSPA/CBSA and a FCA (Vlerick, 2003). At the end of the training (after about eight weeks) the adolescents immediately completed a Satisfaction Questionnaire and a Focusing Checklist for Adolescents (FCL-A). To be able to make a process evaluation for themselves they were given a focusing exercise in which they could create a synthesis of what sort of evolution they had experienced, what they would like to keep from the training and what they might need in the future. In this way they start thinking of their personal development as a continuous process.

Due to lack of time in the last session of the course, the members of the focusing training were given a copy of the CBCL-YSR and the SPPA/CBSA to complete at home and send back by post. As many adolescents did not send back the questionnaire, there was not enough data to compare the changes effected since the beginning of training. In future, enough time will be included to complete all the questionnaires during the training.

# RESULTS

### FOCUSING CHECKLIST FOR ADOLESCENTS

Due to the small number of people tested, no reliable factor analysis of the FCL-A could be made. However, the internal consistency of the scales looks relatively good. For the time being we shall keep the experimental division items/scales and compare the average scale scores between initial and final situation, so we can see that there is an improvement on nearly all scales! (see Table 3). Moreover, the calculations of significance (paired t-keys) show that two scales differ in a significant way – with $p < .05$ and $p < .01$ – namely, scale 1 and 3. Scale 2 shows a 'strong tendency' of change, scale 5 and 6 show a 'tendency' of change.

*Table 3*

Pre- and post-treatment comparisons – Results of T-test pairs

| | Mean (SD) | | | |
|---|---|---|---|---|
| Scales | Pre | Post | *T*-value | *r* |
| Consciousness of one's body | 1.62 (.67) | 2.00 (.57) | -2.63* | .69 * |
| Inviting felt sense / Receiving | 1.24 (.58) | 1.65 (.46) | -2.06 | .11 |
| Finding a handle | 1.33 (.67) | 1.61 (.57) | -3.25** | .90 *** |
| Resonating | 1.54 (.71) | 1.60 (.63) | -0.46 | .76 ** |
| Being with / Questioning | 1.65 (.61) | 1.79 (.49) | -1.01 | .64 * |
| Clearing a space | 1.68 (.68) | 1.90 (.54) | -1.50 | .68 * |

Note: $N = 12$; $df = 11$; *** $p < .001$; ** $p < .01$; * $p < .05$
The above table is based on the scales, including all items without items 15, 16 and 33, which reduced the internal consistency.

### SATISFACTION QUESTIONNAIRE (N = 12)

In a graduation scale with five possible replies (ranging from highly dissatisfied to highly satisfied), this list investigates the satisfaction from an organisational point of view (place, waiting time, information given in advance, cost, etc.) as well as being concerned with content (literature, acquired knowledge and skills, the group aspect, etc.) I shall limit myself to aspects concerning content.

All the adolescents were satisfied with the focusing training. They felt they had learned something about their self-image, were happy with the skills they acquired in the focusing training and thought the training could be used in daily life. Most adolescents didn't feel the need for further therapy at the end of the training. The fact that the training was given in a group produced an even more positive score. What they specifically appreciated was being able to contribute to the group and the extent to which they could learn from each other. This stresses the importance of the peer group in this age category.

## FOCUSING CHECKLIST FOR ADOLESCENTS/QUALITATIVE ANALYSIS

A qualitative analysis of the answers of the participants of the training demonstrates some interesting tendencies. On the level of 'consciousness of the body', adolescents pay more attention to their sensory perception, they notice how their body breathes in and out, and they can focus their attention more easily on their body after the training.

'Inviting a felt sense/receiving' is clearly easier for them than at the outset. After the training, adolescents have less trouble perceiving their own feelings; they prefer to consult their body than rationalise what they feel. In this, they take more time to let a feeling come up, they are friendlier towards their own experiences and they don't push away unpleasant feelings so much. On the other hand, they succeed better in not being submerged by their feelings: they can keep them at a correct distance. In the items concerning the subscale 'finding a handle', it is striking that adolescents have improved their skills in the bodily localising of their own feelings. They are more able to work out the best way to display their feelings and are better at illustrating this with a drawing. During 'resonating', adolescents seem to look more carefully for the most suitable words or images to go with a feeling. The subscale 'being with/questioning' shows specific progress in the curiosity that the adolescents can muster towards what a specific feeling means or needs. In 'clearing a space' the adolescents have learned that drawing how they feel has a liberating effect. Above all they succeed better in ridding themselves of a feeling long-term.

# CONCLUSION

I believe the scheme of this training could be used as the basis for more extensive research. Although we need more research with control groups, the conclusions above confirm former clinical impressions. They suggest that adolescents make use of the offered focusing steps and skills. In this sense, the original purpose of the focusing training seems to have been realised. It appears to show that much can be realised in a first training of only six sessions. But, so far, we are not able to pinpoint the reason for the effects. Is it the training? Is it the trainer? Is it primary/only the group experience? We need better data to make more clear, causal interpretations.

Another interesting thing is the development of the experimental version of the FCL-A. Even with the small sample in this research project, we could see the usefulness of the questionnaire. Until now, there has been no specific instrument for questioning children and adolescents about how they could use the focusing steps and skills in their daily lives. It seems worthwhile to research the subject further and more thoroughly.

# REFERENCES

Achenbach TM (1991) *Manual for the Child Behaviour Checklist/4–18 – Youth Self-Report Form.* Burlington: University of Vermont. Nederlandse bewerking: Verhulst FC, Ende, J van der & Koot, HM (1997) *Handleiding voor de CBCL/4–18 – Zelf in te vullen Vragenlijst voor jongens en meisjes.* Rotterdam: Erasmus Universiteit/Sophia Kinderziekenhuis, Afdeling Kinder- en jeugdpsychiatrie.

Barelds, DPH, Luteijn, F, & Vervaeke G (2004) Pesten op school en persoonlijkheid [Bullying at school and personality]. *Diagnostiek-wijzer, 7* (2), 48–56.

Berzonsky, MD (2003) Identity style and well-being: Does commitment matter? *Identity. An International Journal of Theory and Research, 3,* 131–42.

Buist, L, Dekovic, M, Meeus, W & van Aken, MAG (2004) Gehechtheid en internaliserend en externaliserend probleemgedrag bij adolescenten [Attachment and adolescent internalising and externalising problem behaviour]. *Kind en Adolescent, 25* (2), 132–49.

Deklerck, J (2005) Verbondenheid, kans tot existentieel leren in onderwijs en jeugdhulpverlening. [Connectedness, a chance for existential learning in education and youth assistence]. In L Lacombe, R Loosveldt & L Van der Vorst (Eds) *Grenzen. Begripvolle grenzen – Grenzen aan begrip* (pp. 165–81). Kortrijk: Ipsoc-Bijscholing.

Depestele, F (1995) Het lichaam vóór de 'gevoelde zin' [The body before the 'felt sense']. In G Lietaer & M van Kalmthout (Eds) *Praktijkboek gesprekstherapie* (pp. 109–29). Utrecht: De Tijdstroom.

De Wachter D (2005) Borderline Times. Over vermaatschappelijking van een diagnose [Borderline Times. About the socialibility of a diagnosis]. In L Lacombe, R Loosveldt & L Van der Vorst (Eds) *Grenzen. Begripvolle grenzen – Grenzen aan begrip* (pp. 59–68). Kortrijk: Ipsoc-Bijscholing.

Dierick, P & Lietaer, G (1990) Member and therapist perceptions of therapeutic factors in therapy and growth groups: Comments on a category system. In G Lietaer, J Rombouts & R Van Balen (Eds) *Client-Centered and Experiential Psychotherapy in the Nineties* (pp. 741–70). Leuven: University Press.

Dosamantes-Alperson, E (1986) The interaction between movement and imagery in experiential movement psychotherapy. *The Focusing Folio, 5,* 104–13.

Elchardus, M & Heyvaert, P (1991) *Soepel, flexibel en ongebonden* [Supple, Flexible and Unattached]. Brussels: Globe.

Elliott, R, Watson, JC, Goldman, RN & Greenberg, LS (2004) *Learning Emotion-Focused Therapy. The process-experiential approach to change.* London/Washington: APA.

Erikson, EH (1963) *Childhood and Society.* New York: Norton.

Erikson, EH (1968) *Identity: Youth and crisis.* New York: Norton.

Gendlin, ET (1981a) *Focusing.* New York: Bantam Books.

Gendlin, ET (1981b) Movement therapy, objectivication, and focusing. *The Focusing Folio, 1* (2), 35–7.

Gendlin, ET (1996) *Focusing-Oriented Psychotherapy: A manual of the experiential method.* New York: Guilford.

Gendlin, ET (2005) Bringing focusing into political context. *Staying in Focus. The Focusing Institute Newsletter, 5* (1) 1–4.

Harter, S (1988) *Manual for the Self-Perception Profile for Adolescents (SPPA).* Denver, CO: University of Denver. Nederlandse bewerking: Treffers, A et al. (2002). *Competentiebelevingsschaal voor*

*Adolescenten (CBSA)*. Lisse: Swets & Zeitlinger.

Hendricks, MN (2001) Focusing-oriented/experiential psychotherapy. In D Cain & J Seeman (Eds) *Humanistic Psychotherapy: Handbook of research and practice* (pp. 221–51). Washington, DC: APA.

Horwitz, L (1984) The self in groups. *International Journal of Group Psychotherapy, 34*, 515–40.

Huysmans, H (2007) Tevredenheid over zichzelf, de buurt en met een gevoel van veiligheid op weg naar een hoopvolle toekomst. Jongeren en welbevinden [Satisfaction about themselves, the neighbourhood and a feeling of security towards a hopeful future: Adolescents and wellbeing]. In N Vettenburg, M Elchardus & L Walgrave (Eds) *Jongeren in Cijfers en Letters. Bevindingen uit de JOP-Monitor 1* (pp. 161–74). Leuven: Lannoo Campus.

Huysmans, H, Rutgeerts, E & Sinnaeve, I (2007) Gezocht: vriend (m/v) & lief (m/v). Jongeren, vriendschap en relaties [Wanted: Friend (m/w) & sweetheart (m/w). Adolescents, friendship and relationships]. In N Vettenburg, M Elchardus & L Walgrave (Eds) *Jongeren in cijfers en letters. Bevindingen uit de JOP-Monitor 1* (pp. 147–58). Leuven: Lannoo Campus.

Marcia, JE (1993) The status of statuses: Research review. In JE Marcia, AS Waterman, DR Matteson, SL Archer & JL Orlofsky (Eds) *Ego Identity. A handbook for psychological research.* (pp. 22–41). New York: Springer Verlag.

Morikawa, Y (1997) Making practical the focusing manner of experiencing in every day life: A consideration of factor analysis. *The Journal of Japanese Clinical Psychology, 15* (1), 58–65.

Noel, P & Noel, J (1981) The use of experiential focusing in movement therapy. *The Focusing Folio, 1*(2), 31–4.

Olweus, D (1995) Bullying or peer abuse at school: Facts and interventions. *Current Directions in Psychological Science, 4*, 196–200.

Peters, H (2003) Enkele gedachten over vroegkinderlijk imiteren en intersubjectiviteit in relatie tot aspecten van psychotherapie [Some thoughts about imitation and intersubjectivity in early childhood in relation to aspects of psychotherapy]. *Tijdschrift Cliëntgerichte Psychotherapie, 41* (2), 84–114.

Renders, K (2005) Serie Een Bijzondere Casus: Rocco op de rand. Existentiële thema's in de psychotherapie van een adolescent [Rocco on the edge: Existential themes in the psychotherapy of an adolescent]. *Tijdschrift voor psychotherapie, 31* (4), 273–89.

Rennie, DL (2006) Radical reflexivity: Rationale for an experiential person-centered approach to counseling and psychotherapy. *Person-Centered and Experiential Psychotherapies, 5* (2), 114–26.

Santen, B (1988) Focusing with a borderline adolescent. *Person-Centered Review, 3*, 435.

Santen, B (1990) Beyond good and evil: Focusing with early traumatised children and adolescents. In G Lietaer, J Rombouts & R Van Balen (Eds) *Client-Centered and Experiential Psychotherapy in the Nineties* (pp. 779–96). Leuven: Leuven University Press.

Santen, B (1999) Focusing as a therapeutic technique with children and young adolescents. In S Schaefer (Ed) *Innovative Psychotherapy Techniques in Child and Adolescent Therapy.* New Yrok: Wiley & Sons.

Steinberg, L (2001) We know some things: Parent–adolescent relationships in retrospect and prospect. *Journal of Research on Adolescence, 11* (1), 1–19.

Stern, DN (2000) *The Interpersonal World of the Infant: A view from psychoanalysis and development psychology* (2nd edn). New York: Basic Books.

Tophoff, MM (2006) Sensory awareness as a method of mindfulness training within the perspective of person-centered psychotherapy. *Person-Centered and Experiential Psychotherapies, 5* (2), 127–37.

Treffers, A et al. (2002) *Competentiebelevingsschaal voor Adolescenten (CBSA).* Lisse: Swets & Zeitlinger. (See Harter, 1988 for English publication.)

Van Tilt, E (2005) Grenzen aan het begrijpen. Over de over-rationalisering in onze westerse cultuur en (dus) in het welzijnswerk [Limits in understanding. About over-rationalisation in Western culture and public work]. In L Lacombe, R Loosveldt & L Van der Vorst (Eds) *Grenzen. Begripvolle grenzen – Grenzen aan begrip* (pp. 195–208). Kortrijk: Ipsoc-Bijscholing.

Verhulst, FC, Ende, J van der, & Koot, HM (1997) *Handleiding voor de CBCL/4–18 – Zelf in te vullen Vragenlijst voor jongens en meisjes.* Rotterdam: Erasmus Universiteit/Sophia Kinderziekenhuis, Afdeling Kinder- en jeugdpsychiatrie.

Vettenburg, N, Elchardus, M & Walgrave, L (2006) *Jongeren van nu en straks. Overzicht en synthese van recent jeugdonderzoek in Vlaanderen* [Adolescents from now and then. Overview and synthesis of recent youth research in Flanders]. Leuven: Lannoo Campus.

Vlerick, E (2003) *Focusing Checklist voor Adolescenten* [Focusing Checklist for adolescents]. Eigen beheer [Privately published].

Vliegen, N & Cluckers, G (2001) Babyobservatie en therapeutisch proces [Baby observation and therapeutic process]. In N Vliegen & C Leroy (Eds) *Het moederland? De vroegste relatie tussen moeder en kind in de psychoanalytische therapie* (pp. 21–43). Leuven/Leusden: Acco.

Zimring, FR (1983) Attending to feelings and cognitive performance. *Journal of Research and Personality, 17* (3), 288–99.

Zimring, FR (1985) The effect of attending to feeling on memory for internally generated stimuli. *Journal of Research and Personality, 19* (2), 170–84.

Zimring, FR & Katz, K (1988) Self-focus and relational knowledge. *Journal of Research and Personality, 2* (3), 273–89.

**Endnote**
I want to thank Karla Van Leeuwen of the University of Ghent for her help with the statistics.

# Chapter 7

# PERSON-CENTRED INTERVENTIONS WITH VIOLENT CHILDREN AND ADOLESCENTS

## Klaus Fröhlich-Gildhoff

## INTRODUCTION

Violent children and adolescents offer a specific challenge to both psychotherapists and teachers. Their behaviour often has a long individual history originating in early childhood and is seemingly 'change-resistant'. Though the behaviour and its effects are dramatic, the offenders' motivation to change is mostly low.

The offending behaviour can be explained by a distorted and rigid self-concept. My hypothesis is that to 'reach' the aggressive/violent target group the 'basic' person-centred psychotherapy model needs an extension or specification. On the basis of an empathic and congruent relationship the general therapeutic attitude has to include positive regard *and* the willingness to confront (Carkhuff, 1969). The first step in work with aggressive/violent children or adolescents is to build a motivation for change. It is very important to work with self-responsibility – to change the 'reality-distortion', including the 'aggression-biased' perception patterns. This needs a structured therapeutic procedure involving confrontation.

In order to give reasons for the hypothesis, the development of the 'aggressive-biased' self-concept is shown on the basis of an integrated biopsychosocial model. This model attempts to summarise current empirical results from different theoretical traditions, to lead to a disorder-specific comprehension of violence within the context of broader person-centred theory.

## DEFINITION OF AGGRESSIVE AND VIOLENT BEHAVIOUR; CLASSIFICATION AND FREQUENCY

### DEFINITION

Depending on the theory, there are a number of definitions of aggressive and violent behaviour. Over the past several years, we find a tendency to conclude that 'aggression', or 'aggressive behaviour' involves the specific intention of the aggressive/violent actor or offender:

- *Aggression* is a well mapped-out and intentional verbal or physical activity, which leads to an emotional, psychological, or physical injury.
- The term *violence* is usually used for very intensive or destructive forms of aggressive behaviour (Fröhlich-Gildhoff, 2006a).

In diagnostic systems stronger and persistent aggressive/violent behaviour is classified in the following way:

- Disorders of antisocial behaviour (*DSM-IV*, American Psychiatric Association, 1994): aggressive behaviour against persons and/or animals; disturbance of property; fraud or theft; permanent acting against (social) rules
- Disorders in social behaviour (*ICD-10*, F91 e.g. Dilling et al., 1994)
- Combined disorders of social behaviour and emotions (*ICD-10*, F92)

FREQUENCY/PREVALENCE

Frequency data (prevalence rates) are different, depending on the research methods and instruments, but are often reported to be between 2 and 16 per cent.

*Table 1*
Prevalence rates of disorders in social behaviour

| Study by: | Prevalence | Reference |
|---|---|---|
| American Psychiatric Association, 1994 | 8% of all children and adolescents (6–16% boys, 2–9% girls) | Petermann, Döpfner & Schmidt, 2001 |
| Mannheimer Risiko- Kinder-Studie, Ihle & Esser, 2002 | 14.5% of identified children up to 10 years (70% boys, 30% girls) | Laucht, 2003 |
| Romano, Tremblay & Vitaro, 2001 | 4.2% 14–17 year-old adolescents (self-rating)(5.5% boys, 2.9% girls) | Essau & Conradt, 2004 |
| Lahey, Miller, Gordon & Riley, 1998 | 0–11.9% (4–18 years old, median 2%) | Scheithauer & Petermann, 2004 |

'Disorders in social behaviour' and 'combined disorders in social behaviour and emotions' constitute the highest rates of diagnosis in childhood and adolescence (Scheithauer & Petermann, 2004: 373).

The ratio of boys to girls varies from 2:1 up to 4:1. There have also been found different patterns of violence (boys: more verbal and physical; girls: more relational). There is a high comorbidity with other disorders, especially with ADHD (~ 50%), delinquency (~ 30%), and anxiety disorders (~ 30%) (Scheithauer & Petermann, 2004; Essau & Conradt, 2004).

In Germany, there was a (strong) increasingly observed frequency of 'clear' aggressive and delinquent behaviour until the year 2000. Since then, studies and statistics show a stagnation reflecting a small decrease (Brettfeld & Wetzels, 2003). A small group (5% of the offenders) is responsible for about 50% of the violent acts.

## DEVELOPMENT AND CAUSES OF VIOLENT BEHAVIOUR

It is necessary to distinguish between causes and trigger mechanisms: Violent behaviour usually results when a *person* with a general behaviour and/or disposition pattern, characterised as a higher willingness in violence ('violence standby'), encounters in a *situation* a specific trigger mechanism. The first issue is the development of this general disposition to act in a violent way generally:

### DEVELOPMENT

There is a general development line of aggressive behaviour (Fröhlich-Gildhoff, 2006a; Dornes, 1997; Scheithauer & Petermann, 2004):

- *First Year:* Anger appears as an emotional reaction; reactive-aversive activities are only shown in cases of threat or restriction. These activities are not self-activating in contrast to the assertive motivation system with exploration behaviour. This 'aversion-programme' normally works in three steps: (1) signalling apprehension; (2) trying to avoid or put away the threat; and (3) acting aggressively. If these steps are not successful, decompensation follows, resulting in a 'behaviour collapse'.

- *Second and third year:* Children are testing instrumental-aggressive actions just to reach goals; the highest level of aggressive action is shown at around 24 months. With the ability to verbalise and symbolically process intrapsychic representations, hate can become independent of the specific context/situational trigger.

- *Fourth to sixth year:* There is often a decrease in physical aggression and an increase in verbal aggression.

  Long-term studies show a high stability of aggressive/violent behaviour from the fifth year (Burke, Loeber & Lahey, 2003; Essau & Conradt, 2004; Dornes, 1997; Krahé, 2001; Roth & Seiffge-Krenke, 2005).

- *Early school age:* There are distinct differences between stable aggressive behaviour and spontaneous-reactive aggression; distinct gender differences also appear.

- *Adolescence:* During adolescence, there is a fundamental decrease of aggressive behaviour for most people, but an increase of violence from children/adolescents with unstable self-structures and/or patterns of aggressive behaviour in the past. The peer group has a very important influence; violent adolescents seek others with similar patterns.

## BIOPSYCHOSOCIAL EXPLANATION MODEL

The disposition for a stable violence-biased contact with others is a result of the interaction of biological conditions and lifetime experiences (especially social experiences), specific risk and protection factors, and the characteristics of the individual psychic structure (self). *Biological conditions:* Until now there has been no substantial evidence of a genetic predisposition for violent behaviour (Scheithauer & Petermann, 2004). But children

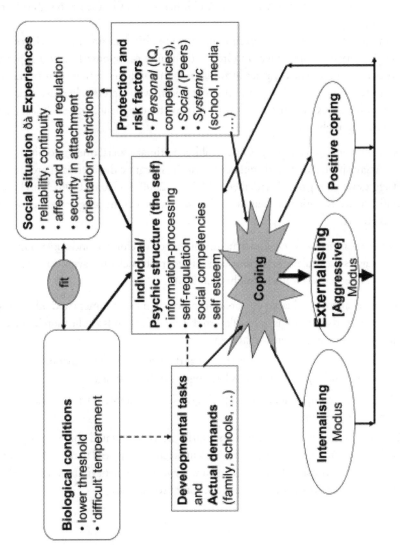

*Figure 1.* Biopsychosocial model of the development of aggressive/violent behaviour.

appear to be born with different levels of activity, abilities of perception and stimulus threshold intensities. There are connections between a 'difficult temperament' – that means lower threshold, higher sensitivity, and lower possibilities for self-regulation (Resch, 2004; Schmeck, 2003) – and the disposition to show stronger aggressive behaviour (Schmeck, 2003; Wurmser & Papousek, 2004; Essau & Conradt, 2004). Whether the 'difficult temperament' leads to aggressive behaviour or not depends on the fit of this temperament with early conditions in the social environment.

• *Early experiences in interaction and attachment*: If young children have changing attachment figures and environments, they often cannot build up secure attachment patterns. This leads to intrapsychic representations (or 'inner working models') of an 'insecure world' and lower self-esteem. Aggressive behaviour is the attempt to find clarity in this insecure and disorganised world. And it helps for a short time to stabilise one's self-esteem.

Another consequence of insecure and unempathic attachment experiences is a restricted ability to regulate affect and arousal (Wurmser & Papouszek, 2004). If parents (or other important persons) react inconsistently to children's testing of instrumental-aggressive action in the first years, this behaviour will increase, because it is only momentarily successful. In this way, it leads to the experience of self-efficacy and, temporarily, to higher self-esteem.

• *Social environment, peer group*: Older children's primary social orientation is the peer group. Aggressive children and adolescents usually integrate themselves in groups with other aggressive young people (Kleiber & Meixner, 2000; McCord, 1998). This leads to a specific, aggressive-oriented 'culture' and these groups become progressively closer and more exclusive.

• *Intrapsychic structure (self)*: The structure of the self of children and adolescents with stronger aggressive/violent behaviour and 'disorders in social behaviour' is shaped by four typical elements (Fröhlich-Gildhoff, 2006a):

1. A limited, aggressive-biased information-processing: Environment and other people are perceived as ominous or hostile – so the individual finds vindication in building up aggression as a 'defensive' strategy.

2. Lower abilities for self-regulation of affect and arousal – for the individual it is harder to control and regulate emotions like anger, trouble and rage.

3. Missing social competences/skills, especially abilities to handle or resolve social conflicts without aggression.

4. Lower self-esteem, which will temporarily be compensated for with aggressive behaviour. Momentarily, aggressive/violent behaviour can lead to the self-perception of efficacy and control. In the long run, however, the behaviour is restricted and punished – the consequence is a reduction of self-esteem.

TRIGGERING CONDITIONS

In (social) situations there are specific conditions that trigger the realisation of aggressive/ violent behaviour:

- Unclear or ambiguous social situations
- Excessive demand or confrontation (without 'flight' possibilities)
- A social atmosphere that tolerates violence (e.g. some schools and other institutions lack clear rules that are consistently followed to deal with violence)
- Presence or use of alcohol and other drugs
- Media (television, computer games) have a triggering influence on unstable children and adolescents (Borg-Laufs, 1997; von Salisch et al., 2005; Selg, 2003)

## THERAPEUTIC INTERVENTION

'Disorders in social behaviour' are particularly resistant to modification because this behaviour has its roots in early life experiences and becomes an important influence in the self-concept. So it needs specific forms of encounter and intervention to modify the rigid developed self.

A conclusion of empirical results of the psychotherapeutic work with aggressive and violent children and adolescents shows:

- Structured therapeutic procedures are more successful than an 'open' process: 'Behaviour and problem orientated procedures ... [and] multimodal methods proved clearly superior by three times higher power of effect against undirected group settings, psychodynamic ... or non-directive concepts and justice measures' (Kleiber & Meixner 2000: 200 [translation KF-G]; see also Essau & Conradt 2004).
- The combination of group and individual therapy/training is more effective than individual therapy (Scheithauer & Petermann, 2004; Borg-Laufs, 2002; Petermann & Petermann, 2005; Petermann et al., 2007).
- Working with the social environment (parents and teachers) is more successful than individual therapy: 'combined schemes which incorporate the individual and the social environment have the greatest chance of success. A purely one-on-one setting achieves – at least from the age of six years – less apparent success ' (Dornes, 1997: 285 [translation KF-G]; see also Borg-Laufs, 1997, 2002; Elsner 2004; Fröhlich-Gildhoff, 2006a).

In person-centred psychotherapy with violent children and adolescents, it is very important to consider disorder-specific characteristics to 'reach' – that means to connect and to understand – this target group and their kind of contact to the world. Five principles describe the general attitude in the contact with the patients/clients:

1. The basis of every therapeutic intervention is a good relationship between the therapist and the client and this includes children and adolescents. It is not easy to build up this sort of relationship because violent children and adolescents are not usually motivated to interact with a therapist or change their behaviour (or themselves); violent children and adolescents are often viewed as resistant or not motivated to engage in the therapeutic process. They have been acting in a 'violent way' for a very long time – it is part of the self-structure – and this behaviour temporarily protects their self-esteem. In the beginning of the psychotherapy, I suggest that there should be:

   a) time to find an access to the child; one possibility is the recognition of the child's strengths, resources, and potential;

   b) a building-up of motivation for change. It is necessary to find little signs of desire for change – in most cases the children might report situations in which they don't want to have any more 'stress with others'; sometimes distinct discussion or reinforcements of these desires are helpful.

   McCulloch (2005) considers that the openness of the person-centred approach, whilst 'clients are accepted as worthwhile, free from rejection and abandonment as persons' (p. 183) builds up a good access to patients with high resistance. Similarly, Greenberg, Elliott and Lietaer (2000) find that 'clients with higher resistance (including high dominance, low submissiveness) appear to do better in client-centered or non-directive therapies' (p. 517).

2. The therapeutic attitude must be characterised by positive regard *and* confrontation. The (violent) person needs the positive regard of the therapist, but the (violent) behaviour should not be accepted. Research with (criminal) offenders shows that a *only* hard, confrontational style has negative effects on the therapeutic outcome. But, although empathy alone does not often lead to a change of the self-concept and behaviour (e.g. Marshall et al., 2002; Elsner, 2004), it should still provide an important base for 'increasing trust and decreasing resistance' (McCulloch, 2002: 12). In this, communication based on the congruence of the therapist is an important element. I propose that it is useful to show – within the context of a supporting therapeutic relationship – disaffirmation, and even, at times, condemnation, of the aggressive and violent acts. Thus, offenders must be confronted with their behaviour and its consequences for other people and themselves. This confrontation should be realised not in a moralistic but in a very authentic way: If a boy boasts about a violent act – for example about him and his friends assaulting another boy – talking about ethics is not recommended. It could be much more meaningful to bring in the feelings of the therapist or the perspective of the victim's mother. ('It sounds like you think you were right to beat up this boy. On the other hand, you talked about how important *your* mother is. I care about the whole you – not just about how good you felt when you beat him up, but also your love for your mother. It strikes me that he has a mother too. She has cared for him for fifteen years just like your mother has with you. How does it feel to wrestle with two different sides of the situation?')

3. It is important to work with the child or adolescent's own sense of compassion, conscience and/or responsibility: Because of their limited perception of self and others, violent children and adolescents delegate the responsibility for their behaviour to other people, very often to the victims themselves. They feel constantly provoked by others and therefore find a rationale or excuse for their own violence. It is very important to help the young person change this kind of 'reality-distortion'.

4. The therapist should work to help the client change the intrapsychic schema: the self-concept, based on developed intrapsychic schemas, changes through reflection on new, inspiring and/or stimulating experiences. This means that it is necessary to consider and organise specific experiences to:

   • change aggression-biased perception patterns; aggression-biased information processing must be explored with confrontation.

   • differentiate the spectrum of emotions, especially by precisely reflecting and 'mirroring' emotions to help the child or adolescent develop more subtle awareness and distinction between emotions (e.g. disappointment, annoyance, hurt, frustration, anger, rage).

   • improve self-regulation processes: children and adolescents need to learn to use a 'filter' between impulse and action. Violent people have to discover their own 'filter' by introjecting the therapeutic situation and learning how to make choices rather than just react. Learning relaxation techniques can be particularly helpful in this process.

   • build up social competencies, especially non-violent coping in social conflicts (e.g. de-escalation strategies). The concrete behaviour should be taught in the therapy, e.g. in role plays (with puppets or real people) or through proven conflict-resolution programs for young people.

   • increase sustainable self-esteem by arranging experiences of self-efficacy and cooperation without aggression.

5. Pedagogic and therapeutic work with violent children and adolescents is very stressful as helpers can feel offended, the disorder is modification-resistant, and the attitudes of violent young people can challenge the therapist's value system. Therefore burn-out prevention is important. Some guidelines for this follow:

   • Try to get feedback and build up support networks for the therapist in the form of a team or with supervision.

   • Share responsibility with clients and other helpers in the clients' lives.

   • Build up support networks for the children and adolescents, including cooperating with youth welfare institutions.

   • Be aware of your own boundaries, setting limits that will allow you to keep therapeutic attitudes.

   • Look for a good 'work–life balance'.

103

Many group intervention programmes can provide an extension to individual psychotherapy. The programs of Olweus (1995), Bieg and Behr (2005) and Steinmetz-Brandt (2006) are made for the institutional context, especially to create a non-violent atmosphere in school. These programmes are based on concepts of humanistic psychology and are particularly relevant for integration with person-centred approaches.

There are confrontation programmes especially for work with juvenile offenders (e.g. Heilemann & Fischwasser-von Proeck, 2001). The theoretical model 'behind' these programmes is more behaviour-orientated; they can be partly successful in a particularly restrictive structure (e.g. prison). Long-term evaluation shows a tendency to an ebbing of the former effectiveness (Ohlemacher et al., 2001).

Additionally, there are holistic (group) programmes that try to change self- and world-perceptions, improve self-regulation, upgrade the social competencies and stabilise the self-esteem of violent children and adolescents, including more behavioural (Petermann & Petermann, 2001) and humanistic (Fröhlich-Gildhoff, 2006b) approaches.

## CONCLUSION

The background to persistent violent behaviour is a rigid and distorted self (-concept), characterised by four central elements: aggression-biased information-processing; low ability for self-regulation of affect and arousal; missing social competencies and skills, especially for the regulation of social conflicts without aggression; and low self-esteem. Because this self-concept appears to develop in the first years, it is highly resistant to modification and the child's motivation to change the 'well-known' and 'secure' behaviour is low.

The person-centred therapeutic paradigm needs some disorder-specific extensions to reach violent children and adolescents: the foundation is the offer of a secure and beneficial relationship. The first part of therapy often involves a struggle to build both this relationship and the child's motivation to engage in the process of therapy. The person-centred approach gives good (common-sense) advice for building this alliance, including the conditions for personality change (Rogers, 1959). However, it is important for the therapist to form their statement (e.g. interventions) from the congruence of the therapist and the combination of empathy, positive regard *and* confrontation (Carkhuff, 1969). This should lead to a greater sense of self-responsibility in the children and adolescents and consequently to better relationships with others.

# REFERENCES

American Psychiatric Association (1994) *Diagnostic and Statistical Manual of Mental Disorders.* (4th edn) *(DSM-IV).* Washington, DC: APA [dt. Bearbeitung von H Saß, H-UWittchen & M Zausig (1996) *Diagnostisches und statistisches Manual Psychischer Störungen. (DSM-IV).* Göttingen: Hogrefe].

Bieg, S & Behr, M (2005) *Mich und Dich verstehen. Ein Trainingsprogramm zur Emotionalen Sensitivität bei Schulklassen und Kindergruppen im Grundschul- und Orientierungsstufenalter.* [Understanding Me and You. A training for emotional sensitivity in school classes and groups of children in elementary school]. Göttingen: Hogrefe.

Borg-Laufs, M (1997) *Aggressives Verhalten: Mythen und Möglichkeiten* [Aggressive Behaviour. Myths and possibilities]. Tübingen: DGVT.

Borg-Laufs, M (2002) Verhaltenstherapie mit aggressiven Jugendlichen. Ableitungen aus der Entwicklungspsychopathologie [Behaviour therapy with aggressive adolescents. Deductions from developmental psychopathology]. In Berufsverband der Kinder- und Jugendlichenpsychotherapeutinnen und Kinder- und Jugendlichenpsychotherapeuten: *Viele Seelen wohnen doch in meiner Brust. Identitätsarbeit in der Psychotherapie mit Jugendlichen* (pp. 107–31). Münster: Verlag für Psychotherapie.

Brettfeld, K & Wetzels (2003) Jugendliche als Opfer und Täter: Befunde aus kriminologischen Dunkelfeldstudien [Adolescents as victim and offender. Results from crimonological field studies]. In U Lehmkuhl (Hrsg) *Aggressives Verhalten bei Kindern und Jugendlichen. Ursachen, Prävention, Behandlung* [Aggressive Behaviour of Children and Adolescents. Causes, prevention, therapy] (pp. 78–114). Göttingen: Vandenhoeck & Ruprecht.

Burke, JD, Loeber, R & Lahey, BB (2003) Course and outcomes. In CA Essau *Conduct and Oppositional Defiant Disorders: Epidemioloy, risk factors and treatment* (pp. 61–94). Hillsdale, NJ: Lawrence Erlbaum Associates.

Carkhuff, RR (1969) *Helping and Human Relations; A primer for lay and professional leaders. Volume 1. Selection and Training.* New York: Holt, Rinehart and Winston.

Dilling, H, Mombour, W, Schmidt, MH, Schulte-Markwort, E (1994) *Internationale Klassifikation psychischer Störungen. ICD-10 Kapitel V (F) Forschungskriterien* [International Classification of Mental and Behavioural Disorders. *ICD-10*, ch. V (F), research criteria]. Bern: Hans Huber.

Dornes, M (1997) *Die frühe Kindheit. Entwicklungspsychologie der ersten Lebensjahre* [Early Childhood. Developmental psychology of the first years]. Frankfurt: Fischer.

Elsner, K (2004) Tätertherapie. Grundlagen und kognitiv-behavioraler Schwerpunkt [Therapy with offenders. Basics and cognitive behavioural focus]. *Psychotherapie im Dialog, 5* (2), 109–19.

Essau, CA & Conradt, J (2004) *Aggression bei Kindern und Jugendlichen* [Aggression of Children and Adolescents]. München/Basel: Ernst Reinhardt.

Fröhlich-Gildhoff, K (2006a) *Gewalt begegnen – Konzepte und Projekte zur Prävention und Intervention* [Surrender Violence – Concepts and projects for prevention and intervention]. Stuttgart: Kohlhammer.

Fröhlich-Gildhoff, K (2006b) *Freiburger Anti-Gewalt-Training (FAGT) – Konzept, Manual, Evaluation* [Freiburger Anti-Violence Training: Concept, manual, evaluation]. Stuttgart: Kohlhammer.

Greenberg, LS, Elliott, RK & Litaer, G (2000) Research on experiental therapies. In AE Bergin

& SL Garfield (Eds) *Handbook of Psychotherapy Change* (4th edn) (pp. 509–39). New York : Wiley.

Heilemann, M & Fischwasser-von Proeck, G (2001) *Gewalt wandeln. Das Anti-Aggressivitäts-Training AAT* [Changing Violence. The Anti-Aggression-Training AAT]. Lengerich: Pabst Publishing.

Ihle, W & Esser, G (2002) Epidemiologie psychischer Störungen im Kindes- und Jugendalter: Prävalenz, Verlauf, Komorbidität und Geschlechtsunterschiede. [Epidemiology of mental disorders in childhood and adolescence: Prevalence, process, comorbidity and gender differences]. *Psychologische Rundschau, 53* (4), 159–69.

Kleiber, D & Meixner, S (2000) Aggression und (Gewalt-)Delinquenz bei Kindern und Jugendlichen: Ausmaß, Entwicklungszusammenhänge und Prävention [Aggression and (violence-) delinquency of children and adolescents: Range, developmental framework and prevention]. *Gesprächspsychotherapie und Personzentrierte Beratung, 31* (3), 191–205.

Krahé, B (2001) *The Social Psychology of Aggression.* Philadelphia, PA: Psychology Press.

Lahey, BB, Miller, TL, Gordon, A & Riley, AW (1998) Developmental epidemiology of disruptive behavior disorders. In HC Quay & AE Hogan (Eds) *Handbook of Disruptive Behavior Disorders* (pp. 23–48). New York: Wiley.

Laucht, M (2003) Aggressives und dissoziales Verhalten in der Prä-Adoleszenz: Entstehungsbedingungen und Vorläufer in der frühen Kindheit [Aggressive and dissocial behaviour in pre-adolescence: Causes and development in early childhood]. In U Lehmkuhl (Ed) *Aggressives Verhalten bei Kindern und Jugendlichen. Ursachen, Prävention, Behandlung [Aggressive Behaviour of Children and Adolescents: Causes, prevention, therapy]* (pp. 47–56). Göttingen: Vandenhoeck & Ruprecht.

Marshall, WL, Serran, GA, Moulden, H, Mulloy, R, Fernandez, YM, Mann, RE & Thornton, D (2002) Therapist features in sexual-offender treatment: Their reliable identification and influence on behaviour change. *Clinical Psychology and Psychotherapy, 9,* 395–405.

McCord, J (Ed) (1998) *Coercion and Punishment in Long-Term Perspectives.* New York: Cambridge University Press.

McCulloch, LA (2002) A person-centered approach to individuals diagnosed with antisocial personality disorder. *Person-Centred Practice, 10,* 4–14.

McCulloch, LA (2005) Antisocial personality disorder and the person-centered approach. In S Joseph & R Worsley (Eds) *Person-Centred Psychopathology: A positive psychology of mental health* (pp. 169–89). Ross-on-Wye: PCCS Books.

Ohlemacher, T, Sögding, D, Höynck, T, Ethé, N & Welte, G (2001) *Anti-Aggressivitäts-Training und Legalbewährung* [Anti-Aggression Training and Legal Probation]. Hannover: kriminologisches Forschungsinstitut Niedersachsen, Eigendruck. Online veröffentlicht unter: www.kfn.de [Zugriff: 25.6.2005].

Olweus, D (1995) *Gewalt in der Schule* [Violence in School]. Bern: Huber.

Petermann, F, Döpfner, M & Schmidt, HM (2001): *Aggressiv-dissoziale Störungen* [Aggressive-Antisocial Disorders]. Göttingen: Hogrefe.

Petermann, F & Petermann, U (2001) *Training mit aggressiven Kindern* 10 [Training with Aggressive Children (corrected edn)]. Weinheim: Psychologie Verlags Union.

Petermann, F & Petermann, U (2005) *Training mit aggressiven Kindern* 11 [Training with Aggressive Children (corrected edn)]. Weinheim: Psychologie Verlags Union.

Petermann, U, Nitkowski, D, Polchow, J, Pätel, S, Roos, F-J & Petermann, F (2007) Langfristige Effekte des Trainings mit aggressiven Kindern [Long-term effects of a cognitive behavioral therapy program with aggressive children]. *Kindheit und Entwicklung, 16* (3), 143–51.

Resch, F (2004) Entwicklungspsychopathologie der frühen Kindheit im interdisziplinären Spannungsfeld [Developmental psychology of early childhood in an interdisciplinary view]. In M Papousek, M Schieche & H Wurmser (Eds) *Regulationsstörungen der frühen Kindheit* [Regulation Disorders in Early Childhood] (pp. 31–48). Bern/Göttingen: Huber.

Rogers, CR (1959) A theory of therapy, personality and interpersonal relationships as developed in the client-centered framework. In S Koch (Ed) *Psychology: A study of a science. Vol. III: Formulations of the person and the social context* (pp. 184–256). New York: McGraw-Hill.

Romano, E, Tremblay, RE & Vitaro, F (2001) Prevalence of psychiatric diagnoses and the role of perceived impairment: Findings from an adolescent community sample. *Journal of Child Psychology and Psychiatry, 42*, 451–61.

Roth, M & Seiffge-Krenke, I (2005) Die Relevanz von familiären Belastungen und aggressivem, antisozialem Verhalten in Kindheit und Jugend für Delinquenz im Erwachsenenalter: Eine Studie an 'leichten' und 'schweren' Jungs in Haftanstallten [The relevance of familial strain and aggressive, antisocial behaviour in childhood and adolescence for delinquency in adult age: A comparative study in prisons]. In I Seiffge-Krenke (Ed) *Aggressionsentwicklung zwischen Normalität und Pathologie* [Development of Aggression between Normality and Pathology] (pp. 283–308). Göttingen: Vandenhoek & Ruprecht.

Salisch, M von, Kristen, A & Oppel, C (2005) Aggressives Verhalten und (neue) Medien [Aggressive behaviour and (new) media]. In I Seiffge-Krenke (Ed) *Aggressionsentwicklung zwischen Normalität und Pathologie* [Development of Aggression between Normality and Pathology] pp. 198–237. Göttingen: Vandenhoek & Ruprecht.

Scheithauer, H & Petermann F (2004) Aggressiv-dissoziales Verhalten [Aggressive-antisocial behaviour]. In F Petermann, K Niebank & H Scheithauer (Eds) *Entwicklungswissenschaft: Entwicklungspsychologie – Genetik – Neuropsychologie* [Developmental Science: Developmental psychology – genetic – neuropsychology] (pp. 367–406). Berlin, Heidelberg: Springer.

Schmeck, K (2003) Die Bedeutung von spezifischen Temperamentsmerkmalen bei aggressiven Verhaltensstörungen [The meaning of specific temperament characteristics for aggressive behaviour disorders]. In U Lehmkuhl (Ed) *Aggressives Verhalten bei Kindern und Jugendlichen. Ursachen, Prävention, Behandlung* [Aggressive Behaviour of Children and Adolescents: Causes, prevention, therapy] (pp. 157–74). Göttingen: Vandenhoeck & Ruprecht.

Selg, H (2003) Mediengewalt und ihre Auswirkungen auf Kinder [Violence in media and its effects on children]. *Unsere Jugend, 55* (4), 147–55.

Steinmetz-Brand, U (2006) In der Krise wächst die Chance. Ganzheitliches Gewaltpräventions- und Interventionsprogramm der Georg Büchner Schule, Schule für Erziehungshilfe und Kranke [From crisis grows opportunity: A holistic violence prevention and intervention programme in a school for special education]. In K Fröhlich-Gildhoff *Gewalt begegnen. Konzepte und Projekte zur Prävention und Intervention* [Surrender Violence: Concepts and projects for prevention and intervention] (pp. 134–51). Stuttgart: Kohlhammer.

Wurmser, H & Papousek, M (2004) Zahlen und Fakten zu frühkindlichen Regulationsstörungen: Datenbasis aus der Münchner Spezialambulanz [Data and facts about regulation disorders in early childhood: Data of the Munich special ambulance]. In M Papousek, M Schieche & H Wurmser (Eds) *Regulationsstörungen der frühen Kindheit* [Regulation disorders in early childhood] (pp. 49–76). Bern/Göttingen/Toronto/Seattle: Huber.

# CHAPTER 8

# PEER GROUP COUNSELLING
## A PERSON-CENTRED AND EXPERIENTIAL TREATMENT
## FOR STRESSED ADOLESCENTS

### ULRIKE BÄCHLE-HAHN

## INTRODUCTION

I first became acquainted with the ideas of positive peer culture (PPC) in 2005 when I embarked upon a new career as a psychologist in residential youth services at St. Augustinusheim in Ettlingen, Germany. Here, I witnessed peer group counselling meetings with so-called 'difficult' (aggressive, delinquent, over-stressed) boys and young men, who were able to show empathy, patience and appreciation towards each other, and I became fascinated by my own experiences in contact with these adolescent groups. I was, at the same time, in training to be a person-centred counsellor and, triggered by the preoccupation with the beliefs and ideas of the person-centred and experiential (PCE) approach, I asked myself how this highly structured course of peer group counselling, including the labels and rules used within PPC, might be compatible with PCE approaches.

Aggressive adolescents with a strong propensity for violence and antisocial behaviour provide a special challenge for residential programmes. Several recent publications (e.g. Fröhlich-Gildhoff, 2006, Chapter 7 this volume) point out the possibility and importance of confrontation and structuring elements for successful, person-centred work with this special clientele. For two decades, the ideas of a positive peer culture (PPC), consisting of a humanistic attitude, confronting elements and structuring rituals, have been practised in American institutions of the youth welfare system as an educational model. In Germany, the realisation is still in its infancy, although the number of publications and applications of this model continues to increase (Opp & Unger, 2006).

## THE IMPORTANCE OF PEERS

Adolescents all over the world implement their own special culture with their own language, fashion, customs, icons and attitudes. This is a natural process of growing up and seeking an identity (Oerter, 1987; Fehringer, 2006). As we get older, parental influence progressively decreases and the influence of a peer culture gains importance. The socialising authority of peers is relevant for the development and consolidation of norms, attitudes and manners and for the development of self-esteem (Holzer, 2006; Gaiser, 1997) but, when embedded in a milieu that encourages aggressive behaviour and delinquency, this process becomes negative.

Generally, the adolescent culture and its values do not differ significantly and are no more threatening than any other social group (Oerter, 1987; Vorrath & Brendtro, 1985). All the same conflicts and misunderstandings may arise between the 'young' and the 'old' based upon whether the values of the 'opponent' generation are seen as acceptable. It is usually in socially disadvantaged contexts that problems arise and from where adolescents frequently become clients of residential care.

## CLIENTS OF ST. AUGUSTINUSHEIM

St. Augustinusheim in Ettlingen is an institution for disadvantaged male adolescents from the ages of 12 to about 20 years and cares for approximately 120 boys and young men. The adolescents live together in groups of about eight and attend the affiliated special education school or do an apprenticeship until they are able to move into their own apartments, where the level of assistance is lower and scheduled to decrease further until they are released. Two of these groups are intensive therapeutic sexual offender groups. There is also a daytime attendance group for 10 adolescents who still live with their families.

About 50 per cent of St. Augustinusheim new entries have already been in residential care, often having experienced several placements in different residential institutions; about 16 per cent have undergone stays at psychiatric clinics. Almost 60 per cent of St. Augustinusheim residents are diagnosed with conduct disorders (*ICD-10*, F91) involving negative social behaviour, low tolerance of frustration, and readiness for aggression and violence. About 50 per cent suffer from developmental disorders (*ICD-10*, F80 – F89) and approximately 60 per cent of the adolescent residents have been delinquent (Bächle-Hahn, 2006). Adolescents admitted into St. Augustinusheim have often received special acknowledgement from their peers for being aggressive, delinquent and violating social norms.

Clients at St. Augustinusheim commonly feel discontented about their environment and themselves – a sign of incongruence – and receive their only acceptance from like-minded peers. Their allegiance to the values and norms of society has often disappeared over time and been replaced by the values of those with the most severe behavioural problems. Vorrath & Brendtro (1985) name this 'Negative Peer Culture'. The positive peer culture tries actively to work within the mechanisms of peer influence but against negative peer culture, thus enabling positive developmental experiences (Brendtro & Ness, 1983).

## POSITIVE PEER CULTURE

PPC is a method of treatment specifically aimed at adolescents who have grown up in the disadvantaged environments mentioned above and who have tended to follow a negative peer culture. It is rooted in experiences with prisoners and adolescent delinquents in residential programmes (Opp, 2006), humanistic beliefs about education (Brendtro & Ness, 1983; Cornelius-White & Harbaugh, in press) and the ideas of pedagogical pioneers such as Korczak (Dauzenroth, 2002) and Makarenko (Brendtro & Ness, 1983). After World War II, Harry Vorrath, a former marine, worked in a peer group oriented intervention programme in a residential institution for delinquent adolescents in Highfields, New Jersey, USA. There, they applied a programme based upon the concept of Guided Group Intervention (GGI), developed in US military prisons during WW II. Group meetings that aimed to support adolescents in helping each other in problem-solving were a central element. Witnessing these difficult adolescents supporting one another inspired Vorrath with enthusiasm about their hidden potential. At the same time, Vorrath distanced himself from aggressive GGI programmes which, in his opinion, mainly demanded obedience to adults. His proposition was that adolescents accept responsibility. His aim was to empower them to discover their own potential, skills and qualities and to foster processes of problem-solving. The term 'positive peer culture' highlights the balance between mutual support, caring and group culture (Opp, 2006).

The basic idea of PPC is easy to understand but difficult to realise. It demands an attitude towards and a communication with the most difficult and disturbed individuals by emphasising their strengths, resources and cooperative desires – not their inadequacies. Thus, the concept requires a deep conviction about each adolescent's potential to grow in a pro-social manner. The adolescent, regardless of his own problems or stresses, must support others in their social and personal developments, and it is through this mutual support that they will progress.

For me, it is fascinating to understand how these assumptions about adolescent development are rooted in the basic ideas of both progressive education and the Rogerian theory of personality. For example, the actualising tendency is an agency for fostering growth if the social environment is supportive; also addressed is the idea of people as dialogical beings. The adolescent clearly has the capacity to let his potential emerge when he is in non-destructive contact with other individuals (Rogers, 1951, 1957).

## INSTITUTIONAL PROCEDURES

Adolescents admitted into institutions of the residential care system have often experienced highly stressful familial situations, including violence, abandonment and loneliness; they may have already been in residential care or even lived on the streets. One common feature of their experience is the absence of boundaries or security, leading to antisocial developments and the vicious cycle of a negative peer culture (Brendtro & Ness, 1983; Adam & Peters, 2003) – many stick to this negative peer culture, paradoxically finding within it security, orientation and the feeling of self-efficacy. Educational interventions that aim to help adolescents escape this vicious cycle should satisfy the basic human need of belonging, of being loved and appreciated. Children and adolescents who grow up under positive conditions experience love and attachment in everyday situations.

Communication within their families and milieus, quality and intensity of time spent with others, frequency of being touched and held – both directly and figuratively – build these conditions. Of course, it is difficult to provide deprived adolescents with these experiences. They have a need for attachment, which cannot usually be met literally because of traumatic experiences of sexual abuse, violence and/or severe physical punishment. Also, adolescents and educators might be close in age, adding a sexualised component to any warm or affectionate physical contact.

Therefore, the following principles are practised to provide a safe and caring environment in the everyday routine:

*Structural elements:* Structure can be described as a precondition for fostering the development of a PPC (see also Fröhlich-Gildhoff, 2006; Weidner, 2001). One of the educational aims is to enable the adolescent to lead a life of self-responsibility and autonomy without getting into trouble with social norms and laws. Many of the adolescents have never experienced the benefits of a daily routine. Basic abilities needed to reach autonomy include getting up in the morning, doing the dishes, getting to school or training on time, keeping to break times, etc., and many St. Augustinusheim clients have to master these basic habits at the beginning of their stay.

*Rules:* In order to provide structure in everyday routines, consistent rules are needed. Therefore, a 'step-by-step plan' derived from behavioural therapy has been created. Correspondent to their behaviour, the adolescent is assigned specific steps. Within this step-by-step model the individual finds himself in a competitive situation. Contrary to former experiences, this competition is not led by those who achieve their objectives by antisocial assertiveness but by those who follow prosocial attitudes. These rules embrace each adolescent's right to feel secure and protected from victimisation and violence.

*Environment:* The atmosphere of buildings and rooms influences the feelings of individuals living and working in them (Breuker, Bächle-Hahn, & Schrenk, 2008; Purkey & Novak, 1995). Therefore, St. Augustinusheim places value on the positive and cherished aura of the buildings and rooms. Posters with sexist, violent, or drug-glorifying illustrations are not tolerated. Damage and vandalism are abolished post-haste. Ambiance is also created by positive communication: adolescents, employees, and guests alike should experience appreciation and respect; the tone is friendly, inviting and civilised. Discriminatory expressions are discouraged and confronted.

*Communication:* The aim is for authentic communication – transparent, unambiguous and, when necessary, confrontational – both in educational terms and in relationship building. Educational demands, like the handling of rules, are initially a real challenge for the adolescent client. At the same time, PPC communication means making the individual feel that he is authentically liked. A precondition to being helpful and beneficial as a staff member is to communicate unconditional positive regard and strive to be congruent at all times. This is sometimes a real challenge for our work.

On the basis of these principles, the staff's main task is to demonstrate, demand and support the growth of a positive culture (Vorrath & Brendtro, 1985). Basic values and general principles of this work on PPC are to:

- communicate and act non-violently,
- interact respectfully,
- not use illegal drugs,
- use legal drugs according the German law for the protection of children and youth,
- be punctual and dependable, and
- be helpful to others.

To most of the adolescents, these values, particularly at the beginning and during the first months of their stay, are extremely challenging. Staff and peers have to tolerate the frustration of dealing with the inconsiderateness of many of the clients, to confront them in their negative behaviour, to stop negative behaviour, and at the same time emphasise their strengths (Weidner, 2001). The PPC approach acts from the conviction that despite the obvious weaknesses, deficiencies and disorders of disturbed adolescents, their strengths and resources can be seen and fostered (Vorrath & Brendtro, 1985). If staff simply focus on trying to minimise bad behaviour, rather than uncovering social strengths and abilities in the adolescents, important opportunities will be lost. While behavioural methods may be necessary or supportive (Fröhlich-Gildhoff, 2006) and used during the daily routine, the building of relationships in a constructive social climate is the core of the PPC approach.

A next step is to encourage adolescents to change their attitudes and to develop more positive identities. In everyday communication staff try to notice and comment on any strengths they perceive and, by confronting and critical renaming, to clearly convey their belief in the competency and potential of adolescents (see Vorrath & Brendtro, 1985). In this way, the incongruence between the adolescents' problematic behaviour and the staff's appreciation and recognition of their 'positive' traits may be highlighted. Both PPC and person-centred thinking assert that adolescents surrounded by an atmosphere of acceptance and warmth – a positive culture – can start to perceive their potential and effect change. And this change, initiated by the individual's own insight and motivation, is consistent change affecting more than just behaviour. Thus PPC demands an attitude that accepts and esteems the client. As in person-centred thinking, the experience of being accepted is a condition for the development of positive self-esteem (Rogers, 1951). This attitude challenges staff to distinguish between the person and his aggressive, antisocial and delinquent behaviour, so all staff members must constantly train their abilities and competencies in communication and perception.

Within this concept, a commitment to conveying unconditional positive regard in a congruent way is obvious. I experience the PPC as highly similar to person-centred ways of relationship building and fostering the development of a congruent self. My training in person-centred counselling has helped me to live these challenging demands of relationship building in my everyday routine. As for the highly structured environment and the rigid rules within this institution, again, I experience no contradiction to person-centred principles. To me, these structures are a prerequisite for our work: we have to set up the first Rogerian core condition (Rogers, 1957). I don't feel that I could make psychological contact with any adolescent without the clear rules which we pursue in the institution – clear communication and the building of relationship within a chaotic situation would be impossible and, consequently, we would all suffer.

## PEER GROUP COUNSELLING (PGC)

Peer group counselling (PGC) is the most prominent element and instrument for the implementation and maintenance of a positive peer culture (PPC). The counselling routinely comprises a meeting of the adolescents centred around their present problems and difficulties and their attempts to achieve their goals. PGC meetings take place once a week in all groups: residential, daytime attendance, school classes and workshops. The group size at the workshops is approximately 12; all other groups consist of six to nine members. Meetings are facilitated by two staff members. At school, teachers function as facilitators of their class peer groups. At the workshops, the facilitators are also carpenters or gardeners, and at the residential and daytime attendance group meetings, the facilitators are youth care workers. Wednesday evening at 6.30 p.m. is PGC time in the residential area and all adolescents living in each of the nine residential groups and those living in the apartments in the city have their weekly meeting then, except the daytime attendance group, which has theirs in the afternoon.

Given the clients' often huge deficiencies in social behaviour, one of the facilitators' aims is to minimise distractions and interruptions. Hence, the doors are locked, the phones are turned off and all the residential groups have one collective appointed time for their meeting to ensure silence in the area. The meetings are high priority events: attendance as well as constructive cooperation is obligatory for the adolescents.

No one is forced to open up, but everyone is expected to react fairly to the contributions of their peers and to be able to take feedback concerning their own behaviour (Vorrath & Brendtro, 1985). There are three different types of PGC meetings: the problem-solving meeting, the life story meeting, and the release or graduation meeting (Vorrath & Brendtro, 1985). At St. Augustinusheim all weekly meetings are problem-solving meetings. The aim of these problem-solving meetings is to help students in understanding their part in their problematic behaviour and to suggest alternative ways of reacting, to cooperate, to train communication skills and to initiate and foster group and personal developmental processes.

Problematic behaviour is defined as behaviour which hurts people (Vorrath & Brendtro, 1985; Brendtro & Ness, 1983). Bit by bit, the group and its members come to understand that behaviour that hurts others is also hurtful to themselves. In contrast, behaviour that does not directly hurt others, but may traditionally be seen as undesirable, can be understood in a new or more benign light. As a strengths-based approach, the intention is not to stigmatise adolescents as carriers of problems but to facilitate their strengths and competencies. Difficulties in accepting instructions given by teachers, educators or parents – something generally seen as problematic – can be viewed as required or positive qualities, perhaps representing determination, courage, independence and assertiveness. For example, adolescents who steal may reveal intelligence and ambition in their delinquent and inadequate behaviour, so that positive qualities can be appreciated alongside the harm that has been done.

One of the aims of counselling is to enable adolescents to analyse their own perceptions so that they can identify the contribution they make to problematic situations: a difficult process since the whole 'us against them' mentality of the gang culture is often needed to maintain a fragile self-concept (Fehringer, 2006). A less distorted view of their own behaviour often emerges in the identification of 'inconsistent thinking' (Kahn, 2001) and 'preferred' perceptual distortions. Within effective working groups, the counselling enables the adolescents to actualise their understanding of themselves and their peers. The meetings enable them to experience a supportive group, mutually committed, all with similar problems and difficulties. In this environment, self-esteem, social competencies and a more adequate system of values can develop as the adolescents learn to convey their beliefs and assume some responsibility for themselves and others.

## THE COURSE OF THE MEETINGS

The following structure is an ideal one, but its realisation needs long-term group cooperation, highly qualified facilitators, and group members who are both motivated and open to change (Vorrath & Brendtro, 1985).

### OPENING AND REPORTING

(a) A few minutes before the meeting starts, the adolescents of the group are responsible for preparing the room by arranging the chairs in a circle. The facilitators open the meeting, remind the group of the meeting rules (Kahn, 2001) or ask members to do so. If there has been homework, members are asked whether and how it could be shared.

(b) Each adolescent group member names a concrete incident, occurring since the last meeting, in which he behaved in a way that was unintentional (e.g. 'I messed up something in the workshop and picked it up and threw it across the room endangering others'). The peers may in turn contribute problems, incidents and situations that have been evoked. Relevant issues for counselling are actual problems and difficulties occurring in everyday life. Besides the criterion of actuality, the issue must be judged to be relevant, for example, if an individual has experienced difficulty in social interactions or is not able to interact appropriately in a problem situation. The group decides whether a named issue has sufficient relevance to become a topic for discussion.

PGC-relevant problems are more *socio*-dynamic than psychodynamic: they are about what an individual does to others or how an individual gets along with others. PGC aims to empower adolescents in areas that relate to appropriate social interaction and communication, empathy and problem-solving.

## AWARDING THE MEETING

After each group member has named a recent incident or a current problem, the group has to decide who they will focus on in the meeting. This decision has to be unanimous, voting is not possible. A person may decide against being the one who is focused on; on the other hand, an individual who is very keen to be the object of attention may find he is unable to be. At this point the facilitator must be attentive to the process of decision-making and highlight possible 'group-think'. This means that some kind of mob mentality or lack of thought is occurring, and this will not be accepted. Disturbances of all kinds are highlighted by the facilitator; any aspect of group dynamics will be brought into focus so that the facilitator can help the adolescents to negotiate in a constructive and respectful manner. Less effective work groups may need a long time to reach a unanimous decision; nevertheless, unanimity is indispensable as the group as a whole faces up to particularly divergent opinions and is encouraged to work through conflicts in a protected and safe structure accompanied by the facilitator.

## PROBLEM-SOLVING

The group's function is – by analysing the problematic situation and understanding the emotions involved – to help each member towards a greater self-awareness and perhaps to suggest alternative behaviour. Initially, groups are markedly dependent on the facilitator but, with appropriate attendance and as experience increases, group members experience themselves as valuable counsellors, effective in their interaction and communication. The structure of detecting the meaning of problems is given by the 'conflict-cycle' (Long et al., 1996; Brendtro & Shahbazian, 2004), a broadly simplified model to explain the psychodynamic connectedness of feelings, valuing and action.

## REPORTING THE PROBLEM

Clarifying the circumstance surrounding a problem means, firstly, clearly and comprehensibly describing the situation. The adolescent presents the problem in as detailed and chronological a way as possible, without interpretations or assumptions. The group's task is to try to fully understand the situation. The facilitator leads and accompanies the group by appropriate and supportive interventions on their way to understanding. Practical experience shows that adolescents who have difficulties with social behaviour often have a severely biased perception of themselves and social processes. External attributions, in particular, bias the identification of any personal or individual contribution to problems. Common issues in peer groups include dealing with dissension between peers and problems with aggression, girlfriends, alcohol or drug abuse.

115

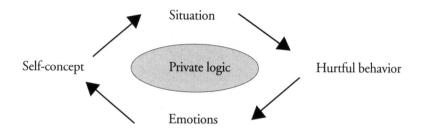

*Figure 1.* Conflict cycle in the process of group work within PGC (Long et al., 1996; Brendtro & Shahbazian, 2004).

### DETECTING HURTFUL BEHAVIOUR

PPC approaches define 'problems' as hurtful behaviour. Once the group has reached an understanding about the incident, they try to support the member concerned in realising the hurt caused by his impulsive actions. The group's job is to enable each other to sense the meaning, motivation, and acceptable aspects of hurtful behaviour.

### DETECTING EMOTIONS

At the beginning of their stay, adolescents often lack empathy (with others and themselves) as, by way of a coping device, they have sometimes found it necessary to sever all connection with feelings, especially their own. Returning to the sort of incident in which the adolescent described hurling something across the workshop, the group tries to understand the feelings involved: a common explanation is 'I felt bad' or 'I was stressed'. They then try to be more concrete about the experience by looking at specific feelings such as disappointment, rage or discontentment rather than generalities like 'stress' or 'bad feelings'. The counselled peer experiences being taken seriously and understood and may come into contact with more actualised feelings.

### REALISING THE SELF-CONCEPT

An effective work group will understand why their peer needed to show destructive behaviour in a certain situation and what he felt like during the incident. The counselled adolescent will understand his actions and feelings and may even come into contact with unknown parts of his self-concept. This sometimes painful process may only evolve in an atmosphere of trust, honesty and prizing.

### TERMINATION OF THE MEETING: FACILITATOR'S SUMMARY

The facilitator summarises the topics and group dynamic processes of the meeting and acknowledges the contributions of the group and individual members. The summary aims to make work more effective. Facilitator's feedback often involves an acknowledgement of courage to talk openly; of resistance or abstinence; of an ability to support others; of prosocial competences, etc. Facilitators strive to emphasise self-reliance and co-counselling abilities. Self-reliance means being able to recognise one's own difficult issues, naming and reporting them, and acknowledging and understanding one's own involvement in incidents. Co-counselling requires the courage to give honest feedback, to empathise with and accept feelings, and the ability to be supportive of others in everyday life.

Another aspect of the summary is to remind the group of any suggestions that arose in the assigning of homework; for example, in response to the workshop incident, possible suggestions generated might have included leaving the room for a few minutes; taking a deep breath; expressing feelings verbally and rationally; or asking a member of staff for support. Specific homework for other group members could involve taking care of their peer and intervening when they see him failing and gently reminding him of the alternatives they discussed.

## FACILITATORS OF PEER GROUP COUNSELLING MEETINGS

The facilitators of the counselling meetings are the staff members with the closest contact to the group in everyday life (see above, Institutional Procedures, p. 110). Their first duty is to maintain the course of the meeting and to ensure the process structure and maintenance of constructive communication. Their role is to be non-directive, present but non-interfering, supportive but not prescriptive; it is not to suggest appropriate incidents to discuss, but to enable the group to work effectively by asking direct questions or making apposite and empathic statements. They will, however, lead the process of the meeting (e.g. decide if particular steps of the process have been handled exhaustively, stop any disturbances, and support counselling). The facilitator's most fundamental activity is to ask simple, brief questions. He or she will also assist group members in their supportive role, guiding them in asking 'necessary' and helpful questions. As PPC aims to emphasise the adolescents' competencies and strengths in supporting each other, the facilitator's role is not to engage in the group process but to foster it. In this sense, it is different from a traditional person-centred encounter group where congruence decrees that facilitators are also participants. This aspect of the role is advanced by addressing the group as a whole instead of individual members: ('Does the group want to …?', 'How does the group hope to …?' etc.), avoiding self-revelations and words like 'we' or 'us', which include the group facilitator.

This task needs high competence in professional communication, in perceiving and affecting group dynamic processes, and the ability to change from the accustomed daily role to the role of a facilitator. Weekly 90-minute meetings for facilitators and staff members, so-called 'Focus groups', provide assistance in and supervision of staff development; maintain competencies relating to PPC and PGC, and offer a forum for facilitator co-counselling and exchange. The first part of the meeting covers topics relating to theoretical information and PPC practices and the sharing of background knowledge and competencies related to communication. The second part of the meeting involves counselling in smaller groups of eight to ten members led by the staff of the psychological service. The counselling meetings have been implemented at the staff's request and express the demand for collegial support in various areas. Within this group work, the paradigm and practice has been further articulated and helpful materials (e.g. study diaries) have been developed.

Additionally, each autumn, the psychological service conducts a workshop for the whole staff with the aim of further implementing PPC ideas, biennially supported by an expert facilitator from Starr Commonwealth, Michigan, USA. Furthermore, the psychologists regularly supervise a sample of PGC meetings to discover possible issues for further staff training.

## OUTCOME

Some objective outcome research was performed by Steinebach and Steinebach (2007) who examined the effects of PPC and PGC at St. Augustinusheim using quantitative and qualitative study from May 2003 until December 2006. Every six months several adolescents and staff members were interviewed and questionnaires were handed out to all adolescents. Additionally, a sample of both parents and consultants of youth welfare offices were interviewed by telephone. Reports from families included the information that fewer fights at home had resulted from their sons being better able to name their problems, to listen to others, and to cope with rules (Steinebach & Steinebach, 2007). Table 1, below, reports the frequency of assessments during the three-year period.

The following findings were reported:

- PPC supports the build-up of a positive self-esteem.

- The readiness to help others increases.

- In the institution, violence and fights decrease.

- Compared to earlier surveys, the adolescents made progress in recognising and tolerating both negative and positive feelings.

- The ease of participation and perceived effectiveness of counselling in the PPC groups distinctly improved during the three years.

- These trends were verified in the longitudinal section and the cross-section analysis using the questionnaires and interviews.

The evaluation thus provides strong evidence for the effectiveness of such an approach with severely distressed male adolescents and young men.

*Table 1*
Issues of the biannual questionnaires and times of assessment

| Questions Concerning: | Spring 2004 | Autumn 2004 | Spring 2005 | Autumn 2005 | Spring 2006 | Autumn 2006 |
|---|---|---|---|---|---|---|
| Age, duration of residential stay | * | * | * | * | * | * |
| Group membership | | | | | * | * |
| Valuation in general | * | * | * | * | * | * |
| Effects of counselling meetings | * | * | * | * | * | * |
| Questions concerning the home | * | | | | | * |
| Desires concerning home life | | * | | | | * |
| Members of the peer group | | * | | | | * |
| Closeness and influence in the group | | | * | | | * |
| Self-image | * | | * | * | * | |
| Values | * | | | * | | |
| Desires and aims | | | | | | * |

# CONCLUSION

Initially, facilitators had no training for PGC. After years of work, several trainings and supervisions distinctly improved the facilitators' competence. Nevertheless, further training for PGC moderators would be an indispensable prerequisite to strengthening competencies and to ensuring the quality of the group processes.

In revisiting the question of how this model of PGC relates to person-centred ideas, several issues emerge. The setting is highly structured and in no way comparable to the very open and unstructured processes which are intended with the Rogerian encounter concept. My training in person-centred counselling certainly helped me to cope with these group processes and to find my role and competencies as a facilitator both in group work and in supervising other facilitators. I cannot think of a better way to facilitate group processes and personal developments with these adolescents. Again, I do not see how I could make psychological contact with so many adolescents without the group, and myself, being bound by these rigid structures.

These adolescents are extremely weighed down by their specific backgrounds and their fragile attachment experiences. They are almost incapable of being aware of their own needs and they attempt to satisfy them in a most distorted manner (e.g. stealing, drug abuse, assault, etc.). The most important and urgent professional task is to somehow meet their unrecognised desire for connection, holding and attachment. Within a structure, I can relate to them and realise a person-centred relationship.

To me, it seems that unconditional positive regard, even in combination with a demanding structure, can be perceived as being taken seriously and valued. This may be the reason that – even though staff members initially receive sparse cooperation – having experienced through PGC that their individual potential is appreciated, the adolescents become increasingly cooperative. Nevertheless, these are adolescents who are only likely to reveal their potential within the provided structure.

Adolescents at St. Augustinusheim are no different from other adolescents with comparable problematic backgrounds. Most of them strongly resist the in-patient treatment and would initially prefer to return to their frequently disastrous but familiar origins – or even to live on the streets. Fear of arrest, the latent hope of graduation, and the lack of alternatives lead them to begin the treatment. We take this chance. As the saying goes, 'You can bring a horse to water, but you can't make it drink.' Insisting on routines, structures and basic values in an empathic framework suggests that we constantly guide them to the source. When I trust in the actualising tendency, I trust that the approach will help these adolescents sense their thirst.

Maybe this is what was meant when one adolescent recently evaluated his development like this: 'It was a bit annoying and wearing meeting every Wednesday for counselling, but it did help me to get along better with myself and with others.'

## REFERENCES

Adam, A & Peters, M (2003) *Störungen der Persönlichkeitsentwicklung bei Kindern und Jugendlichen. Ein integrativer Ansatz für die psychotherapeutische und sozialpädagogische Praxis* [Disorders of Personality Development of Children and Adolescents. An integrative approach for psychotherapeutic and social pedagogic practice]. Stuttgart: Kohlhammer.

Bächle-Hahn, U (2006) Evaluation der teilstationären und vollstationären Unterbringungen im St. Augustinusheim in Ettlingen in den Jahren 2001–2006 [Evaluation of the treatment at St. Augustinusheim in Ettlingen 2001–2006]. Unpublished study. Ettlingen: St. Augustinusheim.

Behr, M, Baegerau, A, Drebes, I, Kunzner, A & Rupieper, M (1997) 'Wenn die Beziehung stimmt, lässt sich pädagogisch alles machen' – Bindungstheorie, Säuglingsforschung und Authenzität der Pädagogenperson ['If the relationship is OK anything is possible': Attachment theory, infant research and the authenticity of the pedagogue ]. In D Deter, K Sander & B Terjung (Eds) *Die Kraft des Personzentrierten Ansatzes. Praxis und Anwendungsgebiete* [The Power of the Person-Centred Approach: Practice and application] (pp. 27–48). Köln: GwG-Verlag.

Brendtro, LK & Ness, A (1983) *Re-educating Troubled Youth: Environments for teaching and treatment.* New York: Aldine Transaction.

Brendtro, LK, Ness, A & Mitchell, M (2001) *No Disposable Kids.* Longmont, CA: Sopris West.

Brendtro, L & Shahbazian, M (2004) *Troubled Children and Youth: Turning problems into opportunities.* Champaign, IL: Research Press.

Breuker, K, Bächle-Hahn, U & Schrenk, A (2008) Positive peer culture im St. Augustinusheim in Ettlingen [Positive peer culture at St. Augustinusheim in Ettlingen]. In G Opp & J Teichmann (Eds) *Positive Peerkultur: Best Practices in Deutschland* [Positive Peer Culture:

Best Practices in Germany] (pp. 103–28). Bad Heilbrunn: Verlag Julius Klinkhardt.

Cornelius-White, JHD & Harbaugh, AP (in press) *Learner-Centered Instruction: Building relationships for student success.* Thousand Oaks, CA: Sage.

Dauzenroth, E (2002) *Ein Leben für Kinder: Janusz Korczak – Leben und Werk* [A Life for Children: Janusz Korczak – Life and works]. Gütersloh: GTB.

Fehringer, C (2006) Ja, so ist die Jugend heute, schrecklich sind die jungen Leute. Personzentrierte Psychotherapie mit Jugendlichen [Person-centered psychotherapy with adolescents]. *Person, Internationale Zeitschrift für Personzentrierte und Experienzielle Psychotherapie und Beratung, 2,* 176–86.

Fröhlich-Gildhoff, K (2006) Personzentrierte pädagogische und therapeutische Arbeit mit aggressiven/gewalttätigen Kindern und Jugendlichen [Person-centered pedagogic and therapeutic work with aggressive/violent children and adolescents]. *Person, Internationale Zeitschrift für Personzentrierte und Experienzielle Psychotherapie und Beratung, 2,* 151–63.

Gaiser, W (1997). Individualisierung und Erwachsenwerden. Biographische und gesellschaftliche Herausforderungen für junge Menschen [Individualisation and growing up: Biographical and social challenges for the young]. In D Deter, K Sander & B Terjung (Eds) *Die Kraft des Personzentrierten Ansatzes. Praxis und Anwendungsgebiete* (pp. 243–66). Köln: GwG-Verlag.

Holzer, A (2006) Jugendliche in der Personzentrierten Psychotherapie. Eine Reflexion der Praxis. [Adolescents in person-centered psychotherapy: A reflection of the practice]. *Person, Internationale Zeitschrift für Personzentrierte und Experienzielle Psychotherapie und Beratung, 2,* 164–75.

Kahn, TJ (2001) *Pathways: A guided workbook for youth beginning treatment.* Brandon, VT: Safer Society Press.

Long, NJ, Morse, WC & Newman, RG (1996) *Conflict in the Classroom: The education of at risk and troubled students.* Austin, TX: Pro-Ed.

Oerter, R (1987) Jugendalter [Adolescence]. In R Oerter & L Montada (Eds) *Entwicklungspsychologie* (pp. 265–38). München: PVU.

Opp, G (2006) Ein Klima der Großzügigkeit schaffen. [To create a climate of generosity] In G Opp & N Unger (Eds) *Kinder stärken Kinder: Positive Peer Culture in der Praxis* [Children Strengthen Children: Positive peer culture in practice] (pp. 86–90). Hamburg: Edition Körber-Stiftung.

Opp, G & Unger, N (Eds) (2006) *Kinder stärken Kinder. Positive Peer Culture in der Praxis* [Children Strengthen Children: Positive peer culture in practice]. Hamburg: Edition Körber-Stiftung.

Purkey, WW & Novak, JM (1995) *Inviting School Success: A self-concept approach to teaching, learning, and democratic practice.* New York: Wadsworth.

Rogers, CR (1951) *Client-Centered Therapy.* Boston: Houghton Mifflin.

Rogers, CR (1957) The necessary and sufficient conditions of therapeutic personality change. *Journal of Consulting Psychology, 21,* 95–103.

Steinebach, U & Steinebach, C (2007) *Positive Peer Culture. Evaluation eines Beratungsmodells für Jugendliche* [Evaluation of a counselling model for adolescents]. Freiburg: Katholische Fachhochschule Freiburg.

Vorrath, HH & Brendtro, LK (1985) *Positive Peer Culture.* New York: Aldine De Gruyter.

Weidner, J (2001) *Konfrontative Pädagogik. Das Glen Mills Experiment* [Confrontational Pedagogy: The Glen Mills Experiment]. Godesberg: Forum Verlag.

# CHAPTER 9

# THE EFFECTIVENESS OF HUMANISTIC COUNSELLING IN UK SECONDARY SCHOOLS
## LITERATURE REVIEW

### MICK COOPER

## INTRODUCTION

In recent years, several studies have been conducted which evaluate the effectiveness of counselling in British secondary schools, including our own evaluation of the first phase of the Glasgow Counselling in Schools Project (Cooper, 2004). In addition, a number of other studies and trials have been conducted in the United Kingdom and the United States that can contribute to an understanding of the potential effectiveness of a school-based counselling service. The findings of these studies, however, have yet to be brought together into a single report. For this reason, this chapter presents a review (conducted in 2005) of recent findings regarding the effectiveness of a humanistic/person-centred counselling in schools service.

## CRITERIA FOR MAIN STUDIES INCLUDED IN THE REVIEW

In order to identify evaluations of counselling in schools to include in this review, a number of criterion were set. These were as follows:

- The evaluation was conducted within the past ten years (i.e. between 1996 and 2005).

- The counselling service was primarily based within secondary schools.

- The practice of the counsellors was primarily 'person-centred' or 'humanistic' (i.e., a client-led approach which views human beings as inherently resourceful and capable of developing their own potential, and in which the counsellor strives to relate to the client in an empathic, valuing and non-directive way, as opposed to a primarily analytical, advice-giving or structured manner).

- The service was based within the United Kingdom (as the practice of 'counselling' within American and European secondary school systems tends to be of a more structured and 'guidance'-oriented nature).

- The counselling was primarily individual.

- There was some quantitative data and/or qualitative data that was collected and analysed in a relatively rigorous way (e.g. thematic analysis of qualitative data rather than 'cherry-picking' of quotes).

On the basis of these criteria, five evaluation studies were identified: Cooper, 2004, 2006a; Fox and Butler, 2003; Loynd, 2002; Sherry, 1999. Background data on each of these studies is presented in Table 1. Where available, data from all pupils attending the services are presented; where not available, data from those completing an evaluation form have been used (and presented in italics).

Across the five services, the average number of sessions offered to pupils ranged from 5.62 to 9.88 (see Table 2).

Attendance rates (i.e. rates of sessions attended as compared to those offered) were reported in just two of the studies, and were both around the 85 per cent mark. This indicates a relatively high level of attendance, particularly when compared with attendance rates at typical adult counselling services, such as the Lanarkshire Primary Care Counselling Service, which has an 80 per cent attendance rate (McGeever, 2006, personal communication).

In terms of gender of clients attending the service, this ranged from 51 per cent female to 63 per cent female, with a median average across the five studies of 56 per cent female.

Ethnic origins of clients were presented in only one study, which reported that 94 per cent of service users were of a British or European background.

Substantial commonality existed across the five studies with respect to the school years of the young people attending counselling. Pupils in the school years S2 to S4 (about 12 to 14 years old) were most likely to attend counselling, with a significant dropping off for both younger and older pupils.

There were also substantial commonalities in terms of the primary presenting problems that the young people tended to bring to counselling. Across the five studies, 'family' was by far the most common presenting problem, with 'school', 'relationships', 'anxiety and stress' and 'anger' also featuring prominently in a number of the reports. Interestingly, the Glasgow Phase I study (Cooper, 2004), the East Renfrewshire study (Cooper, 2006a), the NSPCC study (Fox & Butler, 2003) and the Aberdeen study (Loynd, 2002) all found significant gender differences in the types of issues presented to the counsellor, with females tending to present more frequently with family, relationship and anxiety issues, and males tending to present more frequently with issues related to behaviour, anger and school.

# THE HELPFULNESS OF A SCHOOL-BASED COUNSELLING SERVICE

## OUTCOME MEASUREMENTS

In three of the studies reviewed above (Cooper, 2004, 2006a; Fox & Butler, 2003), clients' levels of psychological distress were measured pre- and post-counselling using

*Table 1*
Background data on evaluations used in review

| | Dudley (Sherry, 1999) (Newton, 2006) | Aberdeen (Loynd, 2003) | NSPCC (Fox, 2003) | Glasgow Phase I (Cooper, 2004) | East Renfrewshire (Cooper, 2006a) |
|---|---|---|---|---|---|
| Period of evaluation | 1998–1999 | 2000–2002 | 2001–2003 | 2002–2004 | 2003–2005 |
| Location of service | School | School | School | School | School and some community |
| School level | Secondary | Secondary (67% of pupils) and primary | Secondary (approx. 50% of schools) and primary | Secondary | Secondary |
| Number of schools | 16 | 1 secondary, 2 primary | Approx. 20 | 3 | 7 |
| Number of counsellors | Approx. 10 | 1 | Approx. 19 | 2 | 4 |
| Pupils seen | 459 | 446 | Not reported | 197 | 115 |
| Length of sessions | 40 mins. | 40 mins. (30 mins. primary) | Approx. 30 mins. | Approx. 40 mins. | 50 mins. |
| Therapeutic modality | Broadly humanistic | Humanistic ('Transactional Analysis') centred | Primarily person-centred | Person-centred | Primarily person-centred |
| Forms of referral | *Mainly teacher-referral* | Mainly self-, some teacher-referral | *Mainly self and some teacher-referral* | Mainly pastoral care teachers (72%), few school self-referrals (4%) | *Primarily person-centred (93% of cases) Mainly teacher and other school staff, some self-referral (13%)* |

*Note.* Data in italics comes from evaluation reports rather than full service audit reports, and represents that sub-sample of pupils who participated in the evaluation procedures

124

*Table 2*
Characteristics of clients used in review

| | Sherry, 1999 | Loynd, 2003 | Fox, 2003 | Cooper, 2004 | Cooper, 2006a |
|---|---|---|---|---|---|
| **Average number of sessions per pupil** | Approx. 9 | Not reported | 7.63 | 5.62 | 9.88 |
| **Attendance rates** | N/A | N/A | N/A | 82% | *Approx. 86%* |
| **Gender (% female)** | *56%* | 51% | 57% | 55% | 63% |
| **Ethnic origin** | N/A | N/A | N/A | N/A | *94% White (British/European)* |
| **School year/age (most frequent, in descending order)** | 12 years old<br>13 years old<br>14 years old | S2<br>S1<br>S3 | N/A | S3<br>S4<br>S2 | *S4*<br>*S3*<br>*S2* |
| **Presenting problems (most frequent, in descending order)** | *School*<br>*Family*<br>*Feeling 'low'*<br>*Relationships*<br>*Physical abuse* | Family<br>Relationships<br>Peers/friends<br>Anxiety<br>Anger/self-control | *Family*<br>*School*<br>*Personal*<br>*Relationships*<br>*Health* | Family<br>Behaviour<br>Anger<br>Anxiety and stress<br>Academic-related | *Family*<br>*Anxiety and stress*<br>*Anger*<br>*Relationships*<br>*School issues* |

*Note.* Figures in italics come from evaluation data rather than full service audit data demonstrably reliable outcome measures. In the Glasgow Phase I (Cooper, 2004) and NSPCC (Fox & Butler, 2003) evaluations, the measure used was a 14-item questionnaire called Teen-CORE (now termed 'Young Person's CORE') (completed by 73 and 114 clients, respectively); and in the East Renfrewshire evaluation (Cooper, 2006a), a 25-item inventory called the Strengths and Difficulties Questionnaire (SDQ) (Goodman, 2001) was adopted (completed by 88 clients). Both questionnaires asked clients to rate, over a specified period of time (one month for the SDQ and one week for Teen-CORE), how they had been feeling with respect to certain items: for instance, 'I have felt a bit nervous and scared' (Teen-CORE) and 'I get very angry and often lose my temper' (SDQ). Higher scores indicate higher levels of psychological distress.

Data from all three studies suggest that clients were significantly less distressed at the end of counselling as compared with the beginning of counselling, with 'effect sizes'[1]

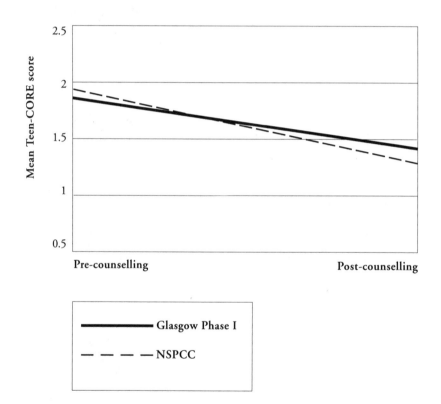

*Figure 1.* Pre- and post-counselling Teen-CORE scores (higher scores = more distressed).

1. Effect sizes (ES) are a way of indicating the magnitude of a treatment effect. They can be calculated in a range of ways, and the ones presented here indicate the degrees of change in terms of numbers of standard deviations (i.e. on average, clients' levels of psychological distress has reduced by 0.65 of a standard deviation).

(*d*) for the three studies of 0.73 in the Glasgow Phase I study (Cooper, 2004), 0.88 in the NSPCC study (Fox & Butler, 2003), and 0.33 in the East Renfrewshire study (Cooper, 2006a). This gives an average effect size of 0.65, which can be considered in the medium range. A graphic representation of the reduction in levels of psychological distress for the two studies that used the Teen-CORE measure can be seen in Figure 1. In a three-month follow-up with 30 clients of the counselling service, Fox and Butler (2003) found that these gains were maintained at a level similar to the post-counselling scores.

With respect to differences in degrees of improvement across sex and age, all three studies failed to find any significant variations. Furthermore, the Glasgow Phase I (Cooper, 2004) and East Renfrewshire (Cooper, 2006a) evaluations failed to find any significant correlation between degree of improvement and the number of sessions that clients had attended.

In addition to pre- to post-effect sizes, outcome measures can also allow for the calculation of the percentage of clients that show 'reliable' change (i.e. change that is probably not due to the unreliability of the outcome measure) and the percentage of clients that show 'clinical' change (i.e. movement from one clinical category – 'normal', 'borderline', 'abnormal' – to another). With respect to reliable change, the NSPCC evaluation (Fox & Butler, 2003) reported that 38 per cent of clients showed reliable improvement, whilst the Glasgow Phase I evaluation (Cooper, 2004) reported that 28.8 per cent of clients showed reliable improvement, 69.9 per cent showed no reliable change, and 1.4 per cent showed a reliable deterioration (this figure includes clients both within and outside of a 'clinical' range prior to therapy). With respect to clinical change, the East Renfrewshire study (Cooper, 2006a) found that 25 per cent of clients had improved (i.e. moved from 'abnormal' to 'borderline', 'borderline' to 'normal', or 'abnormal' to 'normal'), 58 per cent remained in the same range, and 10 per cent had deteriorated (i.e. moved from 'normal' to 'borderline', 'borderline' to 'abnormal', or 'normal' to 'abnormal').

In terms of overall perceived improvement, the SDQ – as used in the East Renfrewshire (Cooper, 2006a) evaluation – also includes an 'impact supplement' which asks clients to directly rate how much their problems have changed since coming to counselling. Here, 52 clients (58%) said that their problems were 'much better' since coming to the clinic, 27 (30%) said their problems were 'a bit better', and nine clients (10%) said that their problems were 'about the same'. No respondents said that their problems were 'a bit worse' or 'much worse'.

RATINGS OF HELPFULNESS

In four of the five studies, clients were asked to indicate on a post-counselling questionnaire how helpful they had found the counselling. In the Glasgow Phase I study (Cooper, 2004) 74 per cent of the respondents said that it had helped them 'a lot' or 'quite a lot' (as opposed to 'a little' or 'not at all'); 97 per cent of the clients in the Aberdeen (Loynd, 2002) study rated it as 'very helpful' or 'helpful' (as opposed to 'not very helpful' or 'not at all helpful'); 54 per cent of clients in the Dudley study (Sherry, 1999) said that the counselling had helped them 'a lot' or 'quite a lot' (as opposed to 'moderate', 'a little' or 'not at all'); and 67 per cent of clients in the East Renfrewshire evaluation (Cooper, 2006a) gave it a rating of '6' or '7' on a 1 ('not at all helpful') to 7 ('very helpful') rating scale. As with scores from the outcome measures, no significant differences in levels of reported helpfulness were found across sex or school year of respondents.

Similar results were obtained from in-depth interviews with clients attending two of the counselling services. The NSPCC evaluation (Fox & Butler, 2003) reported that 'most' of the 16 clients that they interviewed said that the counselling 'had helped' with only one saying that it 'had not helped'; whilst the Glasgow Phase I evaluation (Cooper, 2004) reported that 15 of the 19 clients interviewed described their experience of counselling in predominantly – or entirely – positive terms, with the other 4 describing it as being of limited help.

Because of the different methods and scales used in these studies, it is difficult to amalgamate these findings. However, it would seem that approximately two-thirds of clients attending these services are finding the counselling moderately to very helpful, with only a small minority finding it of no help at all.

## RATINGS OF HELPFULNESS – TEACHERS' EVALUATIONS

Alongside these self-report evaluations of helpfulness, two of the five studies (Cooper, 2004; Loynd, 2002) asked teachers to assess how helpful they felt the counselling service had been to their pupils.

In the Glasgow Phase I study (Cooper, 2004), pastoral-care teachers across the three schools were asked the question, 'Based on any changes that you have witnessed in … pupils [who have attended counselling], overall, how helpful or unhelpful do you think the counselling service has been (1 = extremely unhelpful, 5–6 = neither helpful nor unhelpful, 10 = extremely helpful)?' With a 100 per cent response rate, mean responses from 25 teachers in 2002–3 and 15 teachers in 2003–4 were 7.34 and 8.47 respectively.

In the Aberdeen evaluation (Loynd, 2002), all teachers from across the three schools were asked to rate a number of statements on a six-point scale from 'strongly disagree' to 'strongly agree'. The response rate was just under 50 per cent. Statements which the teachers, on average, strongly agreed with included: 'The counselling service can make a difference in the lives of the students', 'Counselling can help students learn strategies and coping skills for use in difficult situations' and 'The counsellor can help students think about their problems in a more positive way'.

## WILLINGNESS TO SEE THE COUNSELLOR AGAIN

Another standard evaluation question used across three of the five studies was that of how willing the clients would be to use the counselling service again. Here, both the Glasgow Phase I (Cooper, 2004) and Aberdeen (Loynd, 2002) evaluations found that 91 per cent of clients would 'definitely' or 'probably' be willing to reuse it; whilst the Dudley evaluation reports a figure of 84 per cent (Sherry, 1999).

## FORMS OF CHANGE

What kinds of changes did the school-based counselling bring about? The clearest indicator of this comes from the SDQ items used in the East Renfrewshire evaluation (Cooper, 2006a) which are divisible into five subscales. Here, counselling was associated with significant reductions in levels of emotional and peer problems, but not with conduct problems, hyperactivity or levels of prosocialness. Along somewhat similar lines, the greatest pre- to post-counselling reductions on the Teen-CORE items used in the Glasgow Phase I evaluation (Cooper, 2004) tended to be on the emotion-related items: for instance, 'I have felt unhappy', 'I have liked myself', 'I have felt nervous', as compared with more behaviour- and conduct-related items: for instance, 'I have been told off', 'I have done my work'.

## DOMAINS OF CHANGE

As well as providing some indications of the kinds of changes that school-based counselling might bring about, data from three of the five evaluations can provide some initial indicators as to the area of everyday life in which these changes might be most manifest. Again, the most valuable data comes from the SDQ used in the East Renfrewshire evaluation (Cooper, 2006a), whose impact supplement specifically asks clients to rate how much their difficulties interfere with their daily lives in a range of areas. Here, the largest, and only significant, reduction in levels of interference from pre- to post-counselling was in the area of 'classroom learning', whilst 'friendships' and 'home life' showed smaller, and non-significant, decreases in levels of interference. Interestingly, then, whilst the predominant issues brought to counselling are about home life and family relationships, it may be that the greatest positive impact of the counselling is in the classroom. This is consistent with a meta-analysis of research from over 100 studies on person-centred teacher behaviour, which showed that cognitive and behavioural outcomes in the classroom (critical thinking, participation) were significantly more impacted than emotional and social outcomes, though nearly all tested areas showed reliable positive effects (Cornelius-White, 2007). However, in terms of school-based counselling, these findings need to be replicated, and data from both the Glasgow (Cooper, 2004) and the Dudley (Sherry, 1999) evaluations suggest that the counselling impacted on clients' school lives only marginally more than on their home lives, followed by the impact on how they felt about themselves and their relationships.

## HELPFUL ASPECTS OF COUNSELLING

What was it about counselling that the young people found helpful? In four of the studies (Cooper, 2004, 2006a; Fox & Butler, 2003; Sherry, 1999) the young people reported on the aspects of counselling that they had found particularly facilitative, with the Glasgow study producing both questionnaire and interview answers to this question. The findings from these studies are presented in Table 3 with percentages of responses, although these vary considerably according to the method of inquiry used. What is clear from this table is that for many of the clients, the most helpful aspect of counselling was

*Table 3*
Helpful aspects of counselling

| Glasgow questionnaires (n = 117) (Cooper, 2004) | Glasgow interviews (n = 19) (Cooper, 2004) | East Renfrewshire (n = 66) (Cooper, 2006a) | NSPCC (n = 16) (Fox & Butler, 2003) | Dudley (n = 174) (Sherry, 1999) |
|---|---|---|---|---|
| Talking and being listened to (28%) | Opportunity to talk (95%) | Talking and being listened to (59%) | Getting things off chest ('some') | Talking more openly (6%) |
| Specific improvements (24%) | Confidentiality (63%) | Guidance and advice (14%) | Empathy (13%) | Being understood (3%) |
| Getting things off chest (16%) | Suggestions or advice (58%) | Miscellaneous (9%) | Problem-solving ('some') | Specific improvements (3%) |
| Self-esteem (8%) | Reflection on feelings (47%) | Confidentiality (8%) | | Confidentiality (2%) |
| Guidance and advice (8%) | Being asked questions (53%) | Everything (6%) | | |
| Confidentiality (8%) | Getting things off chest (42%) | Specific improvements (6%) | | |

*Note.* Small numbers of participants in the Dudley survey gave a qualitative response, explaining the low response rates having an opportunity to talk and to be listened to. After this, the three other aspects of counselling that were frequently cited as helpful across the four studies were confidentiality, getting things off one's chest, and experiencing guidance and advice from the counsellor.

## UNHELPFUL ASPECTS OF THE COUNSELLING

What aspects of the counselling did the clients experience as unhelpful? Whilst this question was asked across each of the five studies, response rates here were generally low. Whilst 34 of the 90 respondents to the East Renfrewshire post-counselling questionnaire (Cooper, 2006a), for instance, gave a response to the question 'What aspects, if any, of the counselling were unhelpful?', 31 of these responses (91%) were coded under 'nothing' (for instance, 'it was all good') leaving just three (3% of the total respondents) providing genuine criticisms. There were also few commonalities across the aspects identified as unhelpful. However, in the Glasgow Phase I interviews (Cooper, 2004), 16 per cent of the respondents said that they felt the counselling lacked sufficient input or direction, as did 2 per cent of the questionnaire respondents. Two per cent of the questionnaire respondents in the Glasgow Phase I study also said that they felt the service was insufficiently confidential, as did a number of respondents in the Dudley (Sherry, 1999) and NSPCC (Fox & Butler, 2003) evaluations.

## CONTRIBUTIONS FROM THE WIDER FIELD OF COUNSELLING AND PSYCHOTHERAPY RESEARCH

Whilst the findings presented above provide some valuable indicators as to the effectiveness of a person-centred, school-based counselling service, they have some significant limitations. Most importantly, in none of the studies were the changes in levels of psychological distress from pre- to post-counselling compared against changes within a control group in which some other form of intervention, or 'treatment as usual', was undertaken with a similar sample. Hence, it is impossible to ascertain from these studies whether the reductions in levels of psychological distress were specifically brought about by the counselling or by some other factor, such as general improvements over time. In this respect, then, it is useful to briefly consider findings from the wider counselling and psychotherapy research field in which numerous randomised controlled trials – the 'gold standard' of psychotherapy research – have been conducted with young people.

With respect to the impact of counselling and psychotherapy with young people and children as a whole, meta-analyses (i.e. summaries of multiple studies) suggest that it is efficacious, with an average effect size (Cohen's $d$) of around 0.7 (as compared with control subjects) (Fonagy, Target, Cottrell, Phillips & Kurtz, 2002; Kazdin, 2004). This closely parallels the magnitude obtained with adults. Kazdin concludes: 'Psychotherapy appears to be better than no treatment' (2004: 551) and he reports that these treatment gains tend to be maintained at follow-up. A similar finding tends to emerge from meta-analyses of counselling and psychotherapy (Prout & Prout, 1998) and person-centred education (Cornelius-White, 2007) in schools – though not in all instances (e.g. Catron, Harris & Weiss, 1998) – that the treatments are efficacious, with an effect size ($d$) of

0.97 emerging from a pooled analysis of 17 studies. However, Fonagy et al. (2002) report that, in a recent meta-analysis, only 2 per cent of the studies included involved a person-centred approach to therapy, and, in many instances, what is described as a 'non-directive', 'supportive' or 'person-centred' approach to therapy consists, in fact, of the delivery of an 'inert', non-focused intervention, as opposed to the provision of an in-depth person-centred relationship by a practitioner skilled and experienced in this approach.

Despite this, many studies do suggest that a non-directive, supportive approach to therapy may be efficacious in the treatment of a variety of forms of psychological distress, in particular depression. A recent meta-analysis of the efficacy of play therapy also showed that humanistic non-directive approaches can be effective with children with a range of presenting issues (Bratton, Ray, Rhine et al., 2005), at a level superior to the efficacy of non-humanistic directive practices (principally behavioural approaches). Vostanis, Feehan, Grattan and Bickerton (1996a, 1996b) found that a non-focused intervention was as effective as cognitive-behavioural therapy in treating children with depression, and they suggest that 'Non-specific psychotherapy elements, such as empathy, sympathetic listening, reassurance, reinforcement and indirect ways of achieving self-understanding and problem-solving may be involved in the recovery' (Vostanis et al., 1996b: 199). Similarly, Birmaher et al. (2000) found that non-directive, supportive therapy was as efficacious as cognitive-behavioural therapy and systemic-behavioural therapy in treating depression in the long term, though cognitive-behavioural therapy showed superior results at the end of treatment (Brent et al., 1997). In a third study, Fine et al. (1991) found that a person-centred-like therapeutic group was more efficacious than a social-skills group in treating adolescent depressive disorder.

On the basis of findings such as these, the UK-based National Institute for Health and Clinical Excellence (NICE) guidelines for the identification and management of depression in children and young people suggest that, 'After up to four weeks of watchful waiting, children and young people with continuing mild depression should be offered a course of non-directive supportive therapy, group cognitive behavioural therapy (CBT) or guided self-help (National Institute for Health and Clinical Excellence, 2005: 25). Similarly, in their summary of the data, Fonagy et al. (2002) write that, for children and young people with depression, 'it may be wise to offer brief supportive therapy as the first-line of treatment' (p. 104). Along similar lines, there is evidence to suggest that, when a child or young person is exposed to a single, recent undesirable life event, such as bereavement, parental divorce or separation or a severely disappointing experience, a brief supportive therapeutic approach is an appropriate first line of treatment, providing that there are no other risk factors for depression (Fonagy et al., 2002: 391; National Institute for Health and Clinical Excellence, 2005). However, for moderate to severe depression, CBT, interpersonal therapy or shorter-term family therapy were recommended.

Data from randomly controlled trials also suggest that non-directive counselling may not be a particularly efficacious form of treatment for young people with behavioural problems, disturbances of conduct or 'juvenile delinquency' (Fonagy et al., 2002; Lipsey, 1995; McGuire & Priestley, 1995). Here, multimodal, highly structured and skills-orientated programmes, using methods mainly drawn from cognitive and behavioural sources, have been shown to bring about the greatest degree of behavioural change.

As with the findings from the counselling evaluations studies reviewed in this chapter, there are some indications from the wider field that a non-directive, person-centred approach is effective at bringing about change at the emotional – and possibly interpersonal – level, but that it is less effective at bringing about change with respect to conduct and behavioural problems, at least outside the context of play therapy or teacher–student relationships.

## SATISFACTION WITH A SCHOOL-BASED COUNSELLING SERVICE

### CLIENTS' ATTITUDES

How satisfied are clients, teachers and other interested parties with a school-based counselling service? Such a question is important to ask independently of the question of how helpful such a service is, as research suggests that degrees of satisfaction and symptom change can be quite separate dimensions (i.e. someone can feel that a service was very satisfactory even though, personally, they do not feel it helped them much, and vice versa) (Lambert, Salzer & Bickman, 1998).

With respect to clients, 88 per cent of respondents in the Glasgow Phase I evaluation said that they were 'satisfied' or 'very satisfied' with the counselling service, and 91 per cent of the clients in the East Renfrewshire evaluation gave it a score of '6' or '7' on a one-to-seven scale from 'not at all satisfied' to 'very satisfied' (Cooper, 2006a). Across both studies, only two clients indicated that they were dissatisfied or very dissatisfied with the counselling service, and in both instances this was because respondents felt that the confidentiality of the counselling had been breached.

### TEACHERS' ATTITUDES

With respect to teachers, satisfaction with the counselling service was also high. In the Aberdeen evaluation (Loynd, 2002), teachers gave a high positive rating to the statement that 'The introduction of a counselling service was an important development in this school'; and the NSPCC evaluation reported that most teachers were satisfied with the service (Fox & Butler, 2003), with 64 per cent stating that there was 'a lot of need' for such a provision. With specific respect to pastoral care staff, the Aberdeen study reports that, whilst initially doubtful about the service, comments one year on included: 'It's been great, excellent, superb', and 'I think it has been wonderful, super, very, very useful'. Similarly, in the Glasgow Phase I study (Cooper, 2004), all three coordinators of pastoral care were positive about the service: 'It's been absolutely excellent', 'I think, generally speaking, it's going well', 'I think it's an excellent thing'.

In terms of what pastoral and other teachers saw as the 'added value' of a school-based counsellor, a number of points re-emerged across the three evaluation reports

(Cooper, 2004; Fox & Butler, 2003; Loynd, 2002). First, in each of the reports, teachers pointed to the fact that the counsellor was someone 'independent' and 'neutral': 'someone else' other than teachers or parents to turn to (24% of respondents in the NSPCC survey). Second, in each of the reports, teachers highlighted the fact that the counselling service was confidential (10% of respondents in the NSPCC study). Third, the counsellor was seen as an additional resource or support for the school: something that could enhance the quality and diversity of pastoral care services available for pupils (Cooper, 2004; Loynd, 2002). Fourth, the expertise and specialist knowledge of the counsellor was acknowledged by teachers in the Aberdeen and NSPCC studies (13% of respondents in the latter). Three of these points – confidentiality, independence and the counsellors' expertise – were also identified in a recent review of the literature (Cooper, Hough & Loynd, 2005) as the main reasons why teachers valued a school-based counselling service, as well as the fact that counsellors could generally afford pupils far more time than guidance or pastoral care staff had available to them.

In terms of areas of dissatisfaction or suggestions for improvement regarding their school-based counselling service, a number of commonalities also emerged across the three studies (Cooper, 2004; Fox & Butler, 2003; Loynd, 2002). First, a desire to see improved communication and liaison between counsellors and pastoral care staff was expressed by 56 per cent of the pastoral care staff surveyed in the Glasgow Phase I evaluation and two of the three guidance coordinators; by 5 per cent of the teachers in the NSPCC survey; and some of the teachers in the Aberdeen evaluation. In particular, many of these teachers wanted more feedback from the counsellors on the progress that their pupils were making in counselling, and on anything that they could be doing to facilitate their pupils' development. A second concern that was raised by teachers in both the Aberdeen and NSPCC studies (16% in the latter) is that pupils might use the counselling as an excuse to miss lessons or to get out of class. A need for greater promotion and a higher profile to the counselling service was also raised by 2 per cent of the teachers in the NSPCC evaluation and by 12 per cent in the Glasgow Phase I study. Again, a review of related studies (Cooper et al., 2005) suggests that these concerns about counsellor–teacher relationships and of pupils abusing the system are relatively widespread, along with a concern that pupils might feel stigmatised by attending counselling. However, it should be noted that in both the NSPCC and Aberdeen studies, the most frequent response to the question, 'What are the problems of having a counselling service?' was 'there aren't any', and a substantial number of teachers across both these and the Glasgow Phase I studies said that the main problem was that the counsellor was not in the school for a sufficient amount of time. Moreover, a survey of teachers' attitudes towards counselling prior to the establishment of the counselling service in the three Glasgow schools found that they gave it a mean rating of 7.47 on a one-to-ten scale from 'not at all' important to 'essential' (Cooper et al., 2005). As other studies in this area have suggested, teachers generally hold positive views towards counselling and see it as a much needed resource (Cooper et al., 2005).

## LOCATION

How satisfied are pupils with having a counselling service based in their school, as opposed to a non-school environment, such as a community centre or GP practice? In the Glasgow Phase I evaluation (Cooper, 2004), 58 per cent of the clients interviewed said that they preferred that they had seen their counsellor in the school, with 37 per cent expressing no overall preference, and none of the clients expressing an overall preference for seeing a counsellor in a non-school environment. In terms of why they had this preference, the most common response was the 'convenience' of this location, with the familiarity of the setting and the quickness of referral also mentioned by a few clients. In addition to this, 73.4 per cent of the respondents to a school-wide survey of pupils (Cooper, 2006b) said that, if they were to see a counsellor, they would rather see them at the school, as opposed to outside. Further support for the hypothesis that children and young people tend to prefer attending a school-based counselling service comes from the findings of two rigorously controlled studies, which suggest that young people are as much as ten times more likely to access a school-based mental health service as compared with a community-based one (Catron et al., 1998; Kaplan, Calonge, Guernsey & Hanrahan, 1998). Again, the main reasons given for this are ease of access to the service and its familiarity; and a recent pilot study also reports that such a service may be less expensive than a community-based one (American Academy of Pediatrics, 2004). Alan Kazdin, one of the leading researchers in the field of child and adolescent psychotherapy, suggests that mental health services in schools should be increased. 'In fact,' as Prout and Prout (1998: 122) report, 'he notes that the potential for treatment in the schools may be greater than in clinic settings.'

## FORMAT

Finally, there is the question of how satisfied clients are with a one-to-one counselling format, as opposed to a group therapy arrangement. Interviews with clients in the first phase of the Glasgow project found that 63 per cent expressed a preference for this format (Cooper, 2004), with the remainder highlighting advantages and disadvantages of both arrangements, and none expressing an outright preference for group therapy. In terms of reasons for this preference, concerns about feeling nervous and uncomfortable in a group were raised by several respondents, as were fears that a group format would be less confidential. Again, these findings were supported by data from the school-wide survey, which found that 86 per cent of pupils expressed a preference for individual, as opposed to small group, counselling. Interestingly, this preference was significantly more marked in older students (Cooper, 2006b), with younger students somewhat more open to a group format, though still expressing a strong overall preference for one-to-one therapy.

# IMPACT OF A SCHOOL-BASED COUNSELLING SERVICE ON EDUCATIONAL ATTAINMENT

What effect does a humanistic, school-based counselling service have on young people's educational attainment? Here, there is little evidence available – either from the five evaluation studies discussed above or from the wider literature. As discussed earlier, however, the East Renfrewshire evaluation (Cooper, 2006a) did find that the largest improvements from pre- to post-counselling were in the area of 'classroom learning', a finding which received partial support from the Glasgow Phase I (Cooper, 2004) and Dudley (Sherry, 1999) evaluations.

A randomly controlled study by Gerler and colleagues in the United States (Gerler, 1985) also found that counselling brought about significant improvements in under-achieving elementary students' mathematics and language arts grades; and Gerler and colleagues (Gerler, Kinney & Anderson, 1985) reviews a number of further studies which suggest that school counselling can improve the academic performance of elementary-school students as well as their 'classroom behaviour'. More recently, Sink and Stroh (2003) also found that pupils enrolled for several years in elementary schools with comprehensive school counselling programmes showed greater improvements in their achievement test scores than those pupils enrolled in schools without a counselling service. Reviewing the many variables that have been shown to influence academic achievement – behavioural, affective, sensory, imagery, interpersonal and physical – Gerler writes that 'educators and others should not be surprised by counselors' contributions to children's academic success' (Gerler et al., 1985: 156). However, the counselling approach used in many of these studies was of a highly structured, skills-based nature. Moreover, not all studies into the effects of school-based counselling have found such results. Catron et al. (1998), for instance, found that school-based counselling, as compared with academic tutoring, had no effect on grades, though it did bring about a significantly greater reduction in levels of absenteeism. Similarly, Sherr and Sterne (1999) found that counselling interventions within a primary school setting had only a limited effect on discreet educational indicators, as compared with a non-counselling control. As Prout and Prout (1998) state, then, one of the most important priorities for further research in the area of school counselling should be to look at its impact on educationally relevant measures.

## SUMMARY OF FINDINGS

- School-based counselling is associated with significant reductions in levels of psychological distress, with a medium to large effect size.
- School-based counselling brings about reliable and/or clinical improvement in around 25–40 per cent of all clients.
- Approximately two-thirds of clients attending school-based counselling services rate

them as moderately to very helpful, with only a small minority finding it of no help at all.

- A large majority of teachers believe that school-based counselling services are of help to their pupils using the service.

- In contrast to humanistic play therapy and person-centred educational research, findings from both evaluation and controlled studies suggest that humanistic, school-based counselling is most likely to bring about change at the emotional and interpersonal level, as compared with change at the level of conduct or behaviour.

- There are some indications that the greatest impact of school-based counselling is in the classroom, as compared with the home or peer environment.

- For many clients, the most helpful aspect of humanistic, school-based counselling is having an opportunity to talk and to be listened to; followed by confidentiality, getting things off one's chest and experiencing guidance and advice from the counsellor.

- Criticisms of school-based counselling services by clients are rare, though a lack of sufficient input and concerns about confidentiality have been raised by a very small minority of clients.

- The majority of teachers – both pastoral care and otherwise – express positive attitudes towards their school-based counselling services, and particularly valued the independence, expertise and confidentiality of the counsellor.

- Whilst many teachers see a school-based counselling service as unproblematic, some would like to see greater communication between the counsellor and the school staff, and have some concerns about pupils using the service to evade class.

- A majority of pupils would prefer to see a counsellor in their school, as opposed to a non-school location, primarily because of the convenience of such an arrangement.

- A majority of pupils would rather see a school-based counsellor on a one-to-one basis, as opposed to in a group format, primarily because of the increased security and confidentiality of such an arrangement.

## REFERENCES

American Academy of Pediatrics (2004) Policy statement: School-based mental health services. *Pediatrics, 113* (6), 1839–45.

Birmaher, B, Brent, DA, Kolko, D, Baugher, M, Bridge, J, Holder, D, et al. (2000) Clinical outcome after short-term psychotherapy for adolescents with major depressive disorder. *Archives of General Psychiatry, 57* (1), 29–36.

Bratton, SC, Ray, D, Rhine, T & Jones, L (2005) The efficacy of play therapy with children: A meta-analytic review of treatment outcomes. *Professional Psychology: Research and Practice 36* (4), 376–90.

Brent, DA, Holder, D, Kolko, D, Birmaher, B, Baugher, M, Roth, C, et al. (1997) A clinical psychotherapy trial for adolescent depression comparing cognitive, family and supportive therapy. *Archives of General Psychiatry, 54* (9), 877–85.

Catron, T, Harris, VS & Weiss, B (1998) Post-treatment results after 2 years of services in the Vanderbilt School-Based Counseling Project. In MH Epstein, K Kutash & A Duchnowski (Eds) *Outcomes for Children and Youths with Emotional and Behavioral Disorders and their Families: Programs for evaluating best practice* (pp. 633–56). Austin, TX: Pro-ED.

Cooper, M (2004) *Counselling in Schools Project: Evaluation report.* Glasgow: Counselling Unit, University of Strathclyde. Download from http://www.strath.ac.uk/Departments/counsunit/research/cis.html.

Cooper, M (2006a) Analysis of the evaluation data. In *East Renfrewshire Youth Counselling Service (ERYCS): Development and evaluation of a full-time secondary school and community-based youth counselling service in Scotland 2005.* East Renfrewshire: East Renfrewshire Council.

Cooper, M (2006b) Scottish secondary school students' preferences for location, format of counselling and sex of counsellor. *School Psychology International, 27* (5), 627–38.

Cooper, M, Hough, M & Loynd, C (2005) Scottish secondary school teachers' attitudes towards, and conceptualisations of, counselling. *British Journal of Guidance and Counselling, 33* (2), 199–211.

Cornelius-White, JHD (2007) Learner-centered teacher–student relationships are effective: A meta-analysis. *Review of Educational Research, 77,* 113–43.

Fine, S, Forth, A, Gilbert, M & Haley, G (1991) Group-therapy for adolescent depressive disorder: A comparison of social skills and therapeutic support. *Journal of the American Academy of Child and Adolescent Psychiatry, 30* (1), 79–85.

Fonagy, P, Target, M, Cottrell, D, Phillips, J & Kurtz, Z (2002) *What Works for Whom? A critical review of treatments for children and adolescence.* New York: Guilford.

Fox, C & Butler, I (2003) *Evaluation of the NSPCC Schools Teams.* Keele: Keele University.

Gerler, ER, Jr (1985) Elementary school counseling research and the classroom learning environment. *Elementary School Guidance and Counseling, 19,* (39–48).

Gerler, ER, Jr, Kinney, J & Anderson, RF (1985) The effects of counseling on classroom performance. *Journal of Humanistic Education and Development, 23,* (155–65).

Goodman, R (2001) Psychometric properties of the strengths and difficulties questionnaire. *Journal of the American Academy of Child and Adolescent Psychiatry, 40* (11), 1337–45.

Kaplan, DW, Calonge, BN, Guernsey, BP & Hanrahan, MB (1998) Managed care and school-based health centers: Use of health services. *Archives of Pediatrics and Adolescent Medicine, 152* (1), 25–33.

Kazdin, AE (2004) Psychotherapy for children and adolescents. In MJ Lambert (Ed) *Bergin and Garfield's Handbook of Psychotherapy and Behaviour Change* (5th edn, pp. 543–89). Chicago: John Wiley and Sons.

Lambert, W, Salzer, MS & Bickman, L (1998) Clinical outcome, consumer satisfaction, and ad hoc ratings of improvement in children's mental health. *Journal of Consulting and Clinical Psychology, 66* (2), 270–9.

Lipsey, MW (1995) What do we learn from 400 research studies on the effectiveness of treatment with juvenile delinquents. In J McGuire (Ed) *What Works: Reducing reoffending – Guidelines from research and practice* (pp. 63–78). Chichester: John Wiley.

Loynd, C (2002) *Excellence Fund Evaluation of The School Students' Counsellor Programme 2000–2002.* Aberdeen.

McGuire, J & Priestley, P (1995) Reviewing 'what works': Past, present and future. In J McGuire (Ed) *What Works: Reducing Reoffending – Guidelines from research and practice* (pp. 3–34). Chichester: John Wiley.

National Institute for Health and Clinical Excellence (2005) *Depression in Children and Young People: Identification and management in primary, community and secondary care*. London: National Institute for Health and Clinical Excellence.

Newton, J (2006) Personal communication.

Prout, SM & Prout, HT (1998) A meta-analysis of school-based studies of counseling and psychotherapy: An update. *Journal of School Psychology, 36* (2), 121–36.

Sherr, L & Sterne, A (1999) Evaluation of a counselling intervention in primary schools. *Clinical Psychology & Psychotherapy, 6* (4), 286–96.

Sherry, J (1999) *LEA-Organised Counselling in Secondary Schools in Dudley*. Dudley: Dudley Counselling Service.

Sink, CA & Stroh, HR (2003) Raising achievement test scores of early elementary school students through comprehensive school counseling programs. *Professional School Counselling, 6* (5), 350–64.

Vostanis, P, Feehan, C, Grattan, E & Bickerton, WL (1996a) A randomised controlled out-patient trial of cognitive-behavioural treatment for children and adolescents with depression: Nine-month follow-up. *Journal of Affective Disorders, 40* (1–2), 105–16.

Vostanis, P, Feehan, C, Grattan, E & Bickerton, WL (1996b) Treatment for children and adolescents with depression: Lessons from a controlled trial. *Clinical Child Psychology and Psychiatry, 1* (2), 199–211.

CHAPTER 10

# JAPANESE PERSON-CENTRED SCHOOL COUNSELLING
## CASE STUDIES WITH SCHOOL NON-ATTENDEES
## AND JAPANESE-KOREANS

AKIRA KANAZAWA
SATOKO WAKISAKA

## INTRODUCTION

The person-centred approach (PCA) was first imported to Japan in the late 1940s. Carl Rogers himself visited Japan in 1961 and most of his work was translated into Japanese consistently after that. As Rogers (1969, 1983) had great interest in applying the PCA to education and person-centred education has been thoroughly supported by research (Cornelius-White, 2007), the Japanese education system has been adopting PCA ideas.

For instance, problems in school such as bullying, violence and non-attendance became a matter of public concern in the 1980s, therefore the Japanese Ministry of Education increased the importance of 'guidance' and 'guidance counselling' in education in order to develop the ability of teachers to establish a better rapport with maladjusted students, and frequently introduced the concepts of the PCA – particularly 'congruence', 'empathic understanding' and 'unconditional positive regard', known as 'counselling mind' by teachers – into the official curriculum for the teaching profession.

Until the 1980s, only teachers trained in counselling took charge of counselling students in schools. However, in order to deal with increasingly complex problems, the Japanese Ministry of Education introduced a policy of placing professional counsellors in schools, furthering the suitability of PCA for school counselling in Japan. A great variety of therapeutic approaches are used individually by school counsellors, but PCA generally appears in books on school counselling (Oka, 2002).

One of the person-centred approaches most frequently introduced into counselling in education has been the encounter group, and there is some empirical research on the effect of these, especially on university students. Hirayama (1998) composed a scale in order to measure the effect of encounter groups and reported that positive changes in self-concept, concept of others, relationship with self, relationship with others and the development of autonomy, were produced by encounter group experiences. Ito (1989) used personality tests to evaluate the effect of encounter groups and reported that personal integrity increased and dominance over others decreased after students had experienced encounter groups. Kamada (2001) found amongst students who had experienced encounter groups, compared with those who had not, a positive change in self-concept,

140

a reduction in interpersonal anxiety and an increase in an attitude of empathy. This tendency was similar in a follow-up study carried out three months later. Kamada proposed that positive results were produced because encounter groups provided an acceptance by others and an opportunity to express oneself.

This idea that students need to experience the acceptance not only of counsellors but also of other students and staff in their community has led to the active adoption of encounter groups as part of school and campus counselling in Japan. The positive image of encounter groups as an opportunity for personal growth has meant that students find it easier to join them than counselling sessions, which have the somewhat negative reputation among the students of being a treatment for 'dropouts' (Murayama, 2005). However, encounter groups are not easy to implement in Japanese schools, especially in compulsory education, since they require both the permission of the headmaster and the understanding of the staff. Therefore, in the present circumstances, school counsellors mainly practice individual counselling sessions.

## OVERVIEW

The main aim of this chapter is to illustrate how three of Rogers' necessary and sufficient conditions for significant positive personality change – congruence, empathic under-standing and unconditional positive regard (Rogers, 1959) – are effective in supporting incongruent students when practised by therapists in the context of school counselling. School non-attendance and the maladjustment of immigrants (especially those from Korea) are chosen as issues of incongruence in this chapter.

First, we provide some basic information on the Japanese school counselling system and school non-attendance. The therapy process in the latter case is presented to discuss school non-attendance as incongruence; the effectiveness of the three therapist-held conditions in working with school non-attendance, and the importance of families and schools to provide support in making sure that the three therapist-held conditions are met.

Secondly, we introduce school counselling for Japanese-Koreans. These are people who came to Japan (some forcibly) when Japan colonised the Korean Peninsula before World War II; they still face discrimination, poor treatment and deprivation of civil rights; they have often been psychologically damaged and remain deeply incongruent.

### THE SCHOOL COUNSELLING SYSTEM IN JAPAN

In 1995, the Japanese Ministry of Education started a school counselling system as a policy to deal with problems within schools, such as bullying, violence and non-attendance. At first, school counsellors were placed in 154 public elementary, junior high and senior high schools, but, by 2005, school counsellors had been placed in every public junior high school in Japan. School counsellors are employed as part-time local government employees on one-year contracts. Due to the school counselling budget and the aim to preserve the objectivity of school counsellors, they usually work up to eight hours a day, once a week, at one school. Some are placed at only one junior high school and visit elementary schools within that district; others work at several different junior high schools.

## CURRENT BASIC CONCEPTIONS OF SCHOOL NON-ATTENDANCE IN JAPAN

The Japanese Ministry of Education officially defines school non-attendance as the phenomenon where students do not attend school or are not able to attend school for more than 30 days per year due to some psychological, emotional, somatic or social factors, provided that those factors do not include physical illness or financial problems.

There are, however, students whose absences are less than 30 days who also need support. Therefore, school non-attendance is more broadly and commonly regarded as a phenomenon where students are not able to attend school for some psychological, emotional, somatic or social factors. Non-attending students are referred to as 'school non-attendees' in this chapter.

According to the survey by the Japanese Ministry of Education, 122,225 students in compulsory education – 22,709 elementary schoolchildren and 99,546 junior high school students – fell into the category of school non-attendance. In 2005, school non-attendance accounted for 1.13 per cent of all students in compulsory education—0.32 per cent of all elementary schoolchildren and 2.75 per cent of all junior high school students. Education in Japan is compulsory from the age of 6 to 15: six years in elementary school and three years in junior high school. The above numbers include students of both public and private elementary schools and junior high schools.

## SCHOOL COUNSELLING FOR NON-ATTENDANCE

Murayama (2005) reports person-centred therapy cases of school non-attendees, but these took place in a counselling center and were not discussed from the standpoint of a school counsellor. In the following section, the counselling process of a school non-attendee, which the author experienced as a school counsellor, is presented in order to illustrate (a) school non-attendance as incongruence from Rogers' theory of personality (Rogers, 1951) and (b) how Rogers' three core conditions (Rogers, 1959) offer effective suggestions to support a school non-attendee.

## CASE EXAMPLE: ICHIRO

Ichiro, a junior high school student aged thirteen, grew up with his father, mother and a younger brother. In the first semester of the first year he seemed rather quiet but had some friends. His teachers observed no distinct signs of maladjustment at school. However, in the second semester, he started to be absent from school with the excuse of 'feeling unwell'. As his absence continued his parents urged him to go to school, but this led to a situation where Ichiro would run away from both school and home and spend hours in an empty house in the neighborhood. Facing the situation, his parents decided not to force him to go to school and this enabled Ichiro to spend relaxed time at home and to talk to his parents again. After finding a bruise on his body and his belongings broken, his parents suspected that he was being bullied at school. Ichiro confirmed this but refused to give any details. The school investigated the bullying but found no clear evidence to support it. Ichiro's class teacher regularly visited him but, after consultations with me, refrained from pressuring him to go back to school.

At the end of the second semester, at the teacher's suggestion, Ichiro and his mother went to the school to see me. Ichiro stayed nervously close to his mother and didn't speak unless spoken to but he did agree to have regular sessions with me. He didn't want to be seen at school and was worried that he would fall behind in his studies through being absent from classes. Therefore, Ichiro and I decided to have weekly sessions in the evening after which he would study with his class teacher.

From the second session, Ichiro was able to talk with me without his mother but still kept going to school accompanied by her. However, at my suggestion, two months after becoming a second-year student, he started going to school by himself.

In Ichiro's sessions, he talked mostly about his daily life and rarely verbalised psychological conflicts, but he expressed his will clearly by nodding or shaking his head to the suggestions of his class teacher and me for expanding the range of his activities at school.

As the sessions progressed, he started going out more and seemed to have become more active. Hearing him say things like 'I went by myself to see my cousins' confirmed this, so I suggested that he spend more time at school, which he agreed to do. The school accepted my proposal to hire a university student as Ichiro's supporter and allowed both of them to spend time in a spare room. So Ichiro now started going to school for another day every week. Then, in November, he decided to take a job training course in which he worked in a bakery as a shop assistant together with six other students. After the course, however, he didn't try to fulfill the expectations of his parents or class teacher by returning to his class, but continued to go to school two days a week to see his supporter and me. The sessions with Ichiro ended when I was transferred to a different school. He agreed to continue his sessions with my successor once a week, and when he became a third-year student, he started going to school two more days a week in order to study with his supporter.

CASE ANALYSIS: ICHIRO

At first, Ichiro's life at school seemed to be going smoothly but eventually his concept of self, summarised as 'yes, everything's OK at school' became incongruent with his experiences, accompanied by some deterioration in his relationships with other students. His tendency to not verbalise his troubles increased the incongruence, which then created the condition where he 'felt unwell' and 'didn't feel like going to school'.

Seeing him becoming unwell, his parents realised he could be experiencing problems, yet they urged him to go back to school, expecting him to overcome his troubles and be strong. Thus, the incongruence between his concept of self, influenced by his parents own value that 'students must go to school' and his experience of 'I don't want to go to school', kept increasing and enabled him to neither go to school nor stay home.

After facing up to the situation, his parents decided not to press their own values on him and tried to understand his suspected painful experiences at school with empathy. They also tried to give him unconditional positive regard by accepting him at home as 'a son' – not as 'a son who doesn't go to school'. At times, they felt the urge to hasten Ichiro back to school, but consultation with me managed to lessen this. Through experiencing the changes in his parents' attitude towards him, Ichiro became able to spend his days in peace at home and to be congruent.

His peaceful time at home and the space this offered him for introspection enabled Ichiro to regain his vitality. He started to worry about being behind in his studies and wanted to attend classes again, yet he still experienced a fear of going to school. Accordingly, he again became incongruent. To confront this state of incongruence, and with his mother's encouragement, he chose to go to school for counselling.

Rogers (1951) emphasised the importance of the unconditional positive regard of significant others for the process of reintegration; therefore, it was essential for Ichiro's positive progress to acknowledge the acceptance by his parents of himself as a whole person, regardless of his absenteeism from school; otherwise, he might have continued to express his need for his parents' understanding of his inner conflicts in more maladjusted ways, such as withdrawal, self-mutilation or parent (and/or sibling) abuse.

In counselling Ichiro, I accepted his request to meet in the evening after the usual office hours as a part of unconditional positive regard. As they found no clear evidence, teachers cast doubt on the bullying, and some just took it as an excuse for him not to attend school. However, I empathically understood that there was something making him feel anxious about going to school, and I respected his courage to go to school for therapy despite the risk of being seen by other students.

The congruence of school counsellors is another important issue in supporting non-attendees. School counsellors' mission is to promote the positive personality change of school non-attendees, and bringing them back to school is not the primary goal. However, recent government policy places emphasis on decreasing the numbers of school non-attendees, and the pressure on school counsellors to satisfy this policy is likely to create incongruence and increase the risk of hastening non-attendees back to school too soon. Moreover, the implications of offering therapy sessions to non-attendees can be the same, since the sessions take place in schools. Therefore, I paid special attention to congruence, repeatedly considering whether Ichiro was truly benefiting from the therapy sessions and occasionally asking him whether he felt any burden in going to school for the sessions.

Ichiro's class teacher was able to maintain a warm relationship with him and encouraged him to see me. As the class teacher's support related to unconditional positive regard, he regularly visited Ichiro at home when he was not able to attend school and never forced him to go back. When he was able to go to school for counselling sessions he gave his time and energy to individual classes.

Another support related to empathic understanding that the class teacher provided was trying to understand, with compassion, the painful experiences Ichiro had been through at school, even though no clear evidence of bullying had been found and Ichiro never spoke about it. Nevertheless, the teacher did often find himself regarding Ichiro's absenteeism as laziness and becoming impatient for more drastic change in Ichiro, though he intended to respect Ichiro's pace and progress.

In the consultations, I concentrated on conveying verbally my respect for the class teacher's ceaseless efforts to support Ichiro, as well as discussing his psychological state and how to support him. I also placed importance on reviewing together the positive changes he had shown. It was important that the teacher gave the above-mentioned support to Ichiro congruently. The consultations with supportive listening seemed to have helped the teacher to stay congruent.

Having experienced support from his teacher, Ichiro was able to regain trust and a feeling of security towards both the teachers and the school and to regard the school as a resource for self-actualisation, and it was key to Ichiro's self-actualisation that his will to study at school was accepted, and that the means – the supporter and the spare room – were provided, enabling the three therapist-held conditions to be met. The person-centred ideal concept for schools is to help with students' self-realisation; in practice however, schools seem more concerned with making students sit in their assigned classrooms. If schools were more open to different experiences – to allowing students to attend in unconventional ways, such as for therapy sessions; to understanding students' difficulties with empathy; to providing the time, space, and personnel they need with unconditional positive regard – more positive personality change could be created.

In Japan, empathic understanding and acceptance of school non-attendees by schools has made progress, and many schools regard attendance at a therapy session as attendance in a class. Another way for schools to accept school non-attendees is to allow them to use spare rooms to study. The number of schools using this method (known as 'an additional in-school class') is increasing.

To summarise: when supporting school non-attendees it is important that not only school counsellors but their families, teachers and schools try to implement the three conditions to promote students' tendencies for self-actualisation, as illustrated in Ichiro's case.

## SCHOOL COUNSELLING AT SCHOOLS FOR JAPANESE-KOREANS

School counselling for Japanese-Koreans is introduced through the exploration of the counselling process with two adolescents. The Rogerian idea of 'incongruence' is useful for understanding the adolescents' psychological problems, and the idea of 'the necessary and sufficient conditions of therapeutic personality change' is useful in providing psychotherapeutic support. Again, we emphasise the importance of not only the therapist but also the teachers at school embodying the therapeutic conditions in order to support students' growth.

### CASE EXAMPLE: TARO

Taro is a fifteen-year-old boy who complained of problems with his classmates and of both stomach and headaches of unknown origin. His interpersonal relationships were not positive. I counselled him for 50 minutes once a week and during these sessions, I talked about his problems with his classmates in detail. The following quotations are from my notes. He said, 'I have a friend who is very selfish. I'm angry with him. He asks me for advice, but when I ask *him* for advice, he refuses to help me. The other day, I said to him, "I'm finding it hard to live. I want to die". He said, "I don't mind if you do die. Go ahead."' Taro also said, 'When I'm talking, I often panic, suddenly. I can't understand what people are saying. My mind goes blank and I don't know what to do, what to say.' It was clear that he has difficulty in communicating with people.

I was upset by Taro during counselling sessions because he lost control of his emotions when talking; he had sudden outbursts of rage or tears; his speech was incoherent, lacking clear focus and connection between subjects. I suspected that he was psychotic and told him, 'I think you need not just counselling but psychiatric medicine as well, so I suggest you consult a psychiatrist.' Taro replied, 'I don't want to consult a psychiatrist!', vehemently refusing my proposal. I asked him why he was so firm in his refusal and he answered, 'I don't want to talk about myself anymore. I don't want others to know anything about me.' I understood that Taro was mistrustful. I responded to his feelings empathetically and some time later I asked him, 'How do you feel about psychiatry?' He replied, 'If I consult a psychiatrist, everyone will think I'm crazy. It will be impossible to find a job. No one will hire me ... and if I start taking medicine, I won't be able to stop.' This was something that obviously frightened Taro. I counselled him, 'Medicine would help you solve your problems. When you get well, you won't need to take it anymore.' Despite my patient attempts at persuasion, he never accepted my proposal. I felt helpless and irritated. I kept being congruent with what I felt, yet also tried feeling unconditional positive regard towards Taro. As our sessions proceeded, Taro began to talk about what he had experienced in the past and his hopes for the future. He said, 'When I was four years old, I came to Japan from Korea. Japanese people bullied me because I'm Korean. Now I don't want others to know I'm Korean ... I talk to my family in Korean; I speak Japanese with others. So I often feel upset.' Another time, he said hopelessly, 'I want to go to collage and work as a nurse. But now I'm emotionally unstable, so I find it hard to study and my grades are getting worse.'

I then discussed Taro with his class teacher, Mrs. A, because it was important to work in close cooperation for her to support Taro during this fragile time in his life. She felt that he always looked depressed and didn't get along with his classmates. She kept him at a distance because she felt he was keeping her at a distance and didn't want her attention. I told her he might mistrust others and so try to be inconspicuous. As a result of our meeting, Mrs. A began to pay unconditional positive regard to Taro; she had a meeting with Taro and his mother to talk about her concerns about his daily life at school and she also suggested consultation with a psychiatrist.

After the meeting, Mrs. A reported that Taro's mother was a recent immigrant, unable to speak fluent Japanese, which made her reluctant to talk with Japanese people and characterised her as avoidant. Mrs. A considered that the mother did not understand or accept well what was said at the meeting. She repeatedly said 'In Korea, children must obey their parents ... Taro does not obey me. He is troublesome. I do not understand him.' She repeated, 'In Korea, children must ...' on more than one issue. Mrs. A also said Taro's mother appeared emotionally unstable. It transpired that his father was Japanese, his nationality was Japanese, but his family usually talked with each other in Korean.

We met for about one year. Taro ended his therapy because he wanted to spend time studying for an entrance exam. He told me he wanted to go to college and study abroad even though when he first started the therapy, he had lost all hope for his future. He began to study hard, asking his teacher's advice; his mistrustfulness decreased. Then something significant happened. Taro expressed anger to his teacher when, after being kicked by his classmates during a physical education class, she had seemed oblivious to it. He complained frankly to his school about having been bullied and about the carelessness of the teachers. The teachers took his complaints seriously and apologised to him. He was able to express quite openly what he thought and felt.

CASE ANALYSIS: TARO

Here, I assess the psychological struggle of Taro and his family from the perspective of incongruence. Taro's mother insisted he behave as a Korean, making him go to a school for Japanese-Koreans and speak Korean at home, even though his nationality was Japanese. On the other hand, he must have experienced various feelings as a person who lives in Japan, that is, as Japanese. So, the positive regard his mother paid to him was one-sided or conditional.

Taro is troubled by a friend who is selfish and will not listen to him. I consider that the trouble with his friend is related to the problem with his mother. They have both refused to listen to parts of his experience. Because his mother won't listen to either him or his teacher at the meeting, just repeating the phrase 'In Korea ...', Taro feels she doesn't accept his emotional experience. Because of this relationship with his mother, he has experienced discrepancies between what he feels and what she accepts, thus, he has become deeply incongruent. His defense mechanisms have not worked well, his self-structure has collapsed, and he has often become psychotic.

In the counselling session with Taro, I tried to provide the Rogerian 'necessary and sufficient conditions'. It was especially difficult and important for me to keep being congruent with what I felt and to keep paying unconditional positive regard towards him. I felt that providing these conditions enabled me to understand Taro deeply. For example, I felt helpless and irritated when he refused to accept my proposal that he should consult a psychiatrist. I tried being congruent with my opinion and with what he felt and by paying unconditional regard. By holding this ambivalence, I realised that irritation and helplessness were what he too had experienced with his mother, who had never accepted what he felt. Kawai (1970) points out that it is difficult to be congruent and to pay unconditional regard to the client at the same time. This makes therapists ambivalent, but they can achieve deeper understanding of their clients if they can hold this ambivalence – and I felt I could understand Taro more deeply by holding this ambivalence.

Through this process, Taro gradually talked frankly about his past traumatic experiences, his confusion at home and his hope that he would go to a college and become a nurse. That is to say, he gradually became congruent. Had I not been accepting of my own helplessness and irritation, I might have imposed my own opinion on him just as his mother had done.

It is important for school counsellors to work in close cooperation with teachers, to suggest teachers pay unconditional regard to students and understand them empathetically whenever possible. Because Taro was distrustful and avoided communicating with his teacher, she responded by ignoring him. As a result of the meeting, however, she began to pay him more attention and to listen to the feelings he expressed about his daily life. Some time later, Mrs. A had another meeting with Taro's mother. This suggests that the teacher was now paying Taro unconditional positive regard and becoming more accepting of him. She was playing a part in facilitating his emerging congruence.

### CASE EXAMPLE: HANAKO

Hanako is a fourteen-year-old girl who complained of problems with her classmates and physical symptoms of unknown origin. The following quotations are from my notes. She said, 'Everyone speaks ill of me and ignores me and nobody believes what I say.' Descriptions of who she thought was persecuting her were vague and indefinite. I suspected her of being paranoiac and having a persecution complex. I counselled her for 50 minutes, once a week.

As counselling progressed, she began to talk about a particular teacher, Mrs. B, a woman in her forties who taught Korean. She had come from Korea to Japan to teach Korean a few years previously but was not fluent in Japanese. Hanako said, 'She's not good at speaking Japanese and all the students look down on her. She looks continually stressed and on edge. She hasn't adjusted to being in Japan. She's pathetic. I've tried to help her by teaching her Japanese and helping her prepare lessons. I'm anxious about her but she doesn't notice my concern. I suspect she dislikes me. She hates me. I can't help worrying whether she likes me or not and I can't sleep well.' Hanako also asked me, 'Don't tell her what I said.' She was anxious about her privacy. She often complained of headaches and stomach ache. She said 'I often panic suddenly.'

Hanako had a peculiar way of talking, incoherent and lacking subject or object. She talked continuously at a stretch, creating a one-way conversation. I found her speech pattern difficult to follow. I myself began to have a headache listening to her. When I really couldn't understand her I tried questioning her for clarification but she often responded with a frown; I felt she might become angry and walk out of the session so I tried to limit the number of times I did this.

Hanako didn't get along with the teachers at school; she repeatedly complained about her classmates to every teacher until they lost patience with her. After ten months, she developed alopecia areata, a hair loss condition. I chose this time to discuss Hanako with her class teacher as I thought it would be a good opportunity for both her teachers and parents to sympathise and pay her more positive regard. As a result, her teacher, Mr. C, began to increase his unconditional positive regard towards Hanako; he also met her mother to discuss his concerns about Hanako's daily life at school. Mr. C suggested her mother consult a doctor to treat the alopecia areata. As it turned out, she had been anxious about her daughter for some time, so accepted his suggestion and immediately took Hanako to the hospital.

I obtained some information about Hanako's family from Mr. C. Her mother had emigrated from Korea about 20 years earlier and could not speak Japanese well. She seemed worried and depressed. Because Hanako's father was a second-generation Japanese-Korean and physically handicapped, her mother was too busy taking care of him to take sufficient care of Hanako.

Our therapy continues. Hanako's complaints of being criticised by her classmates have disappeared. She now talks about how to have close friendships with boys. Our therapy has alleviated her distrust of others.

### CASE ANALYSIS: HANAKO

Again, I assess the psychological struggles of Hanako and her family from the perspective of incongruence. Hanako was concerned about Mrs. B's lack of confidence and difficulty in adapting to Japan. She desperately wanted Mrs. B's positive regard but did not feel accepted by her. She also worried about whether or not her mother loved her. Since Hanako's mother had also been experiencing problems with language, adjustment and lack of confidence, it seemed likely that Hanako had for a long time been trying to cope with the same feelings about her mother. Hanako's mother could not pay her daughter sufficient positive regard because her own self-regard was underdeveloped. Hanako said, 'Everyone says nasty things' and 'Mrs. B dislikes me': her self-image appeared negative and vague.

In the case of Hanako, it was again important for me to work in close cooperation with the teachers, suggesting they pay unconditional positive regard to students and try to understand them empathetically. Unfortunately, Hanako's teachers regarded her as a nuisance, so this was difficult. But my meeting with Mr. C when Hanako was suffering from alopecia areata led to a discussion between himself and her mother. This suggests that Mr. C had begun to pay unconditional positive regard and to accept Hanako. Hanako's mother talked frankly about her concerns and made the decision to take Hanako to hospital – so Hanako and her mother would have felt positive regard and acceptance by the teacher and school. They became able to be more congruent, paying more positive regard to themselves. Through this process, Hanako is gradually talking about her hope of going to college in Korea. She wants to study and master both the Korean language and Korean traditional dance. In other words, she is gradually becoming congruent.

### DISCUSSION OF SCHOOL COUNSELLING WITH JAPANESE-KOREANS

There are a lot of Japanese-Korean children who are not paid sufficient positive regard or understood empathetically by their parents because of complicated and serious problems in their family. In the two cases above, the students' mothers were recent immigrants. Taro's mother paid him very limited and one-sided positive regard. This suggests that her own structure of self was insecure: a lot of experiences she faced in her daily life in Japan were inconsistent with her self. With her lack of communication in Japanese, the discrepancy between her self and her experiences increased, resulting in maladjustment. In fact, Taro's mother avoided communicating with his teachers at school and remained largely housebound. She frequently experienced discrepancy between her self and her experiences, and her structure of self became insecure; her avoidance protected her from the experience of additional discrepancies. Hanako's mother, too, found it difficult to pay sufficient positive regard because of her maladjustment in Japan.

Finally, it is necessary for both school counsellors *and* teachers of Japanese-Koreans to have the Rogers' idea of 'the necessary and sufficient conditions of therapeutic personality change' in mind. Most importantly, school counsellors need to be congruent, pay unconditional positive regard to, provide empathetic understanding of, and accept, both children and their parents – because it is not only the children but also their parents who are faced with the crisis of the structure of self. In other words, school counsellors, teachers and parents, need to form a cooperative team to increase the necessary and sufficient conditions in students' lives.

## SUMMARY

This chapter discussed the application of three of Rogers' six necessary and sufficient conditions for significant positive personality change in therapists supporting students with incongruence in school counselling. The importance of the three conditions being met not only by school counsellors but also by schools in supporting students and their families was also emphasised.

Kamada (2001) stated in his study on student nurses that it is important for the students to receive acceptance by their group or school community, and encounter groups provide an opportunity for this. However, in present circumstances, it is not easy for school counsellors, especially those who work in compulsory education, to gain the approval of schools for their work. Nevertheless, we practised individual counselling sessions with maladjusted students using Kamada's (2001) viewpoint; we prioritised approaches to parents, teachers and school to gain their acceptance of the students, as illustrated in the case examples. The students' feelings of persecution seemed to diminish as they tried to establish closer relationships with others and, through counselling sessions, to form a more positive self-image for the future. The positive changes observed in the case examples were commensurate with the positive outcome of the study on encounter groups by Kamada (2001).

Murayama (1992) states that therapeutic approaches that focus on curing maladjustment are not best suited to school counselling since it is the school's aim to promote students' growth. If school counsellors also focus on promoting students' growth, their scope will extend, and even those students who are not maladjusted will be able to receive psychological support for better mental health. Ukai (1995) refers to the risk of employing a 'therapist-centred approach' in school counselling by applying one specific psychotherapeutic technique. Using this approach may easily arouse teachers' antipathy towards school counsellors since it would give the impression that the counsellors do not hold teachers' expertise in high regard. Therefore, the person-centred approach, which assigns great importance to the promotion of growth, autonomy and self-actualisation, is generally considered to be well suited for school counselling.

# REFERENCES

Cornelius-White, JHD (2007) Learner-centered teacher–student relationships are effective: A meta-analysis. *Review of Educational Research, 77,* 113–43.

Hirayama, E (1998) *Encouter group to kojin no shinnriteki seichokatei* [Encounter Groups and the Process of Individual Psychological Growth]. Tokyo: Kazamashobou.

Ito, Y (1989) Gakusei encounter group ni okeru syuchuteki group taiken no eikyou ni kannsuru kenkyu [A study of intensive group experiences in students' encounter groups]. Nihon Shinrigakkai dai 53kai Taikaihappyouronbunsyu [A Collection of Papers for the 53rd Annual Congress of Japanese Psychological Association], 353.

Kamada, M (2001) Hissyu jyugyou de okonawareta encounter group no koukasokutei to sono kousatsu [The effect of encounter groups as a curriculum requirement on nursing school students]. *Japanese Journal of Humanistic Psychology, 11* (2), 82–92.

Kawai, H (1970) *Counselling no jissaimondai* [Practical Questions in Counselling]. Tokyo: SeisinShobou.

Murayama, S (1992) *Counselling to kyouiku* [Counselling and Education]. Kyoto: Nakanishiyashuppan.

Murayama, S (2005) *Rogers wo megutte: Rinsho wo ikiru hassou to houhou* [About Rogers: Ideas and ways of living clinical experiences]. Tokyo: Kongoshuppan.

Oka, M (2002) Raidansyachushinryohou [Client-centred therapy]. In M Niregi (Ed) *School counselling no kiso chishiki* [Basic Knowledge of School Counselling] (pp. 185–90). Tokyo: Shinshokan.

Rogers, CR (1951) A theory of personality and behavior. In *Client-Centered Therapy* (pp. 481–533). Boston: Houghton Mifflin.

Rogers, CR (1959) A theory of therapy and interpersonal relationships, as developed in the client-centered framework. In S Koch (Ed) *Psychology: A Study of a Science. Vol. 3: Formulations of the person and the social context* (pp. 184–256). New York: McGraw-Hill.

Rogers, CR (1969) *Freedom to Learn.* Columbus, OH: Charles E. Merrill Publishing.

Rogers, CR (1983) *Freedom to Learn for the 80s.* Columbus, OH: Charles E. Merrill Publishing.

Ukai, Y (1995) School counselor to community shinrigaku [School counsellor and community psychology]. In S Murayama & K Yamamoto (Eds) *School Counselor: Sono Riron to Tenbou* [School Counsellors: Theories and prospects] (pp. 62–78). Kyoto: Minervashobo.

# CHAPTER 11

# REFLECTIONS ON PERSON-CENTRED CLASSROOM DISCIPLINE

## BERNIE NEVILLE

A popular book for newly graduated teachers (Cowley, 2003) devotes a chapter to 'behaviour management'. This is as we would expect, given the title, *How to Survive Your First Year in Teaching*, and the anxiety that the issue arouses in many beginning teachers. The chapter covers such topics as whole school behaviour policy, sanctions, rewards, what to do in a crisis. It distinguishes between low-level misdemeanours (minor rudeness to other students), medium-level misdemeanours (minor rudeness to the teacher) and serious misbehaviour (fighting), and recommends sanctions to be applied in each case. It provides ten 'tried and tested tips' for teachers in their moments of crisis (wait for them; perfect the deadly stare; strike a balance; put yourself in their shoes; avoid confrontation; and so on). There are hints on learning names, developing a teaching style, managing the space and creating groups. None of the advice is bad, and the fact that the book has been reprinted at least once may indicate that many beginning teachers have found it useful in their moments of crisis.

The guiding principle behind the chapter, and the book as a whole, is that teaching is largely a matter of 'management'. Students' learning and their behaviour are to be 'managed' by someone who is wiser and more powerful and has been deputed by society to control and direct children and adolescents for a significant part of their lives. Many approaches to classroom management, especially those rooted in behaviourism, start with this assumption: children who become 'behavioural problems' need to be controlled. In this literature there is a good deal of discussion of 'problem children', however they are labelled. There is far less discussion of 'problem schools', 'problem classrooms' and 'problem teachers'.

Nevertheless, even in *How to Survive Your First Year in Teaching*, there is acknowledgement that students' 'behavioural problems' cannot be attributed solely to the irresponsibility, malice, or sociopathic tendencies of children and adolescents. One 'tried and tested tip' to the beginning teacher who is frustrated by student behaviour is to 'put yourself in their shoes'. Teachers are reminded that the students have a point of view of their own: 'developing this kind of empathy will help you evaluate the work you set, and the way you teach, from a far more objective viewpoint' (ibid.: 41). Unfortunately, this brief paragraph is the only acknowledgement of the students' point of view in 23 pages devoted to behaviour management and it aims for 'objectivity' not subjective understanding.

# MODELS OF CLASSROOM MANAGEMENT

Thankfully, there are more sophisticated approaches to the subject than this (e.g. Cornelius-White & Harbaugh, in press; Wubbels, Brekelmans, den Brok & van Tartwijk, 2006; Freiberg, 1999; Lewis, 1997; Wolfgang, 1999). Burden (2006), writing like Cowley for beginning teachers, suggests that the first step to successful classroom management is selecting a consistent philosophy of teaching. He distinguishes between models of teacher–student interaction in terms of the level of control: low control (e.g. Gordon, 1974; Ginott, 1978; Kohn, 2001), medium control (Glasser, 1998; Dreikurs & Cassel, 1972; Kagan & Lang, 1978), and high control (Canter & Canter, 1992; Jones, 1987). Similar distinctions are made by Lewis (1997) who writes of control, management and influence models of classroom discipline and by Wolfgang (1999) who distinguishes interventionist, interactionist and non-interventionist models.

In the high control or interventionist model, the teacher is in charge and reigns by reward and punishment. In the medium control or interactionist model, power is shared between teacher and class; rules and consequences for inappropriate behaviour are discussed and defined at classroom meetings in which the teacher's voice is but one voice among many. In the low control or non-interventionist model, students are responsible for their own behaviour; the teacher encourages the individual students to find their own way of behaving in a socially responsible manner, does not insist on compliance but trusts in the students' ability to learn by experiencing the consequences of their behaviour.

Proponents of the low control/influence/non-interventionist end of this continuum are inclined to reject the word 'management'. They prefer the word 'discipline', even 'positive discipline' as being more compatible with the educational (as opposed to the management) dimensions of a teacher's work, and because it suggests a choice on the part of the student rather than the teacher's unilateral imposition of control (see Lewis, 1997).

In his advice to young teachers, Burden (2006) locates this discussion in the context of the teacher's efforts to create a learning community. He suggests that the beginning teacher should 'select' a philosophy so there is a fit between the teacher and the philosophy. However, there is also an assumption that a philosophy of teaching grounded in an authoritarian ideology has the same legitimacy as one grounded in an egalitarian and democratic ideology. This second assumption is not an assumption that I share.

We can argue that high control approaches to classroom discipline are inappropriate in a democratic society, and point to the lack of evidence of their long-term effectiveness even by the narrow criterion of improving students' learning and behaviour (see Render et al., 1989). If we look to other criteria, such as developing students' autonomy, creativity and understanding of democratic processes, we will be even more suspicious of the claims of high control, behaviour-modification approaches as either efficient or effective. Unfortunately, 'how to' books for beginning teachers may often continue to take their theory and practice from the Skinnerian, behaviour-modification end of the continuum rather than the Gordonian, non-interventionist end, and teachers will continue to 'manage' students in ways which assume that all power in the classroom rightly belongs to them. Control-oriented approaches to classroom discipline serve to support teachers' tendency to believe that behaviour problems arise because there is something wrong with the children rather than because there is something inadequate about the teaching, schools, or broader non-cooperative, hierarchical society (see Mavropoulou & Padeliadu, 2002).

The language of behaviour management does not have much currency in the world of the person-centred approach (PCA). Nevertheless, even teachers who religiously hold to the conviction that children, in their essence, are good, creative, curious, socially responsible, and needing only the 'freedom to learn' to surge towards the development of their potentials, may occasionally wake up on a Monday morning with a sense of panic at the prospect of spending the day in confrontation with a room full of students, or even one, who seem determined to abuse freedom and make teaching impossible. When negative fantasies of student behaviour are overwhelming, it is difficult to think of teaching in any terms other than control.

# CARL ROGERS' THEORY OF PERSONALITY AND BEHAVIOUR

It has often been said that there is nothing more useful than a good theory. A useful theory which supports non-interventionist and interactive approaches to classroom discipline is Carl Rogers' radical model of personality. In *Client-Centered Therapy* (Rogers, 1951), Rogers laid the foundations of both client-centred therapy and student-centred teaching. Rogers continued to work on his theory in his later writing, but the 19 propositions of his 1951 statement remain a good starting point for a systematic exposition of his theory. Rogers' theory stood in opposition to the deterministic assumptions of American psychology: both the stimulus–response determinism of behaviourism and the libidinal determinism of psychoanalysis. For him, choice and creativity are at the centre of human experience.

In the outline of Rogers' personality theory which follows, I have paraphrased his 19 propositions to make them less abstract and focus specifically on the world of teacher, pupil and classroom. I will illustrate the propositions with the example of David, a fifteen-year-old whom I had the experience of teaching in a Melbourne high school some years ago. My interactions with him remain fresh in my memory. I write this in the present tense, even though David left school years ago, has presumably found a place in the world, and has forgotten all about my brief intervention in his life.

## 1. DAVID EXISTS IN A CONTINUALLY CHANGING WORLD OF EXPERIENCE OF WHICH HE IS THE CENTRE.

In the world of experience of which David is the centre, I am marginal or even irrelevant. It is only for 50 minutes each day that I loom large in his perception, often getting in the way of his wants; I probably am a *management problem* for him.

## 2. DAVID REACTS TO THE FIELD AS HE EXPERIENCES AND PERCEIVES IT. THIS PERCEPTUAL FIELD IS, FOR DAVID, REALITY.

As far as I can ascertain, I (and most other teachers) exist in David's perceptual field as persons who persistently and without provocation 'pick on him', who prefer to give time to other students in the class, who reprimand or punish him for behaviour which they readily tolerate from others, and who want to force him to do tasks which he perceives to be boring and irrelevant. To this picture we must add the factor that David perceives more than he is aware of. He may be receiving non-verbal, subliminal information that is in conflict with his awareness.

## 3. DAVID REACTS AS AN ORGANISED WHOLE TO HIS PHENOMENAL FIELD.

David's behaviour in the classroom is not random. His behaviour is essentially organised and goal-directed. His organism is not integrated yet still systematically interrelated, so that an alteration in any part of it produces changes in other parts.

## 4. DAVID HAS ONE BASIC TENDENCY – TO GROW.

For Rogers, human nature is essentially constructive. He talks about the organism's 'actualising tendency' – 'man's [sic] tendency to actualize himself, to become his potentialities' (Rogers, 1961: 351). We can say of David that all his various needs and motives are aspects of this one fundamental need. David does not just react to stimuli; he is activated by a tendency 'to express and activate all the capacities of the organism' (ibid.) – to become what he potentially can be. Rogers assures us that the actualising tendency persists even in behaviour that I find antisocial and interpret as self-destructive. David will be sometimes insolent, sometimes withdrawn, sometimes ingratiating, all in the interests of survival and growth.

## 5. DAVID'S BEHAVIOUR IS HIS GOAL-DIRECTED ATTEMPT TO SATISFY HIS NEEDS AS HE EXPERIENCES THEM IN THE WORLD AS HE PERCEIVES IT.

While I am on the far side of the room assisting another student, David takes a handful of money from his pocket and starts to count it noisily and ostentatiously. To me, David's behaviour is stupid and counter-productive. It clearly irritates those he wishes to impress, and is likely to lead to him being devalued in some way. Yet when David looks at his world and responds to his needs, counting his money noisily appears to be the most appropriate way to behave.

## 6. THIS GOAL-DIRECTED BEHAVIOUR OF DAVID'S IS ACCOMPANIED BY EMOTIONS. THE INTENSITY OF THESE EMOTIONS DEPENDS ON HOW SIGNIFICANT THE BEHAVIOUR IS FOR SURVIVAL AND GROWTH.

Rogers suggests that the needs of both the 'self' and the 'organism' are sometimes in conflict. It may be 'defence of the self' rather than 'defence of the organism' that is really at issue in the classroom. It seems that David energetically defines himself in a particular way and defends this image, even when this self-image is at odds with his observable behaviour.

## 7. THE BEST VANTAGE POINT FOR UNDERSTANDING DAVID'S BEHAVIOUR IS FROM DAVID'S OWN FRAME OF REFERENCE.

If I could see and feel everything that David sees and feels, his behaviour would immediately make sense to me. If I am to understand David's behaviour in any useful way, I must make the attempt to step into his shoes and see the world as he sees it.

## 8. FROM DAVID'S TOTAL PERCEPTUAL WORLD, HE HAS GRADUALLY SEPARATED A PART WHICH HE PERCEIVES AS HIS 'SELF'.

We seem to distinguish 'self' from 'other' in terms of our degree of control. When David asserts defensively and vigorously that he does not try to disrupt the work of other students, theoretically he is disowning a part of his behaviour which does not fit with his idea of his 'self'.

## 9. THROUGH HIS INTERACTIONS WITH OTHERS, DAVID HAS FORMED A FLUID, CONSISTENT CONCEPT OF HIMSELF.

David's concept of himself acts as a guiding principle of his behaviour. Associated with David's self-concept, and developing with it, is a cluster of values which he attaches to his experiences.

## 10. SOME OF DAVID'S VALUES ARE EXPERIENCED DIRECTLY AND SOME ABSORBED FROM OTHERS. THESE LATTER ARE DISTORTED, SO THAT DAVID ACTUALLY THINKS HE IS EXPERIENCING THEM HIMSELF.

According to this proposition, very early in David's life he began to experience confusion between his natural organismic valuing and the values of others. By the time David reached adolescence he carried, for better or worse, many such introjected values, borrowed from his family, his peers, his teachers or the media.

## 11. THE EXPERIENCES THAT DAVID HAS ARE EITHER (A) PERCEIVED AND ACCEPTED (B) IGNORED OR DENIED, OR (C) DISTORTED, ACCORDING TO THEIR RELATIONSHIP TO THE STRUCTURE OF SELF.

David perceives himself as something of a 'tough guy'. Associated with this image of himself is a sense of his male superiority. He resists any evidence which might challenge this.

## 12. DAVID ORDINARILY ACTS IN WAYS WHICH ARE CONSISTENT WITH HIS SELF-CONCEPT.

When a teacher, attempting to control David's aggressive and disruptive behaviour, puts pressure on him, David is unlikely to act in any way that might give the impression that he is submitting to pressure.

**13. SOMETIMES DAVID'S BEHAVIOUR IS GENERATED BY ORGANIC EXPERIENCES AND NEEDS OF WHICH HE IS UNAWARE. IF SUCH BEHAVIOUR IS NOT CONSISTENT WITH HIS SELF-CONCEPT, DAVID DISOWNS IT.**

Much of David's behaviour seems to be directed against other students. Whatever his conscious motivation, the effect of his actions is to disrupt their learning, and at times it is a direct assault on their rights and feelings. This seems to be in conflict with his self-concept. When challenged about this, he seems genuinely offended. To protect his self-regard, he must continually persuade himself that it is not true.

**14. WHEN THERE IS A SIGNIFICANT CONFLICT BETWEEN WHAT DAVID IS EXPERIENCING IN HIMSELF AND HIS ENVIRONMENT AND WHAT HE IS ACTUALLY AWARE OF, HE MAY BE TENSE.**

Conscious control is difficult when the organism is trying to satisfy needs which are not acknowledged and to react to experiences which are not acknowledged. The tension between organism and self-concept is experienced as anxiety.

**15. WHEN DAVID'S SELF-CONCEPT IS APPROXIMATELY CONGRUENT WITH ALL OF HIS EXPERIENCE, HE WILL BE ADJUSTED OR FEEL OK.**

If David could acknowledge that he is a person who occasionally feels unjustified hostility towards his classmates and his teachers and acts in unacceptable ways, he would no longer be in a state of tension. If David can become non-defensively aware of his aggressive impulses, he could control them rather than be controlled by them. His energy would be freed to express itself in productive and socially responsible behaviour.

**16. ANY EXPERIENCE WHICH IS INCONSISTENT WITH THE STRUCTURE OF THE SELF MAY BE PERCEIVED AS A THREAT. THE MORE PERCEPTIONS OF THIS KIND DAVID HAS, THE MORE RIGIDLY HE HANGS ON TO HIS SELF-CONCEPT.**

When David is informed by teachers that he is immature, lazy, a bully, insolent and arrogant, that he interferes with his classmates' work, that he is wasting his time at school, or that he has been given far more second chances than he deserves, he argues back vehemently. His self-concept hardens to repel the assault. Not only does he refuse to change his attitude and behaviour, he does not even give the teacher the satisfaction of being heard.

**17. DAVID WILL BE ABLE TO TAKE IN NEW INFORMATION ABOUT HIMSELF ONLY WHEN HE FEELS NO THREAT.**

It is clear that people often change their self-concept and behaviour. The key to personality change for Rogers was unconditional acceptance within a relationship. Letting David know that he is a person of worth who is valued absolutely, independently of his behaviour, gives him the freedom to relax the boundaries of his self-concept enough to admit information about himself that has been inadmissible.

**18. WHEN DAVID CAN PERCEIVE AND ACCEPT ALL HIS EXPERIENCING, HE BECOMES MORE ABLE TO ACCEPT AND UNDERSTAND OTHER PEOPLE.**

If David can be more accepting of himself (rather than of an energetically defended self-concept) he will have better relations with others. Attack or defence become unnecessary and it is possible to relate to others as they are.

**19. AS DAVID PERCEIVES AND ACCEPTS INTO HIS SELF-STRUCTURE MORE OF HIS ORGANIC EXPERIENCING, HE WILL REPLACE HIS INTROJECTED VALUE SYSTEM WITH A CONTINUOUS ORGANISMIC VALUING PROCESS.**

As David learns to explore his perceptual world non-defensively, he starts to make value judgements of his own, instead of relying on borrowed values. Valuing becomes a fluid and continuous process, in which both his personal and social needs can be satisfied.

## THE PARADOX OF
## 'PERSON-CENTRED CLASSROM MANAGEMENT'

Rogers was attempting to present a theory that might account for human behaviour as he had observed it in his struggle to formulate an effective and consistent psychotherapy. What he called the 'hypothesis of confidence in the individual' was certainly fruitful in the context of psychological counselling. He believed it could be just as fruitful within the constraints of the classroom.

Rogers applied his theory to the practice of 'student-centered teaching' in a chapter of *Client-Centered Therapy* (1951). In *On Becoming a Person* (1961), in *Freedom to Learn* (1969) and its revision *Freedom to Learn for the Eighties* (1983), and in numerous papers, he outlined the conditions which he saw as facilitating learning. Rogers' approach has been operationalised and researched extensively by Aspy and Roebuck, Tausch and Tausch, McCombs and others, finding strong support in comparison to the traditional classroom for a variety of cognitive, affective, and behavioural student outcomes (see Cornelius-White, 2007). However, I want explore further how to interact when a student purposefully and skilfully appears to resist the teacher's best attempts at facilitation both for him or herself and for the rest of the class.

It is fairly obvious that if I approach the task of classroom management as a confessedly person-centred teacher, I am immediately enmeshed in a paradox. The 'hypothesis of confidence in the individual' leads me to accept that David is doing his best to grow and protect himself in the environment in which he perceives himself to live. It leads me also to the notion that David needs not less freedom but more freedom, and to the contradictions inherent in any attempt to manage his behaviour by confirming his personal power. I can attempt not to control him but rather to empower him, to allow him to take full responsibility for his actions by refusing to exercise power over him in our relationship. I can act on the conviction that self-esteem is a basic human need, that David's manifest need for autonomy and his need for status among his peers must be respected. However, this resides rather uneasily with my need to control David's behaviour, to keep it within boundaries where it will not interfere with my attempts to teach both David and his classmates. It resides even less comfortably with my occasional impulse to punish him, whether out of some abstract notion of justice or from my primitive urge for vengeance. If I am true to my person-centred orientation, I will not want to control or manipulate David's behaviour. On the other hand, I want him to change — for 'his' sake, for the sake of the class he is disrupting and, obviously, for the sake of my own sense of professional competence.

Rogers' ideas are commonly dismissed as naïve and romantic, yet when I try to carry them into my interaction with David I find nothing soft-headed about them. Rather they demand a considerable clarity of thought and toughness of purpose, resilience of my own self-concept, and a heroic respect for the autonomy of the individual. The person-centred approach has nothing to do with *laissez faire* (McKeachie, 1958). While I attempt to understand why David acts the way he does, I do not approve of his behaviour, or even honestly have a neutral attitude towards it. I wish to change it, or rather, I wish to provide the conditions under which David will himself choose to change it.

## PROVIDING THE CONDITIONS FOR GROWTH

If I take the long-term view of classroom discipline, Rogers' theory has application enough. I can offer David and his fellow students a democratic atmosphere with the therapeutic conditions – empathy, congruence and unconditional positive regard – which provide the basic, indispensable ground for a constructive teacher–student relationship, just as they do for a constructive therapist–client relationship. I can progressively abdicate my role of power over them, educating my students to assume full responsibility for their own actions and to develop a mature sensitivity to the needs of others, creating a classroom climate in which David will find that his outrageous and antisocial behaviour simply is not necessary.

I will be clear about what sort of behaviour I consider appropriate in the classroom, yet I will not blame him for acting the way he does, because I will constantly attempt to see the situation from his point of view. I will not threaten or punish him, for I know that even if the threat of punishment changes his perceptual world enough to modify his behaviour in the short term, it will only harden the self-concept which is the source of his actions. However, if his self-concept is so rigid, his defences so strong, that he successfully suppresses any sense of discomfort at his own behaviour and its effect on others, I fear the person-centred approach is not going to generate any change in him.

This may well be the case with David, but I am inclined to think not. His aggression towards teachers in class is coupled with constant attempts to ingratiate himself in and out of class. David's response to me has an element of public performance. His sabotage of other students' efforts to perform well in class is in contrast with his persistent attempts to show off for their benefit. Such behaviour, his evident paranoia about being 'picked on', and the glaring failure of his attempts to be popular with his peers, seem to point to a young man who is at least 'vulnerable to anxiety'. Vulnerability to anxiety is a condition for change (Rogers, 1957).

Unfortunately, no matter how empathic, congruent and accepting or committed to the PCA philosophy I am, I have to face the constant pressure of immediacy. If David is disrupting my class at this moment, I have the interests of the other students to protect, and I must protect them now. I also have to face the constant pressure of dealing with David in the presence of his peers.

## ADDRESSING THE OPTIONS

What did I actually do when, in the middle of a class discussion, David upturned his bag and started noisily sorting through the contents? While I will get to the answer to that question, I'll first start with some possible actions that are consistent with the principles outlined above.

Firstly, I could have taken David seriously as a person who had good reason for choosing this precise time to do a stocktake on his portable property, and suggested that he take his bag to a corner of the room where he could do what he needed to do without disturbing the rest of us.

I could have followed my hunches regarding the symbolic functions of his behaviour and said something like: 'David, you don't seem happy with what is going on here and you are finding something more interesting or useful to do', or if I wanted to be more challenging, 'David, it looks as though you want us to know that you think this discussion is boring', or 'David, you seem to want to get our attention'. I may not have quite hit the spot as far as David's awareness of his intentions was concerned, but I could at least have conveyed to him that I was taking his intentions seriously and making an attempt to understand them. Even if he continued with his activity, I may have succeeded in establishing some credibility with him as someone with at least a faint appreciation of the way he sees things.

If David continued his activity, I could have said something like: 'David, I would really like you to put those things away and join in the discussion, but I appreciate that you might think teachers push you around too much, and so want to continue what you're doing.'

I could have followed Gordon's suggestion (1974, 1991) and acknowledged my own feelings rather than exploring David's: 'David, when you do something like that in the middle of a discussion, I find myself getting really angry with you because your choice to sort through your stuff now interrupts our attention. I don't like getting angry with you, so I'd appreciate it if you stopped doing it.' In Gordon's *Teacher Effectiveness Training*, such I-messages are central to a teacher's way of handling conflicts with students. Such messages make a non-judgemental, non-blaming statement of what sort of behaviour is unacceptable to the teacher, whilst ensuring that the teacher takes responsibility for his or her attitudes and feelings. For Gordon, the rationale in such situations is that it is the teacher who has the problem. No matter how thoroughly I have convinced myself that my insistence that David behave in certain ways is for his own good, I have to acknowledge that in David's world his behaviour may present no problem to him. While I am being driven to frustration by some action of David's, he may be perfectly happy with what he is doing or may be conflicted, wanting more than one thing at a time and making a compromise by emptying his bag. To try to put myself into a counselling-like relationship with David so that he can discuss his 'attitude problem' is to miss the point entirely. It is my problem that has to be dealt with. For Gordon, the most effective way of dealing with the problem I have with David's behaviour begins with my acknowledging that the problem is mine. This awareness is part of being genuine. Gordon advises that if I want David to listen to me I must resist my impulse to tell David that he is bad, and restrict myself to giving a clear message about myself. If David can hear me non-defensively as I state my problem, I have set up the conditions in which we may be able to negotiate a way to solve it.

I could have taken another approach by setting out directly to expand David's awareness of his behaviour, its effect and its inappropriateness. I could have asked David, 'What are you doing?', and if he avoided answering, I could have calmly repeated the question. If my question was a genuine request for information (for David's perception of his behaviour may be very different from mine), and not heard by David as a judgement, a threat or a reprimand, I could expect an answer. I could then ask: 'What are the rest of the class doing?' and when he answered, as he would if I were calm and patient, I could ask: 'Is this a useful way to spend our time right now?' I do not know what David's answer would have been, but I could have taken his answer seriously, and acted on it. Perhaps David would have continued his activity in a corner of the classroom while the rest of us went on with the discussion. Perhaps not. In any case, David's awareness may have expanded a little. At least his humanity would have been respected and his ability to choose would have been confirmed. He would not have been simply a management problem.

So what did I actually do? I shouted at him. Not because I am a particularly brutal person or an incompetent teacher. Not because I think that shouting at students helps them grow into mature and effective adults. Not because I believe that aggression and punishment are effective ways of improving students behaviour and learning; the research makes it abundantly clear that this is not the case (see Freiberg et al., 2007). I shouted at him because, for all my fine words about the person-centred approach, my frustration at his ability to wreck my attempts to make him and his classmates literate got too much for me. Being self-aware and communicating from genuineness in the classroom is a real challenge. Unfortunately, yelling is the default position for most teachers in this situation.

## THE POSITIVE HYPOTHESIS

Interacting with David was a difficult scenario, and I cannot claim that in my brief time as his teacher I dealt with him very effectively. Neither can I claim that I was able to remain consistently person-centred in my dealings with him, though I managed to remain fairly consistently friendly to him outside of the classroom. On one occasion, when I struggled with congruence and his behaviour seemed to me exceptionally outrageous, I was very angry and showed it. David was sufficiently impressed by the possibility of physical violence that he behaved more quietly and passively for the rest of the lesson. Any satisfaction I might have felt in finding an effective way of controlling David's behaviour was destroyed by the discovery that after sitting meekly through my class, he went straight to a class with a female teacher and argued with her arrogantly and insultingly, adding vinegar by abusing her contemptuously in his own (ethnic) language, which she did not understand. From the reactions of the other students, she realised that some of the insults were explicitly sexual. She was reduced to tears.

Fortunately, most children, unlike David, respond better to the teacher who genuinely respects and tries to understand them than to the teacher who bullies and threatens them. It is usually possible to find mutually satisfactory solutions to the conflicts which arise between teachers and students. There need be no calling on authority, threats, warnings, moralising, criticism, analysing, name-calling, sarcasm, or judging. Person-centred classroom discipline involves giving up such strategies, attempting instead to listen to what 'management problems', like David, will tell us when they think we are really listening. If I had really listened to David, I may have found that he was confused by the mixed messages that he was getting from me – on the one hand encouraging the class to 'do their own thing' and at the same time jumping on him whenever 'his own thing' was something of which I disapproved. I may have found him a project that would engage him in the way that official curriculum could never do, and give him a genuine experience of learning. I may even have found that his behaviour in my class was his way of coping with anxiety aroused by my approach to teaching, which conflicted with his notion of how teachers are supposed to behave. I don't know, and it's too late to find out. Of course, I'm a better teacher nowadays, anyway!

If I had my time with David again, I hope I would not experience my interactions with him as persistent low-level tensions interrupted by moments of crisis. I hope that he would not need to behave the way he did, and I would not need to react to his behaviour the way I did. I hope that I would have genuine influence over his classroom behaviour, not by 'exerting my authority' but 'through being credible, attractive, giving students responsibility, and holding [myself] and students accountable for respectful, engaged behaviour in each teachable moment' (Cornelius-White & Harbaugh, in press.

Most critical moments in classroom discipline are small conflicts requiring more finesse than large-scale interventions or negotiations. They do not arise from hostile or violent behaviour but from time-wasting, especially when students are asked to work on their own. Teachers may experience them as 'management problems' but they should more accurately be labelled learning problems. In a person-centred classroom, in which the teacher honestly acknowledges and attempts to understand the grounds for the students 'lack of motivation', restlessness, inertia, or desire to socialise, and adjusts content and process accordingly, 'management problems' will disappear. That's the positive hypothesis.

# REFERENCES

Burden, P (2006) *Classroom Management: Creating a successful K-12 learning community*. San Francisco, CA: John Wiley & Sons.

Canter, L & Canter, M (1992) *Assertive Discipline: Positive behavior-management for today's classroom* (2nd edn). Santa Monica, CA: Lee Canter & Associates.

Combs, A & Snygg, D (1959) *Individual Behavior* (revised edn). Boston: Houghton Mifflin.

Cornelius-White, JHD (2007) Learner-centered teacher-student relationships are effective: A meta-analysis. *Review of Educational Research, 77* (1), 1–31.

Cornelius-White, JHD & Harbaugh, A (in press) Learner-Centered Instruction: Building relationships for student success. Thousand Oaks, CA: Sage.

Cowley, S (2003) *How to Survive Your First Year in Teaching*. London: Continuum International.

Dreikurs, R & Cassel, P (1972) *Discipline Without Tears*. New York: Hawthorn Books.

Freiberg, HJ (Ed) (1999) *Beyond Behaviorism: Changing the classroom management paradigm*. Boston: Allyn & Bacon.

Freiberg, HJ (2007, April) 'A person-centered approach to classroom management.' Paper presented at the International Meeting of of the American Educational Research Association, Chicago.

Freiberg, HJ, Huzinic, CA & Borders, K (2007, April) 'Classroom management as a vehicle for school improvement and student achievement.' Paper presented at the International Meeting of of the American Educational Research Association, Chicago.

Ginott, H (1978) *Between Parent and Child: New solutions to old problems*. London : Pan Books.

Glasser, W (1998) *The Quality School: Managing students without coercion*. New York: HarperCollins.

Gordon, T (1974) *Teacher Effectiveness Training*. New York: Wyden.

Gordon, T (1991) *Teaching Children Self-Discipline at Home and at School*. New York: Plume.

Jones, F (1987) *Positive Classroom Discipline*. New York: McGraw-Hill.

Kagan, J & Lang, C (1978) *Psychology and Education*. New York: Harcourt, Brace, Jovanovich.

Kohn, A (2001) *Beyond Discipline: From compliance to community*. Upper Saddle River, NJ: Merrill/Prentice-Hall.

Lewis R (1997) *The Discipline Dilemma* (2nd edn). Melbourne: The Australian Council for Educational Research.

Mavropoulou, S & Padeliadu, S (2002) Teachers' causal attributions for behavior problems in relation to perceptions of control. *Educational Psychology, 22* (2), 191–202.

McKeachie, WJ (1958) Students, groups, and teaching methods. *American Psychologist, 13*, 580–4.

Rogers, CR (1951) *Client-Centered Therapy*. London: Constable.

Rogers, CR (1957) The necessary and sufficient conditions for therapeutic personality change. *Journal of Consulting Psychology. 21*, 95–103.

Rogers, CR (1961) *On Becoming a Person*. Boston: Houghton Mifflin.

Rogers, CR (1969) *Freedom to Learn*. New York: Charles Merrill.

Rogers, CR (1983) *Freedom to Learn for the Eighties*. New York: Charles Merrill.

Render, G, Padilla, J & Krank, HM (1989) Assertive discipline: A critical review and analysis. *Teachers College Record, 90* (4), 607–30.

Wolfgang, CH (1999) *Solving Discipline Problems: Methods and models for today's teachers* (4th edn). Boston: Allyn & Bacon.

Wubbels, T, Brekelmans, M, den Brok, P & van Tartwijk, J (2006) An interpersonal perspective on classroom management in secondary classrooms in the Netherlands. In CM Evertson & CS Weinstein (Eds) *Handbook of Classroom Management: Research, practice and contemporary issues* (pp. 1161–92). Mawhaw, NJ: Lawrence Earlbaum Associates.

# Chapter 12

# THE USE OF THE PERSON-CENTRED APPROACH FOR PARENT–TEACHER COMMUNICATION

## A QUALITATIVE STUDY

DAGMAR HÖLLDAMPF

GERNOT AICH

THERESA JAKOB

MICHAEL BEHR

## INTRODUCTION

In 2006, two German books were published describing the relationship between parents and teachers: *Schicksal Schule* ('Fate School') and *Das Lehrer Hasser Buch* ('The Teacher-Hater Book'). Without going into the details of the content, one can see from these titles how bad the relationship between parents and teachers is perceived to be, despite constituting a legally based educational partnership. Collaboration between school and parents is hampered not only by a negative view of the profession of 'teaching', but also by the view of some teachers, who see parents as a source of considerable irritation.

## THEORETICAL BACKGROUND

### COMMUNICATION BETWEEN PARENTS AND TEACHERS IN GERMAN SCHOOLS

Communication between home and school normally takes place in a special context: 'the parent–teacher interview'. Fixed consultation hours are part of the official duty of teachers in Germany. However, German universities do not include special training to prepare teachers for such situations, and the prevailing opinion amongst teachers is that their private communication skills are transferable to professional conversations. In a survey of interaction patterns in parent–teacher interviews from a person-centred and systemic view, Behr and Franta (2003) found that teachers predominantly react to parents' behaviour on the basis of their cooperativeness and their attitude towards communication. That is, the communication patterns of teachers are predominantly *reactive* to parents' interaction styles. In this study seven interaction patterns were identified (see Table 1).

Although this study is interesting in many regards, we will, in this paper, concentrate only on Pattern No. 7, as this is the most relevant to our research topic. Also, it corresponds most closely with person-centred communication, an empirically supported approach

*Table 1*

Patterns of interaction (Behr & Franta, 2003)

| Patterns of Interaction | Frequency (n= 88) |
| --- | --- |
| 1. Parents are passive – Teacher gives advice | 27 |
| 2. Mutual directness | 18 |
| 3. Mutual dominance | 9 |
| 4. Mutual open objectiveness | 9 |
| 5. Information – distance | 9 |
| 6. Avoidance – resignation | 8 |
| 7. Exploration – empathy | 8 |

in educational (Cornelius-White, 2007) and parenting (Cedar & Levant, 1990) contexts. In this pattern, the teacher reacts with understanding and tries to verbalise the thoughts of the parent and assist them in continuing the discussion. In Behr and Franta's (2003) study, this pattern occurred in only 9 per cent of interactions. Also, the style of communication is frequently determined by the parents who have less than ideal communication skills, particularly when their children are struggling at school (Rosenzweig, 2000). Without training, with a low frequency of open exploring/ empathic interaction, and with problematic parent communication skills, it appears likely that teachers' communication skills and home–school dialogues need assistance.

Behr (2005) examined the differential effects in parent–teacher communications involving empathic and authentic interventions. The experiments demonstrate the superior effects of person-centred counselling skills when compared with a control group. Gender-specific differences were also apparent, the client-centred approach appealing to women more than men. This gender-specific effect suggests that other factors – for example, the context in which the conversation occurs – may also influence the outcome and affect the appropriateness of the person-centred approach in parent–teacher communication. Nevertheless, as the findings of the current study show, empathic understanding is new to the parents and some say that it seems strange to them. They feel mistrust and need the time and congruence of the teacher to gain confidence in the teacher's sincerity.

## THE PERSON-CENTRED APPROACH ACCORDING TO ROGERS

Rogers' (1957) view is that the client knows his problems best, even though he may not be able to communicate this knowledge. Rogers argues that each person has an innate ability to make appropriate decisions for him or herself. During the facilitative interview the counsellor must hold three attitudes in order to offer a sustainable relationship to his client, and to facilitate the other's growth.

1. *Congruence*: Firstly, the counsellor must be 'real'. Hiding authentic behaviour behind an artificial or professional attitude must be avoided.

2. *Unconditional positive regard*: The counsellor must accept his client unconditionally and as an equal in the interaction. The counsellor should avoid casting moral judgement even though not necessarily agreeing with or condoning all client behaviour.

3. *Empathy*: The counsellor should show empathic understanding, trying to verbalise in his own words the feelings and thoughts of the client.

Using the Rogerian model explicated above through compassion and attention, free from judgemental thoughts, feelings and behaviour, the teacher can help parents to accept themselves as they are. This is the requirement for the sort of sustainable, facilitative relationship that makes solutions possible.

Basically the person-centred approach avoids criticism, demands or coercion on the part of the facilitator. However, an important question is whether and to what extent advice and negotiated compromises may be appropriate in the parent–teacher interview. As a teacher must comply with certain formalities in relation to school concerns, in some situations limits must be imposed. Whilst the non-directive attitude and behaviour in school settings has empirical support, particularly in German classrooms, it almost always involves compromise between the teacher's intention to trust students and parents, and the obligation to provide feedback and suggestions (Cornelius-White & Cornelius-White, 2005). Nevertheless, person-centred values of transparency, clarity of formal rules, democratically negotiated problem-solving when situations fit the rules ambiguously, and general concern with courtesy, can help when limit-setting is required (Cornelius-White & Harbaugh, in press; Rogers & Freiberg, 1994).

## THE STUDY

The project explored the following questions:

- Do productive conversations lead to further collaboration?
- What factors obstruct problem-solving processes during communication between parents and teachers in the school setting?
- What influence does the framework of the conversation, or one person's taking the initiative, have on the course of the communication?
- What advantages and disadvantages do parents and teachers see in the participation of pupils in the dialogue and what is their experience of this involvement?
- In what way do problems between parents and teachers affect pupils?

The aims of the study were to identify problems, needs and expectations experienced in the teacher–parent interview by both parents and teachers; to gather data on dysfunctional communicative processes; and to identify possibilities for optimising the communication process. Another aim was to strengthen the skills of teachers and parents in relation to parent–teacher communication. It was anticipated that the findings of this research could lead to recommendations for the training of both teachers and parents, with the aim of improving communication, leading to more efficient use of the opportunities provided by parent–teacher interviews.

## METHOD

In a first step, needs and problems of parents and teachers in relation to parent–teacher dialogue were identified using semi-structured interviews with an average duration of 45 minutes. Data from the sample of teachers and 'parents representatives' (a representative of parents is a person who is elected by the other parents of the class at the beginning of the school year to support their interests) was collected from a wide cross-section of schools. The teachers and parents took part voluntarily. For convenience, schools closest to the university were initially approached. As there were not enough Gymnasien (secondary or high schools) in the area surrounding the university, we also approached schools from areas responsible to other education authorities. The sample includes a variety of schools ranging from small rural to large urban schools. Of the 26 schools contacted, which included six Grund- und Hauptschulen, eight Realschulen, eight Gymnasien, one Hochbegabten-Gymnasium and three Sonderschulen,[1] 14 schools took part in the study: four Realschulen, five Grund- und Hauptschulen, three Gymnasien and two Sonderschulen.

Both the teachers and the parent representatives were recruited through invitations from the school principals. Appointments for the interviews were made by telephone. Altogether, 17 teachers between the ages of 35 to 58 (five male and twelve female) and 17 parent representatives aged 35 to 60 (three male and fourteen female) were surveyed. The mean age of the teachers was 47. The mean age of the parents was 42. The criterion for the sample of parent representatives was at least one year's experience in the role. The average experience of the parent representatives group was eight years (range 1–17 years' experience). Teachers' experience ranged from 9 to 32 years, with an average of 21 years. The distribution of gender in both groups (with a majority of women) reflected the local gender balance.

---

1. The German school system is divided into three different types of secondary schools. After primary school (Grundschule), an appraisal of aptitude is given for each child by the school. This decides which type of secondary school the child will attend. The 'Hauptschule', lasting five years is attended by pupils showing lower performance. The 'Realschule' lasting six years is attended by pupils showing average performance. The 'Gymnasium' lasting eight or nine years is attended by pupils showing high performance. Only graduation from this school qualifies for university. Furthermore, there are the 'Sonderschule' for retarded and handicapped pupils and the 'Hochbegabten-Gymnasium' for intellectually gifted pupils.

# RESULTS

Results of the interviews with parent representatives are discussed first. The data analysis shows, on one hand, how parents expect teachers to behave in interviews and, on the other, the parents' experience in approaching the interview in person-centred ways.

## PARENT PERSON-CENTRED ATTITUDES AND STRATEGIES

A number of the parent representatives said that *listening* is a basic skill that both parents and teachers should have in order to have a productive conversation. For example, one (Parent representative No.5) said that one 'must have an open ear and should be able to listen'. Listening shows acceptance of the other by allowing them to express themselves. In this way, equal rights are granted to the other, a requirement for parity in any person-to-person encounter. Furthermore, attentive listening is needed in order to receive what is said, enabling empathic reaction.

'Positive regard' towards the teacher was seen as important. Parent representatives said they try not to attack teachers during a conversation even though their opinions may differ greatly from those of the teachers. From their experience, they know that personal attacks are useless and that conversation is hindered by such behaviour. Furthermore, they try to accept the mistakes or misconduct of teachers. Parent representative No. 12 said that 'acceptance is the basis for give and take'. Parent representative No. 2 felt that conversation should take place on a 'respectful' level because personal attacks 'will get you nowhere'. Both regarded it as reasonable to stay calm in emotional situations and considered that outbursts of anger or other emotional expression directed towards the other party were counter-productive. Parent representative No. 4 found 'taking a neutral stand' to be a successful strategy. She believed that 'metaphorically speaking, to observe from a bird's-eye view' is helpful for listening more neutrally. Two other parents (Nos. 6 and 7) said that by addressing problems without attacking or passing judgement on teachers meant that no defensiveness would be necessary and teachers would be able to consider the content of the conversation, be more task-focused and constructive. Parent representative No. 5 expressed herself in a person-centred way: 'People have to try to respect and accept each other; they needn't like and love each other but they must learn to accept every person in his own way: live and let live. However, one has to have a certain love for people; one has to trust oneself and others.'

Statements which belong to the construct 'empathy' are brought together here to show parents' understanding of its importance. Representative No. 5 also mentioned 'that the ability to slip into another's shoes is a basic competence for the honorary post of parent representative'. Parent representative No. 2 saw a difficulty in conversation if one person was unable to be empathic. One of the duties of a representative is to act as a mediator in difficult conversations. In such cases, the representative is expected to be even-handed, to empathise with both parties equally and express the content of the conversation in different words – reflecting and rephrasing.

Sometimes, less eloquent parents ask a parent representative involved in the study to act as supporter and companion in appointments with teachers. Parent representative No. 4 said she finds this awkward if the parent is an acquaintance who expects her loyalty. 'Congruence' (further illustrated in the following paragraph) is demanded in such cases. Representatives must explain to their acquaintances that they have a role to play: they are acting as a mediator and, when expressing the position of the teacher, their relationship to the parent need not be negatively affected. By being empathic, parents may recognise reasons for certain reactions, and knowing these reasons makes it easier to accept the other person. Representative No. 9, for example, said: 'I try to guess and take into consideration what leads them to behave in such a way, so that I can see both my point of view and theirs.' Even though the ability to be empathic was regarded as an important skill by 15 out of 17 parent representatives, only one of them appeared to have any knowledge of the skills required to show this empathy. It can be argued that the 'verbalisation of emotional experiencing' (VEE), or the reflection of the contents of a dialogue, is a helpful strategy for parent representatives in their task, because it is only through such signals that understanding can be demonstrated. Sensing that the parent (or teacher) is empathic towards them enables the other person to avoid potential misunderstandings and correct any assumptions.

The remaining variable in the person-centred approach is 'congruence'. Although it is named last, it is not of less importance in parent–teacher dialogues. Parent representative No. 1 had experienced positive dialogues with teachers when she 'laid her cards on the table', i.e. when she spoke with transparency and authenticity. Parent representative No. 4 had also formed the habit of addressing conflicts and personal problems openly. She said, 'I tried to bring in my own opinion in the process of finding a solution and to remain honest about it.' An attendant risk for the parent representative is being exploited by others. Representative No. 8 said that he tries to avoid this by making his role and point of view clear without discounting the opinions of others.

## PARENTS' EXPECTATIONS OF TEACHERS

Parent representatives also spoke about their expectations of the communication behaviour of teachers in terms which reflect the person-centred approach. Firstly, there is the role of 'appreciation'. Parent representatives said they want to talk about the problems of the child and expect the teachers to acknowledge these problems, even if they themselves regard the situation as unproblematic. They also want the teachers to show a willingness to cooperate in reaching solutions. Parent representative No. 1 said that 'professional behaviour by teachers is shown by the teacher taking parents seriously, even if a parent considers something to be more important than the teacher does.'

A personal relationship and a common interest in the child were regarded as important by parents: they want the teachers to take the time to introduce themselves and to get to know each other. Getting acquainted is one aspect, but parents also want to be able to meet on the same level. This often begins with the seating arrangements. Some parent representatives described it as annoying if they have to sit on the small students' chairs while the teacher sits at their desk looking down on them. Another negative – lack of understanding on the part of the teachers – was often mentioned and, according to representative No. 4, this means 'that in some cases parents don't dare to confront the teachers'. This fear arises from the fact that despite their 'bad' reputation, teachers still have an elevated status in the eyes of some social classes, who are thus reduced to a feeling of helplessness. There is a concern amongst parents that saying anything which might displease the teacher will impact negatively on their child.

Even though five of the seventeen parent representatives spoke of fears and negative experiences, others mentioned positive experiences in dealing with teachers. No. 8, in particular, found it pleasing when teachers were open-minded with parents. His expectations included parents not being devalued by teachers or treated as 'unqualified' just because they hadn't got an educational qualification. However, if a teacher was devaluing or arrogant, he said he tried to explain such behaviour without judging it. His hypothesis that 'a lack of acceptance by some teachers arises out of their own insecurity' helps him to be forgiving. He also expects teachers to admit to their own mistakes and accept the personal opinions of others, a view shared by three other parent representatives (Nos. 6, 7 and 12) who found that some teachers advocate their own position strongly whilst discouraging dissent. Parents expect, as a minimum of acceptance, that teachers listen and at least think about what has been said. Another representative (No. 14) proposed that both teachers and parents leave emotions aside, with no insults or yelling, making the point that, in her experience, emotions are not appropriate to the process of finding a solution.

The researchers don't fully share this opinion. From our point of view, we acknowledge that whilst it may be difficult, emotions can be expressed without damage to communication. When these emotions are verbalised, the teacher must have the professionalism to accept emotional reactions without treating them with disdain. The advantage of expressing emotions such as anger is that, once voiced, the feelings will no longer subliminally obstruct the dialogue. But we also know that this skill makes heavy demands on teachers because they are not sufficiently trained for it. One of the interviewed teachers (No. 8), who has already had communication training, described it as very difficult to draw on learned strategies in emotional situations.[2]

Parents also discussed their expectations of teachers as regards congruence. Teacher (No. 8) said he expected honesty – a teacher shouldn't try to conceal mistakes since, as far as he is concerned, criticism concerning his work is not meant personally. Parent representatives Nos. 6 and 7 said they expected teachers to talk openly and honestly about the weaknesses and strengths of their children. A well-intentioned gentleness is very seldom productive because, eventually, the parents will be confronted with the reality in the child's report. Only one representative (No. 13) wanted a global, not just child-related, unconditional honesty. He said: 'One should allow one's emotions free play. This is the only possible way to have a conversation based on the facts.'

Every parent representative knows of occasions when a teacher's behaviour has been anything but person-centred. One parent (No. 15) reported that he had often

---

2. This is why teachers who understand the advantages of communication training wish to refresh their knowledge and skills continously. Furthermore, they wish to be supported by supervision.

found that teachers became 'enraged' and reacted 'furiously'. In his view such behaviour could be the reason why parents don't dare to meet the teachers in private. In his opinion most teachers are more articulate than parents. In these cases, the teacher could behave in a person-centred way by adapting to the parents' standard of language, thus making it easier for them to express themselves. Parent representative No. 8 sees his presence as, in some cases, offering a form of protection to parents: some parents apparently believe that teachers set out to browbeat them because they, themselves, are scared of being exposed.

## TEACHERS' PERSON-CENTRED ATTITUDES AND STRATEGIES

The following statements by teachers could be assigned to the category of 'positive regard'. Even though teachers sometimes declare unconditional positive regard to be a strategy, they nevertheless speak of this kind of behaviour pattern as an attitude and an offer of relationship. Teacher No. 1 said: 'Basically, all parents want to educate and raise their children in a good way', and this assumption, she believes, gives teachers a reason to control their anger or any other emotional reaction. These considerations help her to find a point of access to parents. In principle, she tries to accept parents by listening to them and giving them space to talk, even though they may be expressing criticism.

Teacher No. 6 admits that he reacts to criticism from parents in an entirely different, less accepting, way. He sometimes experiences them as being too demanding and wishes they would be more trusting and accepting of *him*. Teacher No. 7 agrees: 'If the only reason for coming to a meeting is to attack me [the teacher] I may feel less ready to listen.'

Teacher No. 3 shares Rogers' view concerning each individual's ability to solve their problems. She said: 'Firstly, I let the parents describe the problem from their point of view in order to find a common solution.' She acts non-directively and picks up suggestions for solutions from the parents. In principle, she proceeds on the assumption that she can't change anybody but just wants to help. As she is not passing judgement on the parents, it is easier for her to stay in contact with them. To reduce distrust, she sometimes tells the parents about her own failures in raising children. She regards the devaluation of parents as basically senseless.

All the teachers understand the principle of empathy and try to draw on it during their conversations but, like the parents, most lack the appropriate strategies to signal their understanding. Teacher No. 1 is an exception but, although she knows that reflecting feelings is one way of showing empathy, she says she seldom actually does this, or perhaps only in conversations in which feelings dominate. In other situations she avoids talking about emotions because she fears going too far, but she does try to put herself in the parents' shoes and sometimes verbalises this. For her, a successful conversation is one where she has felt comfortable after, as well as during the conversation, and where the parent has understood a little bit more than before. She doesn't directly touch upon problems such as neglect but tries to find out with the help of empathy 'what makes it so difficult for the mother'.

One of the teachers interviewed (No. 10) was a young school principal who also knew about the possibility of establishing and improving a relationship through empathy and understanding. However, she said that in some cases she has difficulty empathising with parents because their way of life is so unfamiliar to her and, in such cases, finding a common conversational level can be really challenging. Teacher No. 3 said that in parent–teacher interviews she tries to find out whether parents are able to deal with negative feedback about their child. If she thinks that they can't deal with hard facts, she finds a way of talking about positive things in order to establish confidence. This may make it easier for parents to accept negative information. For teacher No. 4, empathy seemed to be a basic and normal communication skill. He claimed that you either have the skill or you don't and, in his opinion, it's impossible to learn it. In his opinion, teachers who don't have this skill are going to have enormous problems in communication.

'Congruence' seemed to be valued by teachers. Teacher No. 2, for example, said that in her experience, parents expect transparency from the teachers. She said that for some parents, honesty seems to be more important than diplomacy. Nevertheless, she still prefers to be friendly and polite. Teacher No. 3 tries to adapt to each parent individually and estimates to what extent they can tolerate honest feedback. Teacher No. 5 also tries to be transparent and hopes for the same from the parents. However, teachers expressed the view that a conversation which is characterised by too much frankness and in which communication is entirely accusatory, is both negative and oppressive. A good relationship was considered a precondition for honest communication.

## THE IMPORTANCE OF A GOOD RELATIONSHIP

In conclusion, we can say that all those interviewed, both teachers and parents, realise the importance to good relationship of both sides contributing easily and confidently. A good relationship between parents and teachers means better understanding and easier collaboration, with less likelihood of conflict arising through statements deemed as personal.

Both parents and teachers spoke of the importance of relationship and the need for straightforward and uncomplicated communication. For many teachers, the parent–teacher conference at the beginning of the school year is an important occasion for establishing an initial relationship with parents. Teachers see it as preparation for private conversation because, ideally at least, it is an opportunity to reduce parents' inhibitions. A personal relationship between parents and teachers, and one that might relieve some tension, can be established through informal conversation. For example, at parent–teacher social events problems can be much more easily articulated and discussed, without the threat of any intervening officialdom. Both groups experienced less formal group situations as more comfortable than private conversations at school.

# DISCUSSION

Our study reinforces the findings of other studies that realisation of the core conditions of the person-centred approach is beneficial to productive communication. They bring about a greater sense of well-being, emotional safety and stability, not only in the psychotherapeutic context but also more generally, as here in the context of teacher–parent interactions. Thinking and acting from the person-centred perspective enables us to design a range of social situations more effectively.

However, specifically, the study shows that more attention should be paid to the scope of the teacher in parent–teacher communication. Commonly, communication between parents and teachers takes place against the background of a specific problem. In addition, a solution has to be found for use within a limited period of time. The consequence, in practice, is that the teacher has to intervene in a much more directive way than is the case, for example, in therapeutic communication, for which the therapist is not as negatively impacted by a problematic student and, even if in brief therapy, a longer time-frame is provided. What can be understood from the interviews is that most parents accept teachers as professionals if they do no more than give honest information, show a willingness to listen to the opinion of the parents concerning an issue, and are willing to be cooperative in solving problems. That is all the parents that I talked with expect from teachers in parent–teacher dialogues. Our view is that advice can be and often is best given in parent–teacher communication, but the variables considered in this study should not be neglected. If given, advice should be offered with emotional warmth and an adequate awareness of parents' perspectives. Teachers need to adjust their behaviour to the needs of the parents, even if they have to consider objective facts and be directive. It is also our view that a teacher acting according to the person-centred approach can be of major assistance to parents in acknowledging and verbalising their feelings, which may help them to release any blockages they experience in such situations.

Despite the conspicuous benefits of the person-centred approach for parent–teacher communication, teachers and parents reported limits, or barriers, in conversation. They are aware of situations in which it has been impossible to find a common ground. Personal antipathies are not uncommon. When children work with a freelance counsellor, parents have a more limited sphere of influence and the counsellor has the option of rejecting a client. Parents and teachers, on the other hand, are forced to attempt to get along with each other and, unsurprisingly, both parties reported that there have been times when it has proved impossible to bridge personal differences.

One of the interviewed teachers (No. 10) expressed the need for a school psychologist to provide support in some parent–teacher interviews, and specific coaching to help her respond properly to parent problems. Such coaching or supervision would be reasonable for dealing with parents who insist on sticking to their preconceived ideas (Schmidt, 2007).

Teachers interviewed also expressed a wish for ongoing training in communication skills. Such training should focus on practical exercises that enable the teacher to become more secure in their practice, more able to stay professional and to withstand aggression in situations where personal attack leaves them emotionally affected (Aspy & Roebuck, 1977). With improved skills in communication strategies, teachers could better influence those parents who seem resistant to counselling. Ongoing access to training would overcome the problem of learned strategies being quickly forgotten.

Even though we have focused on the experience of teachers in the above discussion, we should not forget that there are parents who experience teachers as uncooperative and are therefore intimidated by the possibility of disputes and abuse. In relation to these problems, it would be also desirable to construct a training program for parents; even perhaps combining a program for parents and teachers to create an additional basis for understanding.

The study shows that, without exception, everyone interviewed expressed a desire for positive regard from the other party in conversation. One essential part of the training, therefore, would be for teachers and parents to learn how to give this positive regard, even when disapproving of the other's behaviour. Some of the interviewed teachers mapped out a suitable strategy: try to think positively, see the behaviour shown by the parents as positive in its intentions. Likewise, some parents would be more open if they were not afraid of the teacher's disapproval. This positive regard helps to bring a better dynamic into the conversation. Furthermore, a higher level of empathy would be helpful for the teachers in developing this positive regard. Perhaps, putting themselves in the position of the parents would help them to see that *they* might react in a similar way in the same situation. Congruence also has a part to play in parent–teacher interviews. Honest talk by teachers signals to parents that they are taken seriously if they speak frankly about their own confusion or own up to their mistakes. A relationship based on empathy, authenticity and positive regard leads to more open communication, benefiting children because parents and teachers are working with and not against each other.

## REFERENCES

Aspy, DN & Roebuck, FN (1977) *Kids Don't Learn from People They Don't Like*. Amherst, MA: Human Resource Development Press.

Behr, M (2005) Differentielle Effekte von Eltern-Lehrer-Gesprächen mit empathischen und selbsteinbringenden Interventionen im Rollenspielexperiment [Differential effects in the parent–teacher communication of empathic and authentic interventions]. *Empirische Pädagogik, 19* (3), 244–64.

Behr, M & Franta, B (2003) Interaktionsmuster im Eltern-Lehrer-Gespräch in klientzentrierter und systemischer Sicht [Interactional patterns in parent–teacher dialogue from a person-centred and systemic view]. *Gesprächspsychotherapie und Personzentrierte Beratung, 34* (1), 19–28.

Cedar, B & Levant, RF (1990) A meta-analysis of the effects of parent effectiveness training. *American Journal of Family Therapy, 18* (4), 373–84.

Cornelius-White, JHD (2007) Learner-centred teacher–student relationships are effective: A meta-analysis. *Review of Educational Research, 77* (1), 1–31.

Cornelius-White, JHD & Cornelius-White, CF (2005) Trust builds learning: Context and effectiveness of nondirectivity in education. In B Levitt (Ed) *Embracing Non-directivity: Reassessing theory and practice in the 21st century* (pp. 314–23). Ross-on-Wye: PCCS Books.

Cornelius-White, JHD & Harbaugh, AP (in press) *Learner-Centered instruction: Building relationships for student success.* Thousand Oaks, CA: Sage.

Mayring, P (2003) *Qualitative Inhaltsanalyse* [Qualitative Content – Analysis]. Weinheim und Basel: Beltz.

Rogers, CR (1957) The necessary and sufficient conditions of therapeutic personality change. *Journal of Consulting Psychology, 21* (2), 95–103.

Rogers, CR & Freiberg, HJ (1994) *Freedom to Learn.* New York: Macmillan.

Rosenzweig, CJ (2000) A meta-analysis of parenting and school success: The role of parents in promoting students' academic performance. *Dissertation Abstracts International Section A: Humanities and social sciences, 61* (4-A), 1636.

Schmidt, JJ (2007) *Counseling in Schools: Comprehensive programs of responsive services for all students.* (5th edn). New York: Allyn & Bacon.

**Endnote**

Many thanks to Miss Alexandra Häckel for helpful comments and suggestions on the translation of this article. Address correspondence to: Dagmar Hölldampf, University of Education Schwaebisch Gmünd, Oberbettringer Straße 200, D 73525 Schwaebisch Gmuend, e-mail: dagmar.hoelldampf@ph-gmuend.de

# CHAPTER 13

# THE DIALOGUE BETWEEN TEACHERS AND PARENTS

## CONCEPTS AND OUTCOMES OF COMMUNICATION TRAINING

SUSANNE MÜHLHÄUSER-LINK
GERNOT AICH
SIMONE WETZEL
GEORG KORMANN
MICHAEL BEHR

## INTRODUCTION

The parent–teacher conference is 'an exchange of feelings, beliefs and knowledge between parents and teachers about a particular student' (Manning, 1984: 15). Cooperation between parents and teachers is frequently necessary and the importance of communication between those two partners in education is often emphasised. International studies show the importance of the relationship between the two parties for the development of the child (Henderson, 1987; Day, Henderson & Hunt, 1994; Ramirez, 2002; Konold & Pianta, 2006), including those conducted in German-speaking countries (Knapp 1986; Neubauer & Krumm, 1989; Sacher, 2004, 2005a, 2005b).

New concepts of school development make the collaboration between parents and teachers even more necessary, as the parents achieve a more active partnership in the relationship between schools and parents. Parents should enrich the school by bringing in their own ideas and manpower for learning and creative projects in the school environment. Barron (1996) posits, 'There is a growing awareness that not only the school and parent can form a partnership to enhance learning experience of the children, but parental involvement can be the cementing ingredient for student success' (p. 397).

But what is the reality of parent–teacher partnerships in today's German schools? Very often, the influence of parents is not really appreciated by the teachers. The results of the studies of Sacher (2004, 2005a, 2005b) show that only 17.5 per cent of teachers seek contact with parents and only 10.3 per cent of parents are willing to seek contact with teachers. Others are either unwilling to talk or prefer to adhere to the tradition of the teacher meeting the parents of each class once a year in the evening. Further, these studies show that parents of low-achieving children, in particular, avoid dialogue with teachers.

The studies of Blase (1987) and Stallworth (1981) come to a similar conclusion. The Harvard sociologist, Lawrence-Lightfoot (2004), writes: 'Even teachers that love their job call the contact with parents the trickiest part of their work' (p. 15). Tacke (2004) shows that 47.2 per cent of teachers say that talking to parents is one of the greatest psychological strains of their job. Johns (1992) accentuates, 'Dealing with parents in a formal parent–teacher conference situation can be one of the most difficult aspects of a beginning elementary school teacher's job. It is also one aspect that has an effect on nearly all teachers at one time or another' (p. 147). Huppertz, an expert on parent–school relationships, supposes that there is fear between the two parties that makes them avoid forming a collaborative alliance in support of the children (Huppertz, 1979). And Susteck notes: 'The perennial threat of being accused by parents of unfairness or lack of professionalism leads teachers to a feeling of uncertainty. And parents can be vociferous in their criticism' (Susteck, 1981: 22). This helps to explain why teachers and parents are not enthusiastic about communicating with each other.

When we look at what takes place during conferences we find that, by the standards of counselling, most of the dialogue is very unprofessional. There are many potential reasons for this, and one is certainly structural: in counselling the counsellor's independence separates him from the problem, whereas the teacher, being part of the system, is from a systemic standpoint, necessarily part of the problem. Furthermore, teachers not only have very limited time to talk to parents (Busch & Dorn, 2000), they also often blame their own training, complaining that they have learned neither conflict solving nor parent consultation (Melzer, 1987: 155). So it is hardly surprising that many parent–teacher conferences are disappointing and frustrating – especially for the parents.

A study by Allison (1995) proves that problem-oriented conferences between parents and teachers are mainly dominated by the teachers. Very often, teachers behave as if the parents were their pupils. The teachers' utterances are domineering and confrontational rather than cooperative. During an average consultation, the teachers gave 86.3 per cent of the instructional message. Therefore, parents adopt a position that is passive, disengaged, or try to respond in a neutralising way. Allison (1995) remarks: 'The majority of these messages could be considered as a minimal expression by the parent to encourage the teacher to continue speaking' (p. 25). A study by Behr and Franta (2003) also demonstrates that teachers do not have the professional skills to talk to parents but adapt to the way the parents talk to them. (For example, if the parent appears helpless, the teacher tries to be 'helpful' in giving advice. If the parent is domineering, the teacher tries to sustain and get back to his or her dominant position.)

In summary, whilst we found many studies underline collaboration between parents and teachers, we detected that the two parties are not really interested in talking and listening to each other and that conferences are rather unprofessional, often being dominated by fear and disinclination. As Schaarschmidt (2004) concludes, 'Considering what is required of the teaching profession, this is a serious deficiency' (p. 6). This deficiency was the starting point of our training concept to improve the cooperation and communication between parents and teachers. Being aware of the benefits of person-centred counselling skills in general, we wanted to examine whether communication could also be fostered in such a specialised setting.

## GOALS AND RESEARCH QUESTIONS

Given meta-analyses of person-centred education (Cornelius-White, 2007) and parenting (Cedar & Levant, 1991), the research team at the University of Schwäbisch Gmünd was convinced that the person-centred paradigm is a suitable starting model to understanding interaction and improving cooperation between teachers and parents in schools. A special training concept called the 'Gmünder Gesprächsführungsmodell' ('GGM') [Gmünder concept of conducting dialogues] was developed by the research team. As proof of the effectiveness of that communication training for teachers, 'GGM', is the subject of the following two studies: an experimental and a field study.

The first goal of the research project was to develop a training programme that would enable teachers to improve their behaviour in dialogue with parents in the areas of empathy, unconditional positive regard and congruence. An evaluation of this training for integration into teacher education and other training facilities was a further aim. The eventual publication of GGM, a vocational training for teachers, will endeavour to improve cooperation between parents and teachers in a lasting and concerted way.

The exact research questions are:

- Are trained teachers more empathic and congruent? Do they have more unconditional positive regard for parents than teachers without training?

- If teachers are trained in the core conditions of the person-centred approach, are the achieved solutions better and do parents believe that they have a lasting effect?

- Are teachers appreciated as being more competent and more trustworthy after the training?

- Do teachers feel more confident and more efficient if they are trained?

- Is the climate of conversation better with trained teachers than with untrained teachers?

- Are the outcome expectations better if teachers are trained within the concept of GGM?

These questions are examined within an experimental study (Study I) and a field study (Study II). The data collection within the experimental study was done through role plays with student teachers at the university. The data collection in the field was accomplished with real teachers who came voluntarily to a further vocational training. The teachers wanted to improve their communication and cooperative skills in dialogue with parents. This second study used actual dialogues at school between real teachers and the parents of their pupils.

# THE TRAINING CONCEPT

The communication training for teachers, according to the GGM, is composed of three modules.

The training for teachers in the field study lasts about six months and takes a total of 60 hours; it is intensive and involves ongoing supervision. In contrast, the training for student teachers in the experimental study is shorter, taking a total of 36 hours; there is less detail and no ongoing supervision.

The training is mainly based on the person-centred concept paradigm. It also includes two other theories of communication. The three theories are integrated into the training and are represented in the three modules:

- Module I: Person-centred approach
- Module II: Transactional analysis
- Module III: Systemic theory and stabilisation of the person-centred approach

In Module I, the main focus is on the person-centred approach. Teachers learn the basic conditions of communication: the importance of gestures, eye contact, intonation and body language; Rogers' core conditions of empathy, unconditional positive regard and congruence are taught using examples of direct dialogue with parents; role plays and practice sessions offer consolidation, and a basis for trustworthy and constructive communication is achieved. Teachers learn the importance of transparency, conversational structure, clearness of thought and emotion, and a reflection of power in parent–teacher dialogue. All training elements include self-awareness and personal reflection. Supervision is offered between the modules to improve personal competence in communication.

Module II focuses on the theory of transactional analysis. The main topics, the four basic positions of communication, best known as the 'OK Corral' (Ernst, 1971), are introduced at the beginning of this module to establish and reinforce a position that recognises the value and worth of every person: transactional analysts regard people as basically 'OK' and thus capable of change, growth, and healthy interactions. Here, Rogers' three core conditions are linked together with the theory of transactional analysis. Later, the ego states are taught as an entire system of thoughts, feelings and behaviours from which we interact with one another; basically, students have to learn to recognise which ego states people are transacting from and follow the transactional sequences; they can then intervene and improve the quality and effectiveness of communication. 'Games' are a part of the programme which help the teachers to see their own behaviour patterns in difficult situations or conflicts. The Drama Triangle, for example, is a good tool for analysing such games and helping to find conflict solutions (Aich, 2006). The concept of Satir (1975) describes maladaptive types of communication that are introduced and analysed in the training. When situations result in an impasse, the process can be understood in a person-centred way: the core conditions have not been sufficiently present.

Module III focuses on client-centred aspects of communication and provides an insight into systemic theory; extensive training in person-centred counselling skills takes place and the systemic skills of reframing and problem-solving and techniques of questioning that help focus on new resources, perspectives and options, are also addressed and used in role play exercises. At the end of the training, participants should be able to integrate aspects of all three theories.

Teachers have perceived and reported limitations in the training but, generally, these perceptions appear to be idiosyncratic: what one teacher sees as a limitation, another will dismiss as unproblematic. From this point of view, as proposed by Rogers (1974: 220; 1973: 74), it was very important to introduce ways that teachers could be congruent in interaction with parents whilst being aware of their feelings and subjective limitations.

## STUDY I: EXPERIMENTAL STUDY

### METHOD

#### DESIGN

The evaluation was performed as a three-factor experimental design with repeated measure on one factor. Between initial measurement (t1) and second measurement (t2) no relevant intervention was given, thus creating a baseline. The training group served as its own control group. Between second measurement (t2) and third measurement (t3) the intervention was allocated, thus effects were expected to occur after this period.

#### PARTICIPANTS

Thirty students of a rural teacher training college in south-west Germany took part in a regular class of the psychology curriculum. The attendance was voluntary as alternative classes were provided. The age range was from 21 to 40 with a mean of 27 (SD = 6.3). 80 per cent were women. 55 per cent were trained for primary schools, 45 per cent for secondary schools.

#### MEASURES

A set of questionnaires was provided to assess the experience of teacher, parent and observer during a role play of a typical parent–teacher conversation.

The parent experience scale (PES) is a twelve-item measure. Items are rated on a seven-level Likert scale. This includes three subscales:

• Teacher's competence and trustworthiness: 4 items, alpha = .89. Example: 'The teacher appeared to be most competent.'

• Teacher's positive regard, 4 items, alpha = .89. Example: 'The teacher took me seriously.'

• Outcome expectation, 4 items, alpha = .91. Example: 'The conversation helped to solve the problem.'

The teacher experience scale (TES) is an eleven-item measure. Items are rated on a seven-level Likert scale. This includes three subscales:

- Climate of the conversation, 3 items, alpha = .85. Example: 'I felt good during the conversation.'

- Teacher's view of parent's social competence, 4 items, alpha = .89. Example: 'I think the parent understands what their child feels.'

- Outcome expectation, 4 items, alpha = .90. Example: 'I am optimistic that our ideas are put into practice.'

The observer experience scale (OES) is a thirteen-item measure. Items are rated on a seven-level Likert scale by the participant observers. This is one-dimensional, comprises the above topics and is called:

- Positive counselling process, alpha = .95. Example: 'The parent gained new views of the situation.'

A second source of data was gained by external ratings of the tape-recorded conversations for the Rogerian core conditions.

The Carkhuff (1969) Rating Scales were slightly adapted for this. These are five-level Likert scales scored from one to five. The inter-rater reliability was:

Empathy, $r$ = .82
Genuineness, $r$ = .67
Positive regard, $r$ = .76

PROCEDURE

At each of the three times of measurement, participants had to perform a role play about a typical real situation occurring within a parent–teacher conversation. Therefore, three scenarios were developed with the help of experienced teachers. At each time of measurement participants performed one role play in a group of three people with the second person playing the parent and the third the observer. The duration was limited to five minutes. The scenarios and participants were permutated over time to eliminate effects of possible differences in difficulty. Each role play was tape-recorded. Immediately after the role play, each participant completed the questionnaire about her or his experience during the role play and then participants swapped roles and scenarios twice more. Altogether, one group-work period incorporating all three role plays consumed about 40 minutes. This group work was regularly followed by a plenary discussion and clarification of counselling processes which was helpful on the level of the training process.

The tape-recorded role plays were later rated by 'blind' raters not involved in the training process. The rater training lasted six hours. The raters worked on the tapes of Study I and II in one sitting.

## RESULTS — STUDY I

### ROLE PLAYS

The following table shows results of the study.

*Table 1*

Means and Standard Deviations at three points of measurement on all variables (n = 30)

| Scale | M (t1) | SD (t1) | M (t2) | SD (t2) | M (t3) | SD (t3) |
|---|---|---|---|---|---|---|
| Teacher's Positive Regard (parent rated) | 4.18 | 1.26 | 4.01 | 1.08 | 5.09 | 1.01 |
| Teacher's Competence and Trustworthiness (parent rated) | 4.85 | 0.78 | 3.73 | 0.92 | 5.38 | 1.00 |
| Outcome Expectation of the Parents (parent rated) | 3.91 | 1.50 | 3.65 | 1.51 | 4.30 | 1.42 |
| Climate of the Conversation (teacher rated) | 3.86 | 1.35 | 3.54 | 1.38 | 4.70 | 1.12 |
| Teacher's View of Parent's Social Competence (teacher rated) | 4.07 | 0.86 | 3.60 | 0.66 | 4.71 | 0.59 |
| Outcome Expectation of the Teacher (teacher rated) | 3.86 | 1.35 | 3.58 | 1.33 | 4.42 | 1.15 |
| Positive Counselling Process (participant observer rated) | 3.98 | 1.39 | 4.08 | 1.38 | 4.77 | 0.70 |
| Empathy (external observer rated) | 4.29 | 1.62 | 4.32 | 1.90 | 7.14 | 1.56 |
| Genuineness (external observer rated) | 2.10 | 0.70 | 2.14 | 0.74 | 2.78 | 0.57 |
| Positive Regard (external observer rated) | 2.05 | 0.74 | 1.89 | 0.68 | 2.97 | 0.61 |

*Note.* M = mean; SD = standard deviation.

### ROLE PLAY QUESTIONNAIRES

*Parent experiences*

To examine the efficiency of the training, the scales 'Teacher's Competence and Trustworthiness', 'Teacher's Positive Regard' and 'Outcome Expectations' are of particular interest from the parents' point of view.

The scales 'Teacher's Competence and Trustworthiness' and 'Teacher's Positive Regard' show highly significant effects at three different measuring points (see Fig. 1). About 60 per cent of the variance in scale 'Teacher's Competence and Trustworthiness' can be explained by the factor 'Time'. The scale 'Teacher's Positive Regard' also shows a large effect over the factor 'Time' with the explained variance of 40 per cent. Significance of changes was tested with ANOVA (Analysis of Variance) in SPSS (Statistical Package for Social Sciences).

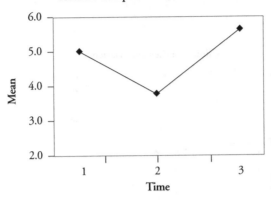

**Teacher's Competence and Trustworthiness**

$F (2, 19) = 12.88$, $p<.001$; $eta^2$ .58, effect size $= 0.8$

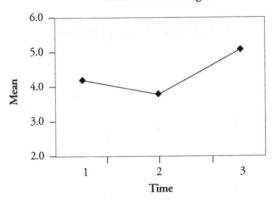

**Teacher's Positive Regard**

$F (2, 19) = 6.30$, $p<.001$; $eta^2$ .40, effect size $= 0.7$

*Figure 1.* Means of parent experiences at three points of measurement. Intervention occurred between points t2 and t3.

For the parent's experiences subscale 'Outcome-Expectation', a significant effect was not found ($F (2, 19) = 1.26$, $p<.31$; $eta^2$ .12, effect size $= 0.3$).

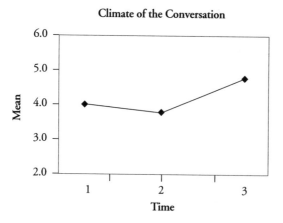

F (2, 19) = 7.05, p<.01; eta² .43, effect size = 0.6

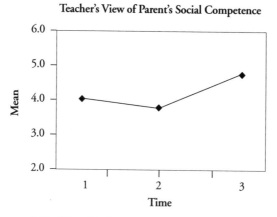

F (2, 19) = 18.51, p<.001; eta² .66, effect size = 0.8

*Figure 2.* Scale means of teacher experience at three points of measurement. Intervention occurred between points t2 and t3.

The scale 'Outcome Expectation' of teachers shows no effects (F (2, 8) = 0.66, p<.55; eta² .14, effect size = 0.3).

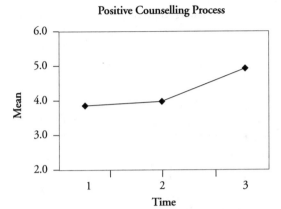

**Positive Counselling Process**

F (2, 17) = 4.31, p<.05; eta² .34, effect size = 0.6

*Figure 3.* Scale means of observer ratings at three points of measurement. Intervention occurred between points t2 and t3.

---

*Teacher experiences*
In this questionnaire, the dialogues were evaluated from the teacher's point of view. Relevant for this measure were the scales 'Climate of Conversation', 'Teacher's View of Parent's Social Competence' and 'Outcome Expectation'.

For the scale 'Climate of Conversation', a significant effect could be observed. The scale 'Teacher's View of Parent's Social Competence' shows a highly significant effect, with a strength of 0.8; 66 per cent of the variance statistically is a result of the treatment.

*Participant observer experiences*
To measure the effectiveness of the training, an additional estimation of an observer is helpful. Therefore the scale 'Positive Counselling Process' was created. This scale also produces a significant effect over the factor 'Time' from an observer's point of view.

ROLE PLAYS – EXTERNAL OBSERVER RATING
The characteristic quality of the ability to communicate in a person-centred way was also measured using the Carkhuff (1969) Rating Scales. Here, the effects for all three core conditions, 'Empathy', 'Genuineness' and 'Positive Regard', were highly significant over the factor 'Time' hence significant increases occur between the second and third measuring points after training has begun.

For the variable 'Empathy', a highly significant value arose. Eighty-three per cent of the clarification of the variance is a result of the treatment. For 'Genuineness' 64 per cent, and for the variable 'Positive Regard', 77 per cent are caused by the effectiveness of the treatment.

185

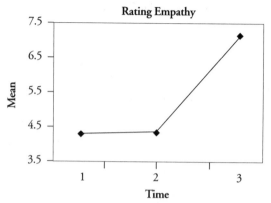

F (2, 19) = 45.31, p<.001; eta² .83, effect size = 1.8

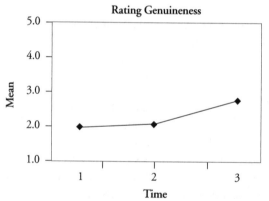

F (2, 19) = 16.80, p<.001; eta² .64, effect size = 2.4

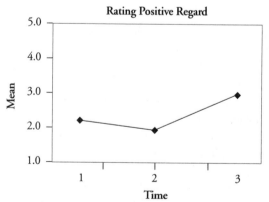

F (2, 19) = 32.53, p<.001; eta² .77, effect size = 1.2

*Figure 4.* Rating of teachers' realisation of the Rogerian core conditions at three points of measurement. Intervention occurred between points t2 and t3.

The figures show that between measuring points one and two there is no relevant change. After the treatment, all scores for the core conditions 'Empathy', 'Genuineness' and 'Positive Regard' increased significantly.

## DISCUSSION

Using the rating process, highly significant values for the variables 'Empathy', 'Genuineness' and 'Positive Regard' were found as a result of the training. According to the person-centred point of view, these three variables indicate the adjuvant behaviour of the counsellor in the counselling process. This adjuvant behaviour affects positively the willingness of a person to change their behaviour. In order to achieve better progress for pupils, the parent–teacher conference should achieve balance through a more equal partnership – beneficial for all parties. It is assumed that the recorded effects of the study show an increased likelihood of a supportive parent–teacher relationship for the sake of the child.

The treatment group did not undergo training between measuring points t1 and t2, and no significant modification was measured here. After the beginning of the training, a significant change of scores in the core conditions was found in a pairwise comparison. Additionally, the efficiency of the GGM is confirmed by the evaluation, which shows that the trained teachers improved their communication skills significantly in the area of the three core conditions of the person-centred approach – this was confirmed via the observer ratings. Again, the scores increased with the beginning of training; thus, it can be said that the changes are caused by the training.

On the other hand, the results of the scale called 'Outcome Expectation' did not show significant changes. Neither parents nor teachers experienced significant effects of the dialogues upon situational resolutions. This could be accounted for by the short length of the role plays. Problems between the two parties simply couldn't be resolved in five minutes. However, the participant observers clearly experienced both parties as interacting more positively towards the expected changes and there was a better atmosphere during the conversation.

Altogether, the significant effects show that the goals of the study have been achieved. The teachers improved their communication skills and thus, the parent experience of the conversation was influenced positively. The role plays proved that cooperation between parents and teachers can be improved by training teachers with the GGM.

Towards the end of the project, new questions arose concerning transferability to real communication in an everyday situation in school:

- Do the same results occur if real teachers do the role plays?
- Could the same results be achieved in real conversations of longer duration between parents and teachers?

To answer these questions further research was undertaken, resulting in Study II.

# STUDY II: FIELD STUDY

Within the communication training, experienced teachers recorded role-playing dialogues as well as real dialogues with parents in school. Both types of conversation were analysed via questionnaires and ratings and evaluated by the use of SPSS.

## METHOD

### DESIGN

Again, the evaluation was performed as a three-factor experimental design with repeated measure on the factor 'Time'. In this second study, relevant trainings were performed between the measuring points t1 and t2. Between the measuring points t2 and t3, further skills were trained with an emphasis on deepening person-centred interventions and including solution-focused interventions.

### PARTICIPANTS

Fourteen teachers, twelve female and two male, from schools of a rural and small town area in south-west Germany took part. The sample was self-selected. Teachers were invited to attend the training which was announced within the further education program of the local school authority. The age range was from 21 to 55 with a mean of 37 ($SD$ = 10.1). Women constituted 86 per cent, 60 per cent worked at primary schools and 40 per cent at secondary schools.

### MEASURES

The same measures were used as in Study I. In addition, two follow-up questionnaires were applied to conversations which the teachers had held with real parents:

- One questionnaire for parents: the 'parent follow-up scale' (PFUS), assessing the verification of planned action; six items to be rated on a seven-level Likert scale, alpha = .98. Example: 'The action we took after the conversation was successful.'

- One questionnaire for teachers: the 'teacher follow-up scale' (TFUS), assessing the same three items to be rated on a seven-level Likert scale, alpha = .87.

## PROCEDURE

Role plays were used and measured as in Study I. In addition, trainees had to apply the measurement procedures to real parent–teacher conversations occurring in their practice. One of these was to be applied before relevant behaviour-shaping training procedures began, another was to be applied in the middle of the training, and another after the training. The same measures were to be applied to the real conversations which, assuming the parent's consent, would be tape-recorded. The follow-up questionnaires were sent to the parents a fortnight after the conversation, with an envelope for posting directly to the researchers. At this point, the teachers also posted their follow-up questionnaires to the researchers.

## RESULTS — STUDY II

### ROLE PLAYS

Table 2 shows results of the study for the role-plays.

*Table 2*

Means and Standard Deviations at 3 points of measurement on all variables (n = 9)

| Scale | M (t1) | SD (t1) | M (t2) | SD (t2) | M (t3) | SD (t3) |
|---|---|---|---|---|---|---|
| Teacher's Competence and Trustworthiness | 4.68 | 1.04 | 3.32 | 0.69 | 5.43 | 1.46 |
| Teacher's Positive Regard | 3.57 | 1.71 | 4.03 | 0.66 | 4.86 | 1.54 |
| Outcome Expectation of the Parents | 3.51 | 1.39 | 3.90 | 0.71 | 4.06 | 1.60 |
| Climate of the Conversation | 2.90 | 1.45 | 3.83 | 1.53 | 4.17 | 1.42 |
| Teacher's View of Parent's Social Competence | 3.82 | 0.67 | 3.95 | 0.82 | 4.50 | 0.70 |
| Outcome Expectation of the Teacher | 3.76 | 1.21 | 3.46 | 1.32 | 4.12 | 1.36 |
| Positive Counselling Process | 4.39 | 0.52 | 4.38 | 1.97 | 4.60 | 0.56 |
| Empathy (rating) | 3.57 | 1.69 | 4.63 | 2.11 | 5.80 | 1.99 |
| Genuineness (rating) | 2.03 | 0.60 | 2.23 | 0.63 | 2.67 | 0.67 |
| Positive Regard (rating) | 2.03 | 0.91 | 2.23 | 0.67 | 3.00 | 0.88 |

### ROLE PLAY — QUESTIONNAIRES

As in Study I, questionnaires were used to evaluate dialogues from different points of view. Real teachers took turns alternating the role of parent, teacher and observer (referred to as a participant observer to show a contrast to the 'blind', external consultants who observed the tapes) in the dialogue.

#### Parent experience

The following scales were shown to have statistically significant changes as a result of training; 'Teacher's Competence and Trustworthiness', 'Positive Regard' of the teacher and 'Outcome Expectation' of the parents.

In the role-playing dialogues performed after the training unit 'Module II', the scale 'Teacher's Competence and Trustworthiness', based on the parents' questionnaire, shows worse values than the evaluation of this scale before the trainings starts. As in Figure 5 'Teacher's Competence and Trustworthiness' increased significantly after the last training unit. Over the factor 'Time' a significant effect has been achieved with an explained variance of 79 per cent based on the treatment.

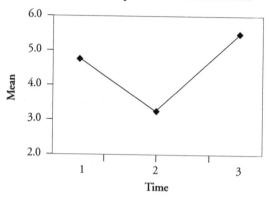

$$F (2, 5) = 9.63, p<.05; \text{eta}^2 .79, \text{effect size} = 0.7$$

*Figure 5.* Rating of parent experience at three points of measurement. Interventions occurred between points t1 and t2 and between t2 and t3.

---

No significant effects were found on the scales 'Positive Regard' ($F (2, 5) = 1.00$, $p<.43$; $\text{eta}^2 .29$, effect size = 0.8) and 'Outcome Expectation' ($F (2, 5) = 0.26$, $p<.78$; $\text{eta}^2 .09$, effect size = 0.4).

---

### Teacher experience

From the teachers' point of view the following scales were evaluated; 'Climate of the Conversation', 'Teacher's View of Parents Social Competence' and 'Outcome Expectation'.

The results of the scale 'Climate of the Conversation' (see Figure 6) just failed to reach statistical significance, but a tendency is observable.

The scale 'Teacher's View of Parent's Social Competence' (see Figure 6) shows a significant effect and an explained variance of 65 per cent, based on the treatment.

### Observer experience

Only a few questionnaires were returned, therefore it was not possible to reach significant results.

### ROLE PLAY — RATINGS

How teachers performed on skills of empathy, positive regard and genuineness in parent–teacher dialogues had been evaluated by the 'blind', external team of three trained experts using the modified Carkhuff scales from tape-recordings.

The statistical analysis of the ratings shows for the variables 'Empathy' and 'Positive Regard' (see Figure 7) significant positive effects over the factor 'Time'.

The significance test of the variable 'Genuineness' barely failed ($F (2, 8) = 2.1$, $p<.19$; $\text{eta}^2 .34$, effect size = 1.1).

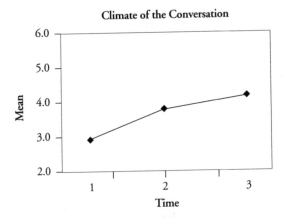

### Climate of the Conversation

F (2, 8) = 3.18, p<.10; eta² .44, effect size = 0.9

### Teacher's View of Parent's Social Competence

F (2, 8) = 7.51, p<.05; eta² .65, effect size = 1.0

*Figure 6.* Rating of teachers' experience at three points of measurement. Interventions occurred between points t1 and t2 and between point t2 and t3.

The increase of the measured values on the scale 'Outcome Expectation' (F (2, 8) = 0.66, p<.55; eta² .14, effect size = 0.3) failed to reach statistical significance.

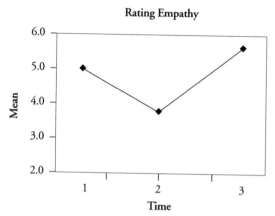

F (2, 8)= 3.45, p<.10; eta² .46, effect size = 1.3

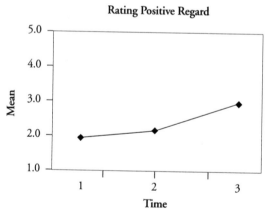

F (2, 8)= 3.32, p<.10; eta² .45, effect size = 1.1

*Figure 7.* Rating of Rogerian core conditions at three points of measurement. Intervention occurred between points t1 and t2 and between points t2 and t3.

## REAL DIALOGUES

Table 3 shows results of the study for the real dialogues.

*Table 3*

Means and Standard Deviations at two and three points of measurement on all variables (n = 4)

| Scale | M (t1) | SD (t1) | M (t2) | SD (t2) | M (t3) | SD (t3) |
|---|---|---|---|---|---|---|
| Teacher's Positive Regard | 5.50 | 0.83 | 6.30 | 0.75 | | |
| Teacher's Competence and Trustworthiness | 5.99 | 1.04 | 6.56 | 0.50 | | |
| Outcome Expectation of the Parents | 5.86 | 0.62 | 5.90 | 0.80 | | |
| Climate of the Conversation | 5.67 | 0.77 | 5.73 | 0.44 | | |
| Teacher's View of Parent's Social Competence | 5.22 | 0.87 | 5.57 | 0.50 | | |
| Outcome Expectation of the Teacher | 4.87 | 0.92 | 5.04 | 0.52 | | |
| Empathy (rating) | 2.80 | 0.61 | 3.83 | 0.71 | 5.53 | 1.49 |
| Genuineness (rating) | 1.90 | 0.33 | 1.77 | 0.33 | 2.60 | 0.55 |
| Positive Regard (rating) | 1.97 | 0.56 | 2.17 | 0.24 | 2.97 | 0.42 |

### REAL DIALOGUES – QUESTIONNAIRES AND FOLLOW-UPS

*Parent experience*

The scale 'Teacher's Positive Regard' (F $(1, 7)$ = 5.40, p<.05; eta² .44, effect size = 1.0) shows a significant effect.

No significant effects were found on the scales 'Teacher's Competence and Trustworthiness' (F $(1, 7)$ = 2.59, p<.15; eta² .27, effect size = 0.5) and 'Outcome Expectation of the Parents' (F $(1, 8)$ = 0.08, p<.43; eta² .00, effect size = 0.1).

*Teacher experience*

The teacher questioning also shows no significance on all evaluated scales.

- Climate of the Conversation: F $(1, 9)$ = 0.10, p<.76; eta² .01, effect size = 0.1
- Teacher's View of Parent's Social Competence: F $(1, 9)$ = 2.86, p<.13; eta² .24, effect size = 0.4
- Outcome Expectation of the Teacher: F $(1, 9)$ = 0.28, p<.61; eta² .03, effect size = 0.2

*Follow-up questionnaires: teacher and parents*

Again, few follow-up questionnaires were returned, so it was impossible to analyse this data.

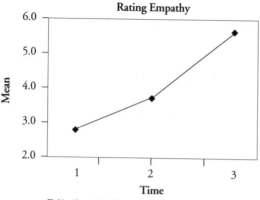

F (2, 3) = 10.34, p<.05; eta² .87, effect size = 4.8

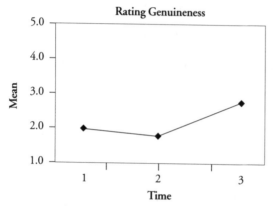

F (2, 3) = 27.78, p<.05; eta² .95, effect size = 2.2

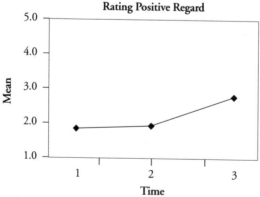

F (2, 3) = 72.38, p<.01; eta² .98, effect size = 1.7

*Figure 8.* Rating of teacher's realisation of the Rogerian core conditions at three points of measurement. Intervention occurred between points t1 and t2 and points t2 and t3.

In all of the three variables 'Empathy', 'Genuineness' and 'Positive Regard' significant effects were indicated.

The results of the explained variance show that the treatment has a great impact on the examined variables ('Empathy' = 87%, 'Genuineness' = 95%, 'Positive Regard' = 98%). Figure 8 shows the effects and the increasing values of the mean.

The changes that took place during the training are remarkable. The training showed significant impact on levels of the core attitudes. Additionally, the high values of explained variances indicate that the training is suitable for helping teachers develop person-centred behaviour in conversation with parents.

## DISCUSSION

During the training, the teachers improved their behaviour in the area of the core variables of the person-centred approach – 'Empathy', 'Positive Regard' and 'Genuineness'. This is supported by the results of the analysis of both the role plays and the real dialogues.

In further studies, researchers should secure more participants. It is interesting to glance at the results of the examined real dialogues. There is clear evidence that in the area of core variables the training had a significant effect. The high values of explained variances are remarkable – also highlighting the effectiveness of the training. The observed difference between the results of role plays and real dialogues may be explained in part by the greater motivation and willingness to perform in real situations. These positive effects also offer evidence for the successful practice of the trained skills in real situations.

In general, practising teachers have significantly lower expectations relating to dialogue with parents when compared to student teachers trained in the experimental study. Training could not change this pessimistic assessment. A possible explanation might be the outcome experiences of practising teachers. But more accrued positive interactions could alter expectations. Range restriction may be another limiting factor in the lack of significant results on this variable.

Evaluation of the follow-up questionnaires was not possible because of the small return. Further studies should give consideration to more effective management of these questionnaires.

## CONCLUSIONS ON THE GGM FROM STUDY I AND STUDY II

In all, the study shows that the 'Gmünder Gesprächsführungsmodell' is suitable for increasing person-centred behaviour. It is not only an evidenced-based training concept for students in educational facilities to develop their professional attitude and tools in conversations, but also an advanced training for experienced teachers to improve their skills in communication in real dialogues with parents.

# REFERENCES

Aich, G (2006) *Kompetente Lehrer - Ein Konzept zur Verbesserung der Kommunikations- und Konfliktloesefaehigkeit* [Capable Teachers – A concept to improve communications and conflict solving]. Hohengehren: Schneider.

Allison, J (1995) A descriptive study of problem-oriented parent–teacher conferences. *Humanities and Social Sciences, 56,* 456–65.

Barron, BG (1996) Parent–Teacher Conference Day: A school plan. *Education, 111,* 396–9.

Behr, M & Franta, B (2003) Interaktionsmuster im Eltern-Lehrer-Gespräch in klientzentrierter und systemischer Sicht [Interaction patterns in parent–teacher conferences from the person-centred and systemic point of view]. *Gesprächspsychotherapie und Personzentrierte Beratung, 34* (1), 19–28.

Blase, JJ (1987) The politics of teaching: The teacher–parent relationship and the dynamics of diplomacy. *Journal of Teacher Education, 38* (2), 53–60.

Busch, K & Dorn, M (2000) *Erfolgreich beraten. Ein praxisorientierter Leitfaden für Beratungsgespräche in der Schule* [Successful Counselling: A guide to counselling interviews in school]. Hohengehren: Schneider.

Carkhuff, R (1969) *Helping and Human Relations. Vol. I. Selection and Training.* New York: Holt, Rinehart and Winston.

Carkhuff, R (1969) *Helping and Human relations. Vol. II. Practice and Research.* New York: Holt, Rinehart and Winston.

Cedar, B & Levant, RF (1991) A meta-analysis of the effects of parent effectiveness training. *The American Journal of Family Therapy, 18,* 373–84.

Cornelius-White, JHD (2007) Learner-centered teacher–student relationships are effective: A meta-analysis. *Review of Educational Research, 77,* 113–43.

Day, R, Henderson, M & Hunt, S (1994) Model for development of pre-service conferencing skills. *Journal of Instructional Psychology, 21* (1), 31.

Ernst, F (1971) The OK Corral: The grid for getting on with it. *The Transactional Analysis Journal, 1* (4), 231–40.

Henderson, A (1987*) The Evidence Continues to Grow: Parent involvement improves student achievement.* Columbia, MD: National Committee for Citizens in Education.

Huppertz, N (1979) *Wie Lehrer und Eltern zusammenarbeiten. Ein methodischer Leitfaden für Kooperation und Kommunikation in der Schule* [How Teachers and Parents Collaborate. A guide to communication and cooperation in school]. Freiburg: Herder.

Johns, K (1992) Lowering beginning-teacher anxiety about parent–teacher conferences through role playing. *School Counselor, 40* (2), 146–52.

Knapp, G (1986) *Beziehungs- und Kooperationsprobleme in Erziehungsinstitutionen* [Relation and Cooperation Problems in Educational Institutions]. Klagenfurt: Hermagoras.

Konold, T & Pianta, R (2006) *Measuring Method Variance in Child Behavior Observations: A comparison of mothers, fathers, and teachers.* San Fransisco, CA: American Educational Research Ass.

Lawrence-Lightfoot, S (2004) *The Essential Conversation: What parents and teachers can learn from each other.* Harvard: Random Books.

Manning, BH (1984) Conducting a worthwhile parent–teacher conference. *Education, 105,* 4, 342–8.

Melzer, W (1987) *Familie und Schule als Lebenswelt. Zur Innovation von Schule durch Elternpartizipation* [Family and School as an Environment for Living: To the innovation of school through parental involvement]. Weinheim: Juventa.

Neubauer, C & Krumm, V (1989) *Die Kooperation von Eltern und Lehrern im Lichte empirischer Untersuchungen* [Parent–Teacher Cooperation in the Spotlight of Empirical Studies]. Salzburg: University Press.

Ramirez, AY (2002) How parents are portrayed among educators. *School Community Journal, 12* (2), 51–61.

Rogers, CR (1973) *Entwicklung der Persönlichkeit* [On Becoming a Person]. Stuttgart: Klett.

Rogers, CR (1974) *Lernen in Freiheit* [Freedom to Learn]. München: Kösel.

Sacher, W (2004) Elternarbeit an bayrischen Schulen. Repräsentative-Befragung zur Elternarbeit [Parents' involvement in Bavarian schools. A representative survey of parents' involvement]. *Schulpädagogische Untersuchungen Nürnberg, 23.*

Sacher, W (2005a) Elternarbeit: Forschungsergebnisse und Empfehlungen. Zusammenfassung der repräsentativen Untersuchung an den allgemein bildenden Schulen Bayerns [Parent's collaboration with schools: Research results and recommendations. Compendium of a representative survey at Bavarian schools]. *Schulpädagogische Untersuchungen Nürnberg, 25.*

Sacher, W (2005b) Erfolgreiche und misslingende Elternarbeit. Ursachen und Handlungs-möglichkeiten [Successfull and failing parent–teacher cooperation: Causes and strategies.] *Schulpädagogische Untersuchungen Nürnberg, 24.* Nürnberg: Uni Press.

Satir, V (1975) *Selbstwert und Kommunikation* [Self-Worth and Communication]. München: Pfeiffer.

Schaarschmidt, U (2004) (Ed) *Halbtagsjobber: psychische Gesundheit im Lehrerberuf – Analyse eines veränderungsbedürftigen Zustandes* [Part-Time Workers: Psychological health of teachers – Analysis of a state that has to be changed]. Weinheim: Deutscher Studienverlag.

Stallworth, JT (1981) *Parent Involvement Training for Undergraduate Elementary Teacher Preparation.* Washington, DC: National Institute of Education.

Susteck, H (1981) (ed) *Schulleben und Elternarbeit* [Schools' and Parents' Collaboration]. Bochum: Kamp.

Tacke, M (2004) Gesundheitsförderung in der Schule. Was können Lehrerinnen und Lehrer für die eigene Gesundheitsförderung unternehmen? [Health promotion in school. What can teachers do for their health promotion?]. *Schulverwaltung, Spezial. 1*, 43–5.

# CAN PERSON-CENTRED ENCOUNTER GROUPS CONTRIBUTE TO IMPROVING RELATIONSHIPS AND LEARNING IN ACADEMIC ENVIRONMENTS?

Renate Motschnig-Pitrik

## INTRODUCTION

Several authors from constructivist, learner-centred and person-centred traditions have argued that learning is most effective if it includes the whole person. This means that for meaningful, deep and persistent learning not only the intellect but also feelings, meanings, ideas, skills and dispositions need to be included. Recently, this has also been voiced in the EU strategic statement of core competencies in our society. According to the European Association for the Education of Adults (2004):

> *There is a need for a new curriculum. Traditionally, the curriculum consisted of three elements: knowledge, skills, attitudes – which tends to value knowledge above skills, and skills above attitudes. Experience of life suggests different priorities: positive attitudes are key to a rewarding life and job, skills are also more important than knowledge. These priorities should be asserted in the development of a new curriculum, which would raise the value of social capital, civil society and the role of non-formal learning.* (p. 2)

But how can these principles and strategies be put into practice? Extensive research (Aspy, 1972; Barrett-Lennard, 1998, 2003; Cornelius-White, 2007; Cornelius-White et al., 2004; Rogers, 1983; Rogers & Freiberg, 1994; Tausch & Tausch, 1963/1998) has proved that the instructor's, or better, facilitator's, attitudes and skills, such as realness, respect and deep understanding, are a key factor for learning at the cognitive, social, as well as attitudinal level. More recent research indicates that technology-enhanced learning settings, for example settings that mix face-to-face and online learning, offer the required flexibility in which resourceful people can foster experiential, whole-person learning that addresses the learner at the level of intellect, social skills and attitudes, including feelings (Holzinger & Motschnig-Pitrik, 2005; Motschnig-Pitrik, 2006a). In this chapter, I share my experience from developing, designing, conducting and evaluating a course on 'Person-Centred Communication and New Media' that includes encounter group sessions and is aimed at significant person-centred learning in the field of communication.

The chapter is intended to share experiences and research findings from a technology-enhanced academic course targeted at experiential, whole-person learning of adolescents and young adults in the area of communication. In other words, what has been my experience on the path towards and through an academic course (within a business informatics curriculum) that aims to make students better communicators? In the spirit of participatory action research, I share some personal thoughts on the course experience and its meaning for continued action and research. Moreover, the chapter raises some methodological questions regarding research design. It illustrates the inadequacy of any single research paradigm to respond to a pool of relevant research questions and suggests a research procedure that integrates various paradigms such as participatory evaluation, qualitative and quantitative analyses (Figl, Derntl & Motschnig, 2005) within an overall participatory action research framework (Motschnig-Pitrik, 2004).

Rather than closing up concepts, the chapter aims to open practice and inspire further research along the paths initiated by our endeavours in the Research Laboratory for Educational Technologies at the University of Vienna (Derntl, 2006; Mangler & Derntl, 2004; Motschnig-Pitrik & Nykl, 2005). This is intended to confirm or inspire readers in facilitating deep, meaningful learning in technology-enhanced environments and thereby provide a basis for effective personal and knowledge development.

The chapter is structured as follows: the next section provides a concise orientation to person-centred learning, followed by its manifestation in the course on person-centred communication (PCC). Section 4 presents the basic research questions and methodological considerations. Section 5 is central in so far as it sketches a whole action research cycle encompassing the analysis of the situation, the planning, including research design, action taking with students' reactions, the evaluation and specification of learning. The final section summarises the chapter and identifies questions for further research.

## EDUCATIONAL BASELINE

Our approach to technology-enhanced learning, i.e. combined face-to-face and online learning, builds upon humanistic educational principles as realised in the person-centred approach (PCA) by Carl Rogers (Rogers, 1961, 1983). Person-centred learning is a personally significant kind of learning that integrates new elements, knowledge or insights into the current repertoire of the learner's own resources so that he or she moves to a higher level of meaning and resourcefulness (Barrett-Lennard, 1998). It can be characterised by the active participation of students, a climate of trust provided by the facilitator, building upon authentic problems and raising the awareness of meaningful ways of inquiry (Rogers, 1983). Research in the PCA has proved (Aspy, 1972; Cornelius-White, 2007; Cornelius-White et al., 2004; Rogers, 1983) that students achieve superior results, along with higher self-confidence, creativity, openness to experience and respect, if they learn in a climate in which the facilitator (instructor, teacher, etc.) holds three core attitudinal conditions and if the learners perceive these, at least to some degree. The core conditions are the *realness* or *congruence* of the facilitator, *acceptance* or *respect* towards the student, and *empathic understanding* of the students and their feelings. The way in which these core conditions can be expressed in technology-enhanced learning situations in general has been discussed in more detail (Bauer et al., 2006; Motschnig-Pitrik, 2006b, and Motschnig-Pitrik & Mallich, 2004).

In Rogers' (1983) own words: 'Significant learning combines the logical and the intuitive, the intellect and the feelings, the concept and the experience, the idea and the meaning. When we learn in that way, we are whole' (p. 20). For didactic reasons, in particular for the sake of transparently specifying learning goals, we deconstruct significant, whole-person learning into three layers (Bühler, 1907; Nykl & Motschnig-Pitrik, 2005). These are the level of intellect or intellectual knowledge, the (social) skills level, and the level of personality, attitudes, dispositions, feelings, and intuitions. The three levels play a guiding role in assigning learning activities (always meant to include personal development) to individual levels and in having students estimate how much they benefited from each of the levels.

## PERSON-CENTRED COMMUNICATION: COURSE DESIGN, INCLUDING ENCOUNTER GROUPS

EU strategies foster the development of skills and attitudes beyond mere knowledge. A key question is:

• Can academic, technology-enhanced courses accommodate this goal and, if so, what are the influential factors that enable whole-person learning?

In the context of the course on person-centred communication, we decided to firstly formulate learning goals at each level and then designed the course to address each level.

*Level of knowledge:*

Knowledge about:
  • Three Rogers' variables
  • Active listening
  • Developmental tendency in the person-centred approach
  • Actualising tendency, self-structure and experience
  • Significant learning
  • Encounter groups: process stages, effects, community building

*Level of skills:*

Improvement of skills regarding:

  • Ad hoc communication and online communication

- Speaking in a group
- Active listening
- Short ad hoc presentations
- Teamwork
- Reflection and feedback

*Level of personality and attitudes or dispositions:*

Development towards:

- Inner flexibility
- Transparent communication resulting from increased congruence between self and experience
- Improved online communication
- Higher acceptance of self and others
- Better understanding of self and others
- Dealing with problems in everyday life more constructively

The next step was to design the course scenario, specify individual activities and allocate activities in face-to-face and online phases. After a brief initial meeting, students were asked to fill in an online questionnaire and to read the initial part of the lecture notes along with articles on active listening. This was to ensure that the first workshop could be spent getting to know one another and elaborating and discussing expectations and resources rather than lecturing. After the first workshop, students are asked to form teams of about three people on the platform and to choose one out of about ten small proposed projects to be elaborated by the team in a self-organised fashion and published in the online course space.

The course was designed to include three basic elements: structured, half-day workshops; unstructured encounter group sessions; and accompanying online activities such as reaction sheets, the submission of team projects and self-evaluations.

The four half-day workshops were intended to be spent elaborating the topics in teams; small and large group discussions and sharing about basic features of the PCA; brief presentations of the students' concept of working on their team projects; an exercise in active listening and its reflection; role play; discussions of students' reactions sheets; and watching a video on Carl Rogers' biography. The fourth workshop exposed the students further to the free and open style of encounter groups and their inherent potential for personal development. In general, the workshops served as practice of concrete communication situations, thereby heightening the sensitivity of students in regard to relationship issues and the difference between face-to-face and computer-mediated communication. In this way, the workshops, team projects and course notes contributed primarily, although not exclusively, to learning at the levels of knowledge and skills.

The two subsequent person-centred encounter groups (Rogers, 1970) were scheduled to last one-and-a-half days each and provide generous space for experiencing one's own and the group's communication behaviour. The groups were expected to develop, in the first place, the level of feelings, attitudes, and dispositions (Nykl, 2005). The lack of structure in such groups requires participants to co-construct meaning by relying solely on their personal resources. Each encounter group and workshop was intended to be followed by writing personal reaction sheets that were uploaded on the platform and could be read by all participants to allow for continuous development of the course. After the deadline for uploading the team projects, students were asked to evaluate themselves and each student was supposed to read and comment upon the project work of any two other teams. The final, fifth workshop was devoted to reflecting the students' personal experience in the course process, as well as collectively reflecting on the person-centred encounter group process (Rogers, 1970). At the end, students were asked to fill in the final online questionnaire, including questions on teamwork, interpersonal relationships, course elements, learning at each of the levels, etc.

Since academic courses require grading, we looked for a grading procedure that would allow us to include as many facets of learning as possible in the final grade. Currently, the final grade takes into account students' self-evaluation, the evaluations of the students' project work by peers and by the facilitator, and the facilitator's assessment of each student's participation in face-to-face and online activities.

## RESEARCH QUESTIONS AND METHODOLOGICAL CONSIDERATIONS

Given that academic courses are adequate settings to address all three levels, a follow-up question is:

- Do students perceive the planned focus on the individual levels and in what way do they actually benefit at each of the levels?

It should be noted that qualitative methods are required to find out about the quality of students' learning at individual levels. Thus, besides questionnaires, we employ student-reaction sheets and self-evaluations as a source of potential learning at each of the levels (Motschnig-Pitrik & Nykl, 2005). Excerpts from these sources will be provided in this chapter. The content analyses of the course instance described here are in progress. Whereas quantitative methods have proved useful for comparing the amount of learning at each of the levels, qualitative analyses and action research have the potential to find out more about individual factors and actions that influence the course process.

If the course goal is to address the whole person, another question that arises is:

- Does taking part in the course cause changes in the basic personality dimensions and/or attitudes of students?

Another class of questions addresses the blended course design. We are interested in finding out:

- To what degree the course elements – workshops, online activities, and person-centred encounter groups – are perceived as important to support learning?
- Whether at all, and/or in what way, the online interactions influence the group and community building processes?

Furthermore, since the course aims to develop transparent communication by way of addressing interpersonal attitudes, we are interested in the course's influence on interpersonal relationships.

Last but not least, to obtain constructive comments and improve my communication, action and the course, I am highly interested in the following:

- How do students perceive each workshop and encounter group meeting?

Open reaction sheets, in which students reflect on their experience in each unit, have proved highly valuable to support me in this endeavour.

In general, we have observed that pure action research from the participating researcher appears insufficient to cover the whole range of specific questions posed in researching students' learning at three levels. Consequently, our approach has been to use qualitative and quantitative methods to complement action research as the overall, driving paradigm (Motschnig-Pitrik, 2004). For example, an online questionnaire has been designed to address the perceived quality of interpersonal relationships by structured questions with nominal scales and free-text fields allowing students to supply further comments on their structured and quantitative responses. This extended procedure, described below, appears to be best suited to meeting the needs of a practising, facilitating researcher who wants to improve his or her interventions and at the same time develop a mature course paradigm.

## EXTENDED ACTION RESEARCH PROCEDURE AND RESULTS

Action research is gaining recognition in accompanying the introduction of new media into innovative teaching styles (Baskerville, 1999). This can be understood from the fact that pioneering teachers and facilitators aim to enrich their courses by introducing new media and are likely to combine research with practice in acting as reflective practitioners in their own courses. In this chapter, we take up Susman and Evered's (1978) proposal that suggests that action research typically proceeds in cycles (here, each course instance forms one cycle) that consist of five phases: diagnosing; action planning; action taking; evaluation; and specifying learning. In the following, we discuss selected issues of one action research cycle, more precisely, the third, of the course on person-centred communication.

### DIAGNOSING

Diagnosing refers to setting goals for learning. Currently, most academic courses tend to emphasise the level of knowledge or intellect. However, several sources indicate that this focus is questionable and that deep, persistent learning needs to include attitudes and skills. This demand tends to be shared by the vast majority of students who indicate that they benefit more from significant, whole-person learning when compared with traditional courses (Motschnig-Pitrik, 2006a). Furthermore, in a recent study (Motschnig-Pitrik, 2002), managers of Information and Communication Technology (ICT) enterprises were asked about the required qualifications of business informatics graduates: 'social skills' and 'ability to work in teams' headed the list. As discussed earlier, the EU strategic statement on key competencies clearly states that, within the new curriculum, skills and attitudes will be addressed in addition to knowledge (EAEA, 2004). Keeping these insights and statements in mind, we felt the need to design a course that explicitly integrates all three levels of learning in the context of communication and new media.

## ACTION PLANNING AND RESEARCH DESIGN

Since the course design has already been discussed above, here we describe the participants, instruments and procedures. Sixteen students, one facilitator and one advanced student as co-facilitator participated in the course intervention. In the beginning and at the end of the course students were asked to fill in an online questionnaire, however its submission was voluntary. Eight students filled in the questionnaire at the beginning of the course, fifteen submitted it at the end.

The questionnaire used in a pre-test, post-test design, contained ordinal scales (1 = very low; 5 = very high) to establish the amount of learning (subsuming personal development) students attributed to each of the three levels. At the beginning of the course, students were asked to estimate the amount of learning on the individual levels in a typical, traditional course in their study of business informatics. At the end of the course (starting some days after the final workshop and lasting a further four weeks), the amount of learning was estimated for the particular intervention, namely, the course on person-centred communication. T-tests (statistical comparison between groups) were intended to be used for finding out whether there were significant differences between traditional courses and the course on person-centred communication in the amount of learning allocated to each of the levels. Since only eight students had returned the initial questionnaire, the t-tests used a larger sample size including students from other courses who responded to the same questions, namely the amount of learning on each of the three levels in a typical, traditional course.

In order to respond to the question of whether the course had any effect on students' communicative attitudes, we chose to formulate five indicative items. In the final questionnaire, we asked students to what degree they felt that the statements reflecting particular changes in attitudes were applicable as an effect of participating in the course. An ordinal scale was used with 1 standing for 'not at all' and 5 meaning 'applies fully'. This procedure, with specific, self-formulated items regarding flexibility, sensitivity, and openness in communication, was intended primarily to illustrate potential effects in a purely descriptive form. This approach was taken since, in earlier course manifestations, we had used selected dimensions of the NEO-Five Factor Inventory (NEO-FFI) and had tested the students before and after the course. As hypothesised, no significant changes had been found. We believe that the time span of the intervention is too short and sample sizes too small to indicate changes. However, we hypothesised that specific items relating to a person-centred intervention could, nevertheless, reflect changes in attitudes. It should be noted that earlier we had found that quantitative results stemming from pre- and post-testing on attitudes need to be interpreted with great care since changes in either direction may also be caused by greater sensitivity to individual 'issues' as an effect of the course. For example, a course experience in which a student perceives that he or she is less open to some situations than others may alter their initial self-perception regarding openness – despite the fact that, during the course, he or she actually becomes more open. In this context, we found that quantitative data clearly needs to be complemented by qualitative student reactions to allow for a proper interpretation of the quantitative questionnaire data.

Regarding the importance of course elements, students were asked to estimate the importance of online elements, structured workshops, and encounter groups. A post-test design was used in order to determine whether there were differences in the students' perception of the importance of individual course elements. The questionnaire contained ordinal scales (1 = very low; 5 = very high) to establish the perceived importance of the three course elements. A multivariate analysis of variance was used to find potential differences in the importance of course elements.

In order to establish whether the online reaction sheets had an influence on the group process, we reflected on the process phases (Rogers, 1970) during the final workshop. We also shared the students' perceptions on writing and sharing reactions online. Any hypotheses reported in this article are based solely on my subjective impressions resulting from group dialogue and my understanding of students' sharing in the reaction sheets. The same holds true for the description that I give with respect to the individual workshops and group sessions.

Regarding students' interpersonal relationships, a post-test design was used in which students were asked what effect the course had on their interpersonal relationships with study and work colleagues, superiors, friends, partners, parents, and others in general. An ordinal scale ranging from 'negative effect' to 'positive effect' was used to estimate the effect. Furthermore, a free-text field was provided in which respondents were asked to supply examples illustrating their rating. Since the facilitator's person-centred attitudes are known to be primary influence factors in students' learning and growth, we mention that at the end of each course instance we allow students to grade the three person-centred attitudes of the facilitator(s). So far, the results have tended to lie between 4.3 and 4.7 on scales where 1 means 'very low' and 5 'very high', with the exception of one course instance where the results were generally about 0.5 lower.

*ACTION TAKING*

About thirty students participated in the initial meeting, from which twenty were selected on the basis of their advancement in the study of business informatics. From these, sixteen students attended the initial workshop and all sixteen completed the course successfully.

A student wrote in his reaction sheet, as a response to the initial workshop:

*I liked the first workshop and appreciate a course in which students get the chance to openly talk to one another, discuss, and share their views. Sitting in a circle was a well-planned setting that has facilitated face-to-face communication. I consider it very appropriate to work in teams and subsequently present the ideas. This allows us to learn how to present our views effectively. The feedback after each presentation helps to see the strengths and weaknesses and to work on overcoming the weaknesses later.*

Another student commented:

*I found this workshop very interesting. It made me realise how important communication is in our private lives and jobs. I found the climate in the group very pleasant. As I had heard that we were going to sit in a circle I could not imagine it. But it was not inconvenient and I even preferred it, because in this arrangement one can talk more honestly with one another. I hope the course will remain as thrilling and interesting as it started.*

In a subsequent workshop, we practised active listening and elaborated on factors that contribute to effective speaking and good listening. In order to provide a glimpse of the character of the workshop, consider another excerpt from a student's reaction sheet:

*I consider talking about the reaction sheets at the beginning of the workshops as very meaningful. This way, we can discuss and put into practice comments and suggestions, such as the idea to use name cards which, in my view, contributed considerably to creating a relaxed atmosphere. The moderation cards regarding the themes 'What is important for me as a speaker/listener' enabled one to identify issues of common concern as well as issues that one had not considered oneself. During the discussion we came across the terms 'I-message' and 'you-message'. I would be eager to learn more about these, in particular, why 'you-messages' are problematic and what one can say instead of them.*

Another student valued the group effort, noting:

*I was surprised about how well we cooperated as a large group and how many creative ideas we produced. As a single person I would most probably have needed ten times more time for producing ten per cent of the ideas and would not have had nearly as much fun in doing so.*

To summarise, the workshops aimed to build knowledge about communication by means of elaborating material to be further studied and applied in the team's projects. The consequences of online media in reducing many essential aspects of communication, possible solutions and their potentials and limitations were thoroughly addressed, so that students could continue observing the different modes while meeting online and/ or face to face to work on their projects.

I introduced the person-centred encounter groups (see e.g. Barrett-Lennard,1998, 2003, 2005; Rogers, 1970) as invitations to explore one's communication skills in 'natural' situations as they arise, i.e. in situations that are not constrained by some predetermined, constructed context or task proposed by the facilitator, as was often the case in the workshops. I also made clear that everybody was co-responsible for the outcome of the groups and that it was up to us what we chose to make of the whole experience. In facilitating encounter groups, I see my primary task as providing an open, respectful and understanding atmosphere in which participants and the whole group can move forward in a constructive process to build a community and at the same time develop as individuals.

The groups experienced periods of silence and intense sharing as well as discussion. Interestingly, those who talked a lot in the beginning and complained about the less vocal people learned to give space to the quieter ones, many of whom took the opportunity to share personal issues in the group. This, and the open sharing amongst all participants, contributed to the perception of deep personal learning in the majority of participants. Personally, I believe that the transparency and openness expressed in the reaction sheets significantly contributed to building a safe and trustful climate in the group that allowed for deep learning at all levels. A similarly positive effect of written feedback, although in a different context (therapy) was observed by Reinhard Tausch (2006) who also refers to Berking, Orth and Lutz, 2006. In our course, I felt that participants who talked less during encounter sessions often wrote insightful reactions and thereby became 'known' to the group. This, in my view, built trust in the group and accelerated the group process so that the initial, often tense phases almost disappeared and the group moved quickly to the later, constructive phases, in which the expression of positive feelings, respect and change towards more openness and transparency dominated. The following excerpts from students' reactions after the first and second group meetings are intended to serve as an illustration of the encounter group process. Note also the more personal style in writing when compared with the reaction sheets following the initial workshops.

Following the initial one-and-a-half day encounter a student wrote:

> *I really liked the first encounter group. I didn't expect there to be no schedule at all, but that worked really well. I was surprised by the way in which themes appeared. Also, it was cool how the exchanges became more personal and meaningful and I could 'see' the increase of trust among us. What I really appreciated was that people who tended to remain silent, finally contributed a lot more. Jean\* really impressed me in this respect and I had the impression that she felt encouraged and profited a lot. All in all I hope that it stays as interesting as it is.*

Another student noted:

> *Today's group was really thrilling, especially as we experienced a real conflict or, more precisely, misunderstanding. The discussion developed smoothly and I was enthusiastic about the quiet and caring atmosphere in which a solution to the misunderstanding was*

---

\*All names have been changed.

*sought for. What I appreciated in particular was the way my friend Stefan tried to explain what he thought Austin wanted to get across, and this shows how well we understand each other in the group. Also, I felt the communication and relationships among individual group members improved gradually. In my view, the reason for this was our open sharing of personal experiences. I believe that openness and trust truly facilitate communication.*

After the second encounter group, the same student wrote:

*The breaks were another essential element in supporting our communication. Away from the atmosphere of the seminar room, conversations became even more direct. Without spending breaks together, our relationships would not have evolved so well. During the last meeting, I discovered that our group was open to everything. We talked about alcohol, drugs, faith and cultures, without any fear or reservations. This acceptance increased openness and mutual trust.*

Another student remarked:

*Personally, the encounter groups made me confront myself about things I had never considered before. Moreover, they helped me to think about certain aspects of my life and gain new insight. I got impressions from other cultures and learned to consciously listen to others attentively and to accept and respect their meanings.*

In her final reaction sheet after the final workshop, a student wrote:

*The final workshop was a nice ending. We talked about the reaction sheets and their meaning and importance, and reflected upon the encounter group phases as we lived through them. Before and during the break we shared what conflict type we belong to and, subsequently, we summarised important steps in conflict resolution. It was interesting to see how many people would be willing to participate in an encounter group again – quite a lot! However, I found the last hour a bit sad because it won't ever happen again in quite the same way … It has been really exciting for me to get to know you, to work with you and to spend time with you! I'd like to say thank you for the pleasant atmosphere, which I had hoped for at the start. Also, many thanks to our facilitator for giving us the chance to participate in such a unique course and thanks for your evident interest and engagement. Thank you, it was great and I enjoyed it very much!*

The projects were completed on time by all teams. All of them used a blended way of cooperation interweaving face-to-face meetings with online communication. The topics that were selected and adopted dealt with: communication situations online, conflict situations and potential resolutions, case studies of personal communication situations, person-centred communication with non-native speaking partners, communication in partner, job, and parent–child relationships. The peer evaluation allowed the recipients to gain various perspectives from their colleagues. Frankly, this variety of viewpoints could not have been achieved by me on my own. Also, some comments seem more effective when made by peers rather than the facilitator. For example, a student expressed a requirement for literature references, saying: 'I would like to read more in the professional literature about the cultural differences you have addressed. Unfortunately, a lot of interesting statements have been made without giving references for further reading.'

EVALUATION

In the initial online questionnaire we asked students (on several courses) to indicate the degree to which they felt they had benefited from the three levels of learning in a typical, traditional course in their studies. In the final questionnaire, we asked the same question but in relation to the course on person-centred communication. Figure 1 shows the perceived amount of learning on the three levels in a traditional course (depicted by the dark-grey bar in Figure 1) and the perceived amount of learning in the course on person-centred communication (the light-grey bar). The figure illustrates that students felt that they 'learned' more on the level of skills and personal attitudes in the blended course on person-centred communication, while the perceived degree of learning at the intellectual level was just slightly beneath that of conventional courses.

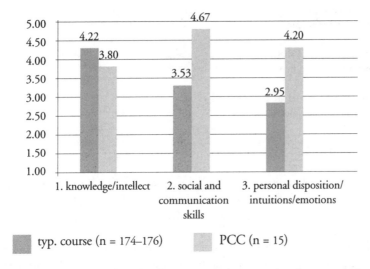

*Figure 1.* 'Learning' on three levels in a typical conventional course in business informatics and the course on person-centred communication (n = 15 out of 16 participants).

T-tests showed that on the level of skills ($T_{30.87}$ = -7.44, p = 0.000) and on the level of attitudes ($T_{17.43}$ = -4.22, p = 0.001) students benefited significantly more in the course on person-centred communication than in conventional courses. On the level of intellect, a trend to learning more in traditional courses ($T_{16.8}$ = 2.02, p = 0.059) was found. We believe, however, that if desired, more intellectual learning could easily be integrated into the course, for example by motivating students more strongly to read and learn from the resources provided. How much learning to aim for at each level appears to be a question of priorities within the curriculum. The whole finding indicates that all three levels of learning can be accessed in academic courses. Furthermore, the different emphasis given to individual levels, as expressed in the course goals, was reflected in the students' perceptions. From this, we conjecture that a thoughtful consideration of course goals and scenarios has the potential to significantly influence the students' whole-person learning (Derntl, 2006; Motschnig-Pitrik & Mallich, 2004).

As a consequence of participating in PCC …

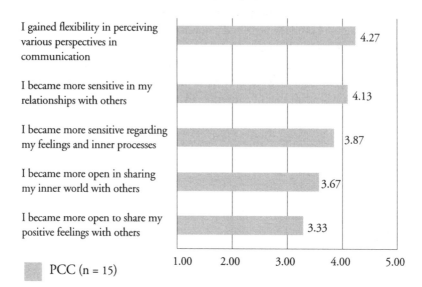

PCC (n = 15)

*Figure 2.* Results of students' responses when asked to what degree the following statements hold true (scales from 1 = 'not at all' to 5 = 'applies fully').

A related question concerned any effect of the course on students' attitudes that might have been influenced by an intervention taking place in a person-centred atmosphere. In this respect, Figure 2 illustrates some consequences of the course as perceived by students at the end of the course. The results can be seen as confirming that the course goals on the level of skills and attitudes have been met to a satisfactory degree. Interestingly, as mentioned above, no significant changes in personality items as reflected by NEO-FFI scales have been found in earlier courses. Hence, we stopped asking students to fill in the respective lengthy questionnaires and instead looked for more specific, indicative items to reflect results from our intervention.

A question of interest regarding course design concerned the students' perception of the importance of individual course elements, particularly the online phases, the structured workshops and the unstructured encounter group session. Approximately the same amount of course time was scheduled to these three course segments, whereas online tasks ran in parallel to the face-to-face processes. As expected from the students' feedback in face-to-face meetings and online reaction sheets, the encounter groups were perceived as the most meaningful. Interestingly, the same results have been found in another group on the same course. Figure 3 illustrates the results of the questionnaires. The three course elements have also been found to be different in their importance ($F_{2.26} = 11.79$, p = 0.000, partial eta-square = 0.48) by employing a multivariate analysis of variance. The pairwise comparisons show that all three elements were perceived as different in their importance, more precisely that the encounter groups were perceived as more important than the structured workshops and the online elements were perceived as least important in relation to workshops and encounter groups.

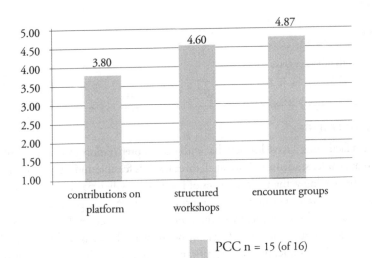

*Figure 3.* Perceived importance of course elements in the course on Person-Centred Communication (PCC). The Figure illustrates to what degree students agreed when asked to rate importance: the contributions from the platform, the structured workshops, the encounter groups respectively, were all important.

Table 1 below indicates the course's effect on interpersonal relationships. It shows that the course's influence on all kinds of relationships was positive, or rather, positive in the vast majority of students and neutral in far less cases. When asked to provide specific examples for the rating, a student wrote: 'Conflict resolution with my partner and my parents works better, in general we are more open with each other and there are fewer conflicts.' Another student commented: 'Maybe I am more accepting of the opinions and feelings of others, but I don't think the course has really affected my behaviour towards others.'

211

*Table 1*

Effects of the PCC course on interpersonal relationships (n = 14)

| | Negative effect | Rather negative effect | No effect | Rather positive effect | Positive effect | Not applic- able |
|---|---|---|---|---|---|---|
| Study colleagues | | | 1 | 7 | 7 | |
| Work colleagues | | | 1 | 3 | 6 | 5 |
| Superiors | | | 3 | 2 | 5 | 5 |
| Friends | | | 1 | 5 | 9 | |
| Partner | | | 1 | 5 | 7 | 2 |
| Parents | | | 3 | 3 | 9 | |
| Contact with others in general | | | | 6 | 9 | |
| All | 0 | 0 | 10 | 31 | 52 | 12 |

SPECIFYING LEARNING

Firstly, as a facilitator, I have learned that with careful preparation and design, a blended course that enables students to learn at all three levels is feasible and truly appreciated by students. Interestingly, the typical phases of resistance – when participants realise there is no structure – were very short and comprised of students' suggestions about how to provide structure (for example, by doing exercises). I conjecture that the preparatory cooperation and motivation of students during the workshops, as well as the reading of materials provided online, played a significant role in accelerating the group process. I felt that the initial phases were significantly shortened, however, without being left out completely. Another factor that may have accelerated the group process was the online reaction sheets written by all participants and published in our interactive space, allowing each participant to read the reactions of their colleagues. In this way, even the less vocal students were able to express themselves and become better known to the group, and this tended to increase trust amongst us.

In one instance, the group started discussing the legalisation of drugs from a third-person perspective. For me, this purely intellectual discussion began to be awkward and I was on the point of interrupting, but then I observed that the students seemed to have a real interest in the subject and its political considerations. So I thought hard about how to accept the students' interest and at the same time to satisfy my own desire to inspire more personal expression. Suddenly, I found myself asking a student what potential legalisation of drugs would mean to him as a person. This altered the scenario and the students started to express themselves on a much more personal level, but with equal engagement. Retrospectively, I can see that they needed some kind of warming up on a hot topic, and that nothing would have been more harmful than cutting them off. I learned to trust the group process, yet also to listen to my own feelings and find expression for them when appropriate. As a facilitator, I confirmed my style of participating actively and visibly, but without taking charge. Also, I found it important to consciously balance taking care of the individual with considering and involving the group (Barrett-Lennard, 2003).

The decision to conduct a structured workshop at the end of the course – not part of the course in the preceding year – proved successful. The structured workshop was definitely different from those held before the encounter sessions. Students cooperated even more intensively. In particular, the collaborative reflection upon the 15 phases of the group process (Rogers, 1970) in terms of experiences that we assigned to individual phases that we had lived through together gave us a feeling of unity that is hard to characterise in words.

From my experience in other course instances, including encounter groups that I have co-facilitated with my colleague Ladislav Nykl, and that included less structured workshops and no reaction sheets between encounter group blocks, it needs to be said that a few students seem not to benefit much from the encounter group experience. I conjecture that technically oriented students with no prior idea of self-experience tend to benefit from structured workshops, sharing in small teams, and cognitive inputs that 'prepare' and motivate them for the unstructured group experience. Also, occasional conflicts in group sessions alert me to the fact that allowing free expression is potent but equally risky in academic institutions. Therefore, skilled facilitators with a good understanding of group dynamics, a thoughtful course design, and administrative support are necessary for conducting courses that include encounter groups.

Finally, students occasionally remark in their concluding reaction sheets that the course on person-centred communication would be better held at the beginning rather than the end of their studies. This would give them ample opportunity to continue friendships, keep in touch with the community that formed during the course, and live the experiences and insights they gained in the structured workshops and encounter groups.

## CONCLUSION AND FURTHER WORK

If interpersonal attitudes and improved interpersonal relationships are to be developed along with subject knowledge, action research supports earlier research (Tausch & Tausch, 1998) in finding that person-centred encounter groups have their place in higher education. More than that, students tend to view person-centred encounter groups as the most important feature in a course targeted at improving communication. This appears to confirm Rogers' view of encounter groups as a highly potent social invention of the twentieth century. Interestingly, from two course instances, I have gained the impression and hypothesis that online journal sheets, submitted and shared after each

213

session, have the potential to accelerate the group process. As a consequence, early phases can be passed through more quickly and later phases, with more trust, deeper expression and more understanding, can start earlier. Whether this increases or diminishes personal learning and development and whether it also applies within other contexts, remain questions for further research.

In summary, person-centred encounter groups enriched by online sharing and projects, and preceded by structured workshops, have proved to be highly effective settings for significant learning for a vast majority of students. However, skilled facilitators and thoughtful course designs are needed, as well as understanding and support from administration, because there is some emotional and/or interpersonal risk attached to facilitating the free expression of students' feelings and meanings.

Further work will proceed with empirical action research to interweave the rich presence, typically found in person-centred encounter groups, with online elements for reflection and cooperation in order to confirm or modify the initial findings reported in this chapter. We also intend to transfer the course concept developed at the Research Lab for Educational Technologies at the University of Vienna to organisations and other institutions for higher and adult education. A complementary research track will investigate and compare the influence of online communication on group processes and teamwork in professional and learning communities. With our work we aim to contribute to a thoughtful blending of face-to-face and online settings for facilitating improved interpersonal understanding and effective, significant learning.

## REFERENCES

Aspy, DN (1972) *Toward a Technology for Humanizing Education.* Champaign, IL: Research Press Company.

Barret-Lennard, GT (1998) *Carl Rogers' Helping System: Journey and substance.* London: Sage.

Barret-Lennard, GT (2003) *Steps on a Mindful Journey: Person-centred expressions.* Ross-on-Wye: PCCS Books.

Barret-Lennard, GT (2005) *Relationship at the Center: Healing in a troubled world.* Philadelphia, PA: Whurr Publishers.

Baskerville, RL (1999) Investigating information systems with action research. *Communications of the Association for Information Systems, 2.* http://cais.isnet.org/articles/2-19/

Bauer, C, Derntl, M, Motschnig-Pitrik, R & Tausch, R (2006) Promotive activities in face-to-face and technology-enhanced learning environments. *The Person-Centered Journal, 13* (1&2), 12–37.

Berking, M, Orth, U & Lutz, W (2006) Wie effektiv sind systematische Rückmeldungen des Therapieverlaufs an den Therapeuten? *Zeitschrift Klinische Psychologie und Psychotherapie, 36* (1), 21–9.

Bühler, K (1907) Tatsachen und Probleme zu einer Psychologie der Denkvorgänge: I. Über Gedanken [Facts and problems of a psychology on mental processes]. *Archiv für die gesamte Psychologie 9*, 279–305.

Cornelius-White, JHD (2007) Learner-centered teacher–student relationships are effective: A meta-analysis. *Review of Educational Research, 77,* 1–31.

Cornelius-White, JHD, Hoey, A, Cornelius-White, C, Motschnig-Pitrik, R & Figl, K (2004) Person-centered education: A meta-analysis of care in progress. *Journal of Border Educational Research, 3* (1), 81–7.

Derntl, M (2006) *Patterns for Person-Centered E-Learning.* Berlin: Akademische Verlagsgesellschaft Aka GmbH.

Derntl, M & Motschnig-Pitrik, R (2005) The role of structure, patterns and people in blended learning. *The Internet and Higher Education, 8* (2), 111–30.

European Association for the Education of Adults (2004) Strategic statement on key competencies. Retrieved from http://www.eaea.org/doc/Strategic_document_2004.doc

Figl, K, Derntl, M & Motschnig, R (2005) Assessing the Added Value of Blended Learning: An experience-based survey of research paradigms. Proceedings of Interactive Computer-Aided Learning. Villach, Austria.

Holzinger, A & Motschnig-Pitrik, R (2005) Considering the human in multimedia: Learner-centered design (LCD) & person-centered e-learning (PCeL). In P Micheuz, PK Antonitsch & R Mittermeir (Eds) *Innovative Concepts for Teaching Informatics* (pp. 102–12). Vienna: Carl Ueberreuter.

Mangler, J & Derntl, M (2004) CEWebS – Cooperative Environment Web Services. Proceedings of 4th International Conference on Knowledge Management (I-KNOW '04) (pp. 617–24) June 30–July 2, Graz, Austria.

Motschnig-Pitrik, R (2002) Anforderungsanalyse an Wirschaftsinformatiker(innen) aus der Sicht der Wirtschaft [An economic perspective on the qualification profiles of business informatics graduates]. *OCG Journal, 1,* 8–11.

Motschnig-Pitrik, R (2004) An Action Research-Based Framework for Assessing Blended Learning Scenarios. Proceedings of ED-MEDIA 2004: World Conference on Educational Multimedia, Hypermedia & Telecommunications (pp. 3976–81). June 21–26, Lugano, Switzerland, AACE Press.

Motschnig-Pitrik, R (2006a) Two technology-enhanced courses aimed at developing interpersonal attitudes and soft skills in project management. In W Neijdl & K Tochtermann (Eds) *Innovative Approaches for Learning and Knowledge Sharing. Proceedings of the 1st European conference on technology-enhanced learning* (pp. 331–46). Berlin, Heidelberg: Springer-Verlag.

Motschnig-Pitrik, R (2006b) Web-Technologie begegnet personzentriertem Lernen. *Zeitschrift der GwG, Gesprächspsychotherapie und Personzentrierte Beratung, 4,* 212–20.

Motschnig-Pitrik, R & Mallich, K (2004) Effects of person-centered attitudes on professional and social competence in a blended learning paradigm. *Journal of Educational Technology & Society, 7* (4), 176–92.

Motschnig-Pitrik, R & Nykl, L (2005) Was hat Carl Rogers Wirtschaftsinformatikern im Zeitalter des Internet zu sagen? *Gruppendynamik und Organisationsberatung, 36* (1), 81–102.

Nykl, L (2005) *Beziehung im Mittelpunkt der Persönlichkeitsentwicklung –C Rogers im Vergleich mit Behaviorismus, Psychoanalyse und anderen Theorien* [Relationships at the Centre of Personal Development – C Rogers in comparison with behaviourism, psychoanalysis and other theories]. Münster, Berlin, Hamburg, London, Wien: LIT Verlag.

Nykl, L & Motschnig-Pitrik, R (2005) Encountergruppen im Rahmen des ganzheitlichen Lernens an den Universitäten Wien und Brünn – Motivation, Kontext, Prozesse, Perspektiven. *Zeitschrift für Hochschuldidaktik,* (4), 36–62.

Rogers, CR (1959) A theory of therapy, personality, and interpersonal relationships, as developed in the client-centered framework. In S Koch (Ed) *Psychology: A Study of a Science. Vol. 3: Formulations of the person and the social context* (pp. 184–256). New York: McGraw-Hill.

Rogers, CR (1961) *On Becoming a Person: A therapist's view of psychotherapy.* London: Constable.

Rogers, CR (1970) *Carl Rogers on Encounter Groups.* New York: Harper & Row.

Rogers, CR (1983) *Freedom to Learn for the 80s.* Columbus, OH: Charles E Merrill Publishing.

Rogers, CR & Freiberg, HJ (1994) *Freedom to Learn* (3rd edn). Upper Saddle River, NJ: Prentice Hall.

Susman, GI & Evered, RD (1978) An assessment of the scientific merits of action research. *Administrative Science Quarterly, 23* (4), 582–603.

Tausch, R (2006) Promoting health: Challenges for person-centered communication in psychotherapy, counseling and human relationships in daily life. Presentation at the 7th International Conference of the World Association for Person-Centered and Experiential Psychotherapy and Counseling, Potsdam, Germany. *Person-Centered and Experiential Psychotherapies, 6* (1), 30–44.

Tausch, R & Tausch, A-M (1963/1998) *Erziehungs-Psychologie.* Göttingen: Hogrefe.

**Acknowledgments**

Sincere thanks to Ladislav Nykl, who initially brought up the idea of including person-centred encounter groups in courses within the business informatics curriculum. The 'we' in the chapter refers to the faculty at the Research Lab for Educational Technologies at the University of Vienna and Ladislav Nykl as a facilitator and mentor in the realm of encounter groups. Sincere thanks also to Godfrey Barrett-Lennard, Robert Hutterer, Antonio Santos, Peter Schmid and Keddie Wanlass for their encouragement and insightful dialogue, and to Kathrin Figl for co-developing and evaluating the online questionnaires. Michael Behr's constructive comments on an earlier version of this chapter opened up valuable perspectives and helped to clarify ideas for further research. Last but not least, I appreciate Jef Cornelius-White's persistent engagement, cooperation and stylistic support.

# CHAPTER 15

# THEMES AND CONTINUING CHALLENGES IN PERSON-CENTRED WORK WITH YOUNG PEOPLE

JEFFREY H.D. CORNELIUS-WHITE
MICHAEL BEHR

## INTRODUCTION

This book has aimed to bring together international contributions from four continents to explore how the person-centred approach is evolving in work with young people and the significant others in their lives. New concepts, new research and new views on person-centred work are exposed in a way that clearly identifies the approach to be grounded in empirical research and in connection to the theories of general psychology (Behr, in press; Cornelius-White, in press; White, 1997). At the same time, being person-centred is sometimes viewed as the disciplined practice of compassion (Cornelius-White, in press). For example, Schmid (2002) looks at it as 'an ethical enterprise, an ethical discipline and profession. ... A decision is made to respond to the misery, to the grief, to the life of another person, to share their joys and sorrows. It derives from being addressed by the other, from being touched, from being asked, being called, from being appealed to' (p. 66).

Certainly the combination of an empirical and a philosophical-ethical basis marks one of the greatest strengths of person-centred work and gives it a unique position. We feel this can be experienced within this book. To make this more transparent, this chapter endeavours to synthesise some common themes and continuing challenges that emerge from our understanding of the collective work. In our view, four themes that weave through this book might be identified:

### 1. CORE CONDITIONS: REACHING OUT FOR CONNECTION, CHALLENGES AND EXTENSIONS

The core of the person-centred approach is the connection between people. Rogers' (1957, 1959) three attitudes of empathy, unconditional positive regard and congruence describe the experience of the relationship from the therapist's view. Whether in therapy or any other setting, fundamentally, person-centred work is about reaching out to the humanity of others and in turn to ourselves (Cornelius-White, in press; Rogers, 1959). Several chapters, especially those by Renate Motschnig-Pitrik on encounter groups in academic environments and Klaus Fröhlich-Gildhoff on common factors, highlight how relationship remains a central focus of person-centred work with young people.

Some concepts address implicitly the question of whether Rogers' (1957, 1959) hypothesis about the six conditions of psychotherapeutic change might be extended. In fact, it has become common in eclectic training programmes in the US and Europe to teach the practice of the core conditions as necessary but not sufficient. This is in contrast to Bozarth (1998) who has argued that the research shows that the conditions are nearly always sufficient but not necessary, since people change in response to a wide variety of situations, including self-help and cognitive-behavioural approaches, without obvious facilitative relationships present. A first proposition for this is marked by Klaus Fröhlich-Gildhoff's research on effective factors in psychotherapy with young people. In part, these common factors represent the Rogerian core conditions, but they also suggest further aspects, which might result in psychotherapists' action beyond the offering of an interpersonal relation. There is strong evidence that psychotherapy might be more effective if additional factors are focused on (Elliott, 2007).

The chapters of Dorothea Hüsson, concerning work with sexually abused children; Klaus Fröhlich-Gildhoff, about work with violent youngsters; Bernie Neville, on classroom management; and Ulrike Bächle-Hahn, with violent and delinquent juveniles, go further to expose a practice that clearly goes beyond the offer of a facilitative interpersonal relationship and suggests that these extensions are necessary in specific circumstances. For example, in the work with juveniles, the behaviour of the therapist includes confrontation, which has been well discussed by Carkhuff (1969). It might be subsumed under condition three: the congruent therapist, who many believe would no longer be congruent if he or she did not address and confront. Furthermore, these interventions often seem to support the establishment and communication (condition 6) of a psychological contact (condition 1) (Behr, 2003). Finally, the therapist might hypothesise that a child or adolescent is incongruent, even though they do not feel vulnerable or subceive problems within their self-concept. Instead, they may be extensionally incongruent (Cornelius-White, 2007b; Rogers, 1959), or out of synch with their context (Cornelius-White, 2007c; Seeman, 2001), not just within the world (condition 2). Thus, confronting interventions might yield some kind of increased congruence within both the therapist's and young person's field of perception.

If the conditions are sometimes necessary but not sufficient and other times sufficient but not necessary, are the fundamentals ever optimal? When is something else better? We believe that further investigation through a variety of methods can help clarify these remaining questions. However, we also believe the actual practice of person-centred work with young people inevitably involves balancing situational, developmental and ideal aspects of the lived person-centred work, resulting in an ever-changing, flexible approach.

## 2. SKILLS FOR YOUNG PEOPLE

Despite the debate on the sufficiency of the core conditions, some authors argue that in addition to experiencing the therapists' core conditions, the learning of some basic skills, particularly by younger people, is necessary for improved social functioning. Again, the

Rogerian core conditions were hypothesised to be central to but not definitively applicable to the work with young people in the whole broad field of possible problems. This includes psychotherapy settings as shown by the chapters of Klaus Fröhlich-Gildhoff, with his fifth principle (increase of competencies) and Erwin Vlerick, with his conviction and focusing example. A further significant example is Renate Motschnig-Pitrik's unique concept, which follows the EU's new, broader goals for education consistent with learner-centred instruction (Cornelius-White & Harbaugh, in press). Her concept can be regarded primarily as an experiential encounter approach rather than a psycho-educational one, but at the same time it is consistent with a holistic skill-development approach.

Dynamic skill theory (e.g. Fischer & Yan, 2007), an influential brain-based approach, and learner-centred instruction (Cornelius-White & Harbaugh, in press), offer some clarity on this seeming controversy of whether basic skills and competencies need to be taught. Fischer and Yan's analyses revealed that 'most psychopathology involves distinctive developmental pathways, not primitive ones', suggesting that the 'skill level [of persons with psychopathology] was not retarded, fixated, or regressed' (p. 24). In other words, psychopathology involves idiosyncrasy, not deficit. Likewise, dynamic skill research has refuted the idea of a 'fixed competence' or 'unitary skill level', offering instead a dynamic range of competencies, stating that context, particularly 'immediate context contributes directly to skill level as evidenced in optimal [high] and functional [low] levels [of support]' (p. 21). In other words, the degree of optimal support directly influences the level of skill observed; skill levels are often inaccurately inferred. 'Most psychological and educational assessments give grossly inadequate portraits of people's skills because they assume one level of competence and ignore the developmental range and the several different upper limits for each person' that vary with the degree of optimal support (Fischer & Yan, 2007: 16). Optimal support to Fischer and Yan is characterised by a positive emotional valence and close relationships: 'Emotions and close relationships are major contributors to the dynamics of growth and variation and primary influences in shaping [neural and behavioural] pathways for both macrodevelopment and microdevelopment. Indeed, emotions *in* close relationships have especially powerful effects' (p. 23). However, optimal facilitation is also characterised by 'High support [which] involved priming the gist of a task – its key components – and then asking the person to perform the task on his or her own [whereas] low support involved simply asking for a performance on the same task without any priming' (p. 14). Hence, dynamic skill theory supports elements of both views, suggesting that understanding of psychopathology and skill-level assessment by clinicians is usually poor, positive relationships are pivotal for optimal development, but direct instruction in skills followed by learner attempts at skill demonstration is helpful.

Likewise, learner-centred research has shown some disparity regarding degree of direct instruction may be best, depending on the type of skills being facilitated. Some guidance and structure appears better for facilitating skill development than no structure (Bohart, in press), particularly in cognitive (den Brok, Brekelmans & Wubbels, 2006) and discrete skill development, if not necessarily abstract, existential (Cornelius-White & Cornelius-White, 2005) or emotional development (den Brok et al., 2006), but only within the context of positive relationships (Cornelius-White & Harbaugh, in press). Again, as Nel Noddings (personal communication, 2007) often says, 'Reasonable people disagree on controversial topics,' here implying that whether skills are seen as needing to be taught directly, or as resulting from facilitative relationships, many of the contributors in this book appear to agree on their importance.

### 3. COMMUNICATION BETWEEN PEOPLE IN CONTEXT

In some ways, the person-centred approach has been extended from basically being an approach to personal development within an individual therapy setting, to a flexible developmentally appropriate encounter with children, groups and the management of communicative and conflictual systems (Rogers, Cornelius-White, & Cornelius-White, 2005). Thus, some chapters of this book represent an extension of the basic rationale of person-centred psychotherapy. The unique unfolding of a person's experience and gaining of growth is embedded in a process of emerging congruence broader than the person alone (Cornelius-White, 2007a, b, c, in press). More and more concepts and more and more fields of work are implicitly grounded on an additional rationale. Small groups, families, couples, and people in conflict base their development and conflict resolution on the use of the three therapist core conditions for optimising their communication and smoothing their interpersonal relation (Behr, 1987, 1989, 2005). Personal development of individuals certainly is not excluded in this process but the focus is on the functioning of group process, communication, conflict resolution and relationship building. Nearly all contributions concerned with school applications in this book represent this additional rationale.

Compassionate and relevant communication processes are vital, not just between therapists and their young clients but also between the people in the systems in which young people live (Cornelius-White & Harbaugh, in press). This includes counsellors, teachers, parents, agency and legal personnel, and young people. Cooper's findings on teachers' preferences, Hölldampf et al., Mühlhäusser-Link et al., Kanazawa and Wakisaka's work with parent–teacher conferences, and Kominkiewicz's concerns with welfare investigations, all articulate this theme.

However, with regard to this rationale, the challenge to develop a theoretical model with a similar depth and complexity as exists for individual growth seems as yet unresolved. One of the greatest strengths of this rationale seems to be the possibility of finding compromises between the classical approach and the demands of particular situations and fields of work. What compromises are necessary in person-centred applications outside of voluntary, traditional child-centred play therapy or adolescent psychotherapy? Likewise, there may be an ever-diminishing 'pure therapy' context in today's world. In some countries, more regulations by insurance, licensing, or specific settings encumber the direct relationship between therapist and client. What are the necessary adjustments based on context? How should practitioners balance multiple goals and multiple interactions with systems, often involving third (or fourth or fifth) parties, like insurance, schools, government, and the influence of international and cultural variations that may conflict with the moment-to-moment self-direction of the child.

A further strength may be seen as the merging of the roles of counsellor and recipient. All individuals within the counselling process gain an orientation towards the core conditions and experience them in reciprocal manner. In highlighting potential roles for reciprocity and encounter, not just facilitation, some authors (e.g. Carkhuff, 2000) have argued that it is actually the learning by the helpee of how to be empathic, unconditional and congruent – as modeled by the helper – that helps creates change, just as much as the receipt of these conditions. Perhaps it is the training of parents (Gordon, 1970; Guerney & Guerney, 1989; Landreth & Bratton, 2006), students (Carkhuff, 2000; Johnson & Johnson, 2001), teachers (Aspy & Roebuck, 1977; Cornelius-White & Harbaugh, in press; Tausch & Tausch, 1991) and others, in the core conditions that is necessary, sufficient or optimal. Perhaps it is just the creation of community and encounter that happens with facilitation coming from any direction. Integrating and grounding research and models on these extensional settings back into the core theories of the person-centred approach remains an ongoing task (Cornelius-White, in press).

## 4. PROVEN EFFECTIVENESS

Person-centred work with children is supported by hundreds of studies and numerous meta-analytic approaches (see Behr and Cornelius-White, this volume). Child-centred play therapy and learner-centred educational approaches perhaps have the largest, strongest findings, showing potentially larger efficacy than other validated approaches (Bratton et al., 2005; Cornelius-White, 2007). While several chapters reference additional research, this book presents further syntheses of research in three areas: a focus on common factors with young people (Fröhlich-Gildhoff,) school-based counselling in UK (Cooper), and parent–teacher interaction (Mühlhäuser-Link et al.; Hölldampf et al.). These contributions stand for a quality standard under which the development of new concepts for person-centred work includes outcome studies and proven effectiveness.

## CONCLUSION ON THEMES AND CHALLENGES

This book has aimed to explore the international, multi-context approaches to person-centred work with young people, including scientific evidence, case studies, practice descriptions, and theoretical arguments and grounding. While authors have written convincingly about the inconsistencies of the person-centred interdisciplinary systems and phenomenological methods with mechanistic science (e.g. Elliott, 2007; Kriz, 2006), others have argued their necessity, both offering alternative methods (Elliott, 2007) and advocating from traditional approaches (Elliott, 2007; Tausch, 2001). Regardless of readers' inclinations, the practicality of existing in a political context, where mechanistic science is viewed as 'reality' and superior to ethical propositions or qualitative research, seems to require further explorations of person-centred work in all contexts, with all 'disorders' and all cultures. We hope that each chapter has stimulated further questions for readers, and challenges for researchers and authors, including this short concluding chapter. In this spirit, we leave with you some additional considerations and challenges and invite you to pursue your own questions:

1. Though we attempted to do so in the introductory chapter, it remains a great challenge to develop and bring together differentiated person-centred concepts of incongruence with the major diagnostic systems of the *ICD* and *DSM* to the extent necessary for the global political context.

2. A further necessity will be the development of more specific knowledge and concepts for relationship building and interventions with adolescents, including outcome research, which appears true for all psychotherapeutic approaches.

3. Although the person-centred approach is a wonderful concept for working with families in the form of encounter sessions, the majority of trainings and work for this has been based on systemic theory in the last decades. Why? Continuing revisions of concept building might be considered.

4. How can person-centred approaches to counselling in schools be better integrated in societies that do not have established school counselling professions, and how can the relationship building expertise of counsellors be used to help teachers develop, and in more structured guidance systems?

5. How can teacher and parent preparation and development projects based on person-centred thinking be better integrated into higher education, social agency, and other settings?

## REFERENCES

Aspy, DN & Roebuck, FN (1977) *Kids Don't Learn from People They Don't Like.* Amherst, MA: Human Resource Development Press.

Behr, M (1987) Carl R Rogers und die Pädagogik [Carl R Rogers and Educational Science]. *Neue Sammlung, 27,* 425–39.

Behr, M (1989) Wesensgrundlagen einer an der Person des Kindes und der Person des Pädagogen orientierten Erziehung [Basic ideas of a child- and educator-centred education]. In M Behr, F Petermann, WM. Pfeiffer & C Seewald (Hrsg) *Jahrbuch für personenzentrierte Psychologie und Psychotherapie, Bd. 1* (pp. 152–81). Salzburg: Otto Müller.

Behr, M (2003) Interactive resonance in work with children and adolescents: A theory-based concept of interpersonal relationship through play and the use of toys. *Person-Centered and Experiential Psychotherapies, 2* (2), 89–103.

Behr, M (2005) Differentielle Effekte von empathischen und authentischen Eltern-Lehrer-Gesprächen im Rollenspielexperiment [Differential effects of empathy and authenticity during parent–teacher conferences in role play experiments]. *Empirische Pädagogik, 19* (3), 244–64.

Behr, M (in press) Schemas and personality change. *Person-Centered and Experiential Psychotherapies.*

Bohart, A (in press) Clients: The neglected common factor in psychotherapy. In M Hubble, B Duncan, S Miller & B Wampold (Eds) *Heart and Soul of Change* (2nd edn). Washington,

DC: American Psychological Association.

Bozarth, JD (1998) *Person-Centered Therapy: A revolutionary paradigm.* Ross-on-Wye: PCCS Books.

Bratton, SC, Ray, D, Rhine, T & Jones, L (2005) The efficacy of play therapy with children: A meta-analytic review of treatment outcomes. *Professional Psychology: Research and practice, 36* (4), 376–90.

Carkhuff, R (1969) *Helping and Human Relations. Vol. I. Selection and training; Vol. II. Practice and research.* New York: Holt, Rinehart and Winston.

Carkhuff, R (2000) *Human Possibilities: Human capital in the 21st century.* Amherst, MA: Possibilities.

Cornelius-White, JHD (2007a) Congruence. In M Cooper, M O'Hara, PF Schmid, & G Wyatt (Eds) *Handbook of Person-Centered Psychotherapy and Counseling* (pp. 168–81). New York: Palgrave MacMillan.

Cornelius-White, JHD (2007b) Congruence as extensionality. *Person-Centered and Experiential Psychotherapies, 6* (3), 196–204.

Cornelius-White, JHD (2007c) A five-dimensional model of congruence. *Person-Centered and Experiential Psychotherapies, 6* (4), 229–39.

Cornelius-White, JHD (in press) Re-examinations of the Rogers' (1959) collection of theories of the person-centered approach. *Person-Centered and Experiential Psychotherapies.*

Cornelius-White, JHD & Cornelius-White, CF (2005) Trust builds learning: Context and effectiveness of non-directivity in education. In B Levitt (Ed) *Embracing Non-directivity: Reassessing theory and practice in the 21st century* (pp. 314–23). Ross-on-Wye: PCCS Books.

Cornelius-White, JHD & Harbaugh, AP (in press) Learner-Centered Instruction: Building relationships for student success. Thousand Oaks, CA: Sage.

Den Brok, P, Brekelmans, M & Wubbels, T (2006) Multilevels in research using students' perceptions of learning environments: The case of the questionnaire on teacher interaction. *Learning Environments Research, 9* (3), 199–213.

Elliott, R (2007) Person-centered approaches to research. In M Cooper, M O'Hara, PF Schmid & G Wyatt (Eds) *Handbook of Person-Centered Psychotherapy and Counseling* (pp. 327–40). New York: Palgrave MacMillan.

Fischer, KW & Yan (2007) Development of dynamic skill theory. In R Licktler & D Lewkowicz (Eds) *Conceptions of Development: Lessons from the laboratory.* Hove: Psychology Press.

Gordon, T (1970) *Parent Effectiveness Training.* New York: Wyden.

Guerney, LG & Guerney, BG Jr (1989) Child relationship enhancement, family therapy and parent education. *Person-Centered Review, 4* (3), 344–57.

Johnson, DW & Johnson, RT (2001) *Teaching students to be peacemakers: A meta-analysis.* Minneapolis, MN: University of Minneapolis. (ERIC Document Reproduction Service No. ED 460178)

Kriz, J (2006) *Self-Actualization.* Hamburg: Books on Demand.

Landreth, G & Bratton, S (2006) *Child Parent Relationship Therapy (CPRT): A 10-session filial therapy model.* New York: Routledge.

Rogers, CR (1957) The necessary and sufficient conditions of therapeutic personality change. *Journal of Consulting Psychology, 21,* 95–103.

Rogers, CR (1959) A theory of therapy, personality and interpersonal relationships, as developed in the client-centered framework. In S Koch (Ed) *Psychology: The study of a science. Vol. 3: Formulations of the person and the social context* (pp. 184–256). New York: McGraw-Hill.

Rogers, CR, Cornelius-White, JHD & Cornelius-White, CF (2005) Reminiscing and predicting: Rogers' Beyond Words speech and commentary. *Journal of Humanistic Psychology, 45*, 383–96.

Schmid, PF (2002) Knowledge or acknowledgement? Psychotherapy as 'the art of not-knowing': Prospects on further developments of a radical paradigm. *Person-Centered and Experiential Psychotherapies, 1* (1&2), 56–70.

Seeman, J (2001) On congruence: A human system paradigm. In G Wyatt (Ed) *Rogers' Therapeutic Conditions: Evolution, theory and practice. Vol. 1: Congruence* (pp. 213–28). Ross-on-Wye: PCCS Books.

Tausch, R (2001) Wirkungsvorgänge in Patienten/Klienten bei der Minderung seelischer Beeinträchtigungen durch Gesprächspsychotherapie [Processes in clients when reducing mental disorders with person-centred psychotherapy]. In I Langer (Hrsg) *Menschlichkeit und Wissenschaft* (pp. 523–48*)*. Köln: GwG-Verlag.

Tausch, R & Tausch, A-M (1991) *Erziehungspsychologie* [Educational Psychology] (10. Auflage). Göttingen: Hogrefe.

White, J (1997) Core constructs, nondirectivity, and theory-integration in client-centered therapy. Unpublished Master's thesis, Illinois School of Professional Psychology, Chicago, IL.

# CONTRIBUTORS

GERNOT AICH teaches and undertakes research projects at the University of Education in Schwäbisch Gmünd, Germany. His main research interests are communication and conflict resolution between teachers, parents and pupils, the parent–school relationship and classroom discipline. He also works as a coach, supervisor and counsellor for schools and other institutions.

ULRIKE BÄCHLE-HAHN has been a psychologist, and since 2005, a member of psychological services at St. Augustinusheim in Ettlingen, Germany. Main work areas: counselling and therapeutical support of aggressive, disadvantaged and addictive drug-consuming juveniles and young men; staff trainer for Peer Group Counselling; evaluation of the educational and therapeutical process.

MICHAEL BEHR is Professor of Educational Psychology at the University of Education Schwäbisch Gmünd, Germany. His research topics are person-centred counselling, child and adolescent psychotherapy, young people's emotions, and parent–school relationships. He has written several books about school development and person-centred work in education. He is the Director of the person-centred play therapy training course at the University of Education in Schwäbisch Gmünd and at the Stuttgart Institute for Person-Centred Therapy and Counselling, which he co-founded and where he works as a therapist, supervisor, and facilitator.

MICK COOPER is a Professor of Counselling at the University of Strathclyde and a UKCP-registered psychotherapist, whose work is informed by person-centred, existential, interpersonal and postmodern ideas. Mick is co-editor of *The Handbook of Person-Centred Psychotherapy and Counselling* (Palgrave, 2007); co-author of *Working at Relational Depth in Counselling and Psychotherapy* (Sage, 2005); and lead researcher on a number of evaluation projects into person-centred counselling in schools, receiving in 2005 the BACP Recognising Achievements in Counselling and Psychotherapy Award for this work.

JEFFREY H.D. CORNELIUS-WHITE, PsyD, LPC is Dean's Fellow for Teaching and Learning, Associate Professor of Counseling, and former Director of School Counseling at Missouri State University and Adjunct Assistant Professor for the Cooperative EdD Program in Educational Leadership and Policy Analysis University of Missouri-Columbia, USA. He is also Co-Editor of the *Person-Centered Journal*, Content Editor of the *Journal of Border Educational Research*, and a World Association for Person-Centered and Experiential Psychotherapy and Counseling board member. He is co-author of the forthcoming 2008 book with Sage entitled *Learner-Centered Instruction*. His work usually concerns person-centred and social justice issues in counselling psychology and education.

ELSE DÖRING has been a psychotherapist for 30 years, working with children, adolescents and adults. She has been a trainer in person-centred play therapy for many years and runs workshops in Germany. She has a private practice in Frankfurt with children and adults, and specialises in psychotherapy with traumatised children, adolescents and adults. As well, she works with patients with dissociative disorders. She is the director of training courses for person-centred child and adolescent psychotherapy in Berlin and at the Person-Centred Institute in Frankfurt, Germany.

KLAUS FRÖHLICH-GILDHOFF is Professor for Developmental and Clinical Psychology at the Protestant University of Applied Sciences in Freiburg, Germany (EFH). He is the Director of the Center for Research in Childhood and Adolescence at the EFH; with research projects in Early Childhood Education, Youth Welfare and Psychotherapy with children and adolescents. He also works as a psychotherapist and supervisor.

DAGMAR HÖLLDAMPF works as a scientific assistant at the University of Education Schwäbisch Gmünd, Germany. She is involved in research projects in person-centred work with children and parents and in teacher training. As well she works as a play therapist at the Centre for Educational Counselling, Schwäbisch Gmünd and in private practice in Stuttgart.

DOROTHEA HÜSSON is the Director of the Counselling Centre for Sexual Violence in Esslingen, Germany. There she works as a person-centred therapist with children and adolescents. She is also involved in training kindergarten teachers. She is a trainer for person-centred child and adolescent psychotherapy at the Person-Centred Institute in Stuttgart, Germany.

THERESA JAKOB is doing her Masters degree in Educational Sciences at the University of Education, Schwäbisch Gmünd, Germany. As a student assistant she works in several projects relating to person-centred work and parent–teacher communication. She is also in training as a person-centred therapist.

AKIRA KANAZAWA is a graduate student of Clinical Psychology at the Graduate School of Human Science, Osaka University, Japan. He runs research projects in psychotherapy with adolescent Japanese-Koreans and consultations with their parents. He is engaged in school counselling, dealing with issues such as personality disorders, eating disorders, psychosomatic disorders in a hospital setting. He is also interested in the development of the infant and is engaged in observation of interactions between mother and infant.

FRANCES BERNARD KOMINKIEWICZ is Associate Professor in the Department of Social Work, as well as the Director of the Social Work Program at Saint Mary's College, Notre Dame, Indiana, USA. Her research has focused on child abuse/child welfare, and she has published in such areas as sibling abuse organisational policy, organisational response to child welfare, grief counselling, and domestic violence educational curriculum. Dr Kominkiewicz is very involved in international cross-cultural comparisons of organisational child abuse policy and definitions. She is also a licensed clinical social worker and marriage and family therapist specialising in person-centred therapy with children and families.

GEORG KORMANN works at the University of Education Schwäbisch Gmünd, Germany as a lecturer and also in research projects concerning the person-centred approach. Additionally, he works as psychotherapist and teaches person-centred psychotherapy.

RENATE MOTSCHNIG-PITRIK is Professor of Computer Science at the University of Vienna. Since 2005 she has been head of the Research Lab for Educational Technologies where she cooperates with psychologists and educational scientists. In her teaching and research she promotes technology-enhanced, person-centred learning. Renate has participated in several international PCA-related conferences, workshops, and encounter groups. Currently, her major interests lie in international, person-centred communication and cooperation and in a smooth integration of cognition and affect in learning.

SUSANNE MÜHLHÄUSER-LINK has a Masters degree in Educational Sciences and works at the University of Education Schwäbisch Gmünd, Germany. Additionally she is a teacher in primary and secondary schools and is a person-centred therapist for children and adolescents. She is mainly interested in combining her long experience with children and their parents and the demands of evaluation in school to improve the quality and effectiveness of communication and cooperation.

BERNIE NEVILLE is Associate Professor of Education at La Trobe University, Bundoora, Australia, where he teaches courses in both education and counselling. He is author of *Educating Psyche: Emotion, Imagination and the Unconscious in Learning* (Flat Chat Press, 2005) and numerous papers on both counselling and education.

ERWIN VLERICK, PhD, focusing trainer and supervisor. He is a clinical psychologist and experiential therapist working in Belgium with children, adolescents and their families and has run many groups for adolescents on personal skills training. He works partly in a centre for mental health, partly in private practice. As a certified focusing trainer and supervisor, he is attached to a training programme for future experiential child and adolescent therapists. He also runs focusing training courses for social and mental health workers and, of course, adolescents.

SATOKO WAKISAKA studied experimental psychology as an undergraduate at Doshisha University but made a shift and got a Masters degree in Clinical Psychology at Kansai University. She is engaged in school counselling, consulting on the development of infants, and deals with issues such as school non-attendance, delinquency, bullying, developmental disorders and various family problems.

SIMONE WETZEL is a teacher in primary and secondary schools. She worked as scientific assistant at the University of Education, Schwäbisch Gmünd, Germany.

# INDEX

# Making and Breaking Children's Lives

## Edited by Craig Newnes
## & Nick Radcliffe

ISBN 978 1 898059 70 7

Are we confident that current services to children and families do more good than harm? *Making and Breaking Children's Lives* examines how children are hurt in modern society and how our concept of 'childhood' serves to exclude children from participating meaningfully in decisions about their care. After paying lip-service to the effects of early abandonment and trauma, children's experiences are sanitised through medical diagnoses, and neatly treated with prescription drugs. Nowhere is this more evident than in the current trend to label children with ADHD. The authors' careful and critical examination of ADHD as a diagnosis and the damaging side-effects of drug therapies on developing children make for disturbing reading.

In this excellent book a plurality of voices return to one consistent theme— the importance of psychosocial context, which has become increasingly dismissed as irrelevant in the rush to label and prescribe. The final chapters describe inspiring examples of how services and communities can be developed which give both children and their families a chance to prosper— evidence that there is nothing remotely inevitable about the breaking of children's lives.

**Sami Timimi writes:**

*... what's happening with child mental health services is negative. Perfectly healthy kids are being labelled and medicated and grow up believing there is something very wrong with them, and our professions are silent about this and silent about the adverse social circumstances that often accompany those who end up labelled.*

**Contents**

Gerrilyn Smith, *Construction of Childhood*; Jonathan Calder, *Histories of Child Abuse*; Elina Baker and Craig Newnes, *The Discourse of Responsibility*; Freddy Brown, *ADHD and the Philosophy of Science*; Geraldine Brady, *ADHD Diagnosis and Identity*; Sami Timimi and Nick Radcliffe, *The Rise and Rise of ADHD*; Dorothy Rowe, *ADHD—Adults' fear of frightened children*; Arlene Vetere and Jan Cooper, *The Effects of Domestic Violence*; Grace Jackson, *Cybernetic Children*; Helen Rostill and Helen Myatt, *Constructing Meaning in the Lives of Looked After Children*; Katherine Weare, *The Holistic Approach*; Raj Bandak, *Empowering Vulnerable Children and Families*; Carl Harris, *The Family Well-Being Project*; Bliss W. Browne, *Imagine Chicago: Cultivating hope and imagination*.

Available with discounts from www.pccs-books.co.uk

# PERSON-CENTRED WORK WITH CHILDREN AND YOUNG PEOPLE

UK PRACTITIONER PERSPECTIVES

EDITED BY
SUZANNE KEYS &
TRACEY WALSHAW

ISBN 978 1 906254 01 8

The first of its kind, this is a book by practitioners for practitioners. Love, respect and time for listening to children and young people are what the person-centred psychotherapists and psychologists contributing to this volume have in common. They do this in a multiplicity of settings including primary and secondary education, a pupil referral unit, voluntary agencies, adoption services, hospital, hospice, community and the streets.

All contributors give examples of their work with particular children and young people, aged from two to eighteen. They all share something of how they embody person-centred theory in their work, often engaging with the systems which impact on their work in the therapy room. They are all imbued with person-centred qualities, values and principles including respect, acceptance, empathy, awareness and self-questioning. All describe how much they have learnt from working with children and young people.

The inherent political and systemic aspects of this work are highlighted throughout the book, which we hope will encourage and inspire all those interested in what person-centred practice with children and young people might look and feel like.

**Suzanne Keys** works as a counsellor with young people in a sixth form college in East London. She has also worked in private practice and as a supervisor and trainer. She has published and edited on person-centred therapy and love, ethics, politics, prayer, human rights, gender and idiosyncratic practice.

**Tracey Walshaw** is a person-centred practitioner, trainer and artist. Play and creativity are at the centre of her work with children and young people. As well as being an independent counsellor and supervisor, she is a Director of PCCS Training Partnership in Manchester.

Available with discounts from www.pccs-books.co.uk